Innovation, organizational change and technology

The Management of Technology and Innovation Series

Series editors: David Preece, *Portsmouth Business School* and John Bessant, *Brighton Business School*

This series offers groundings in the central elements of the Management of Technology syllabus. Designed specifically to introduce students to the area, they present stimulating approaches to a range of technology issues, placing them in the context of management problems and solutions. Using case studies to illustrate the topics together with summaries on the key points, these texts can build together to cover a management of technology course.

The series will be an excellent resource for advanced undergraduates, postgraduates and MBA students.

Other titles in the series:

Organizations and Technical Change
David Preece, University of Portsmouth

Technology Strategy for Business
David Ford and Mike Saren

Technology and Quality: Change in the Workplace
Patrick Dawson, University of Adelaide

Forthcoming titles:

Creative Technological Change: Modern and Postmodern Images of Technology and Organization
Ian McLoughlin, Brunel University

Technology Assessment
Ernest Braun

Innovation, organizational change and technology

Edited by
Ian McLoughlin and Martin Harris

INTERNATIONAL THOMSON BUSINESS PRESS
I ⓣ P An International Thomson Publishing Company

London • Bonn • Boston • Johannesburg • Madrid • Melbourne • Mexico City • New York • Paris
Singapore • Tokyo • Toronto • Albany, NY • Belmont, CA • Cincinnati, OH • Detroit, MI

Innovation, Organizational Change and Technology

Copyright ©1997 Ian McLoughlin and Martin Harris

First published by International Thomson Business Press

 A division of International Thomson Publishing Inc.
The ITP logo is a trademark under licence

British Library Cataloguing-in-Publication Data
A catalogue record for this book is available from the British Library

First edition 1997

Typeset by J&L Composition Ltd, Filey, North Yorkshire
Printed in the UK by the University Press, Cambridge

ISBN 0-41513-034-4

International Thomson Business Press
Berkshire House
168–173 High Holborn
London WC1V 7AA
UK

International Thomson Business Press
20 Park Plaza
13th Floor
Boston MA 02116
USA

http://www.itbp.com

Preface and acknowledgements

The idea for this book emerged out of one of the many lunch time, office, tea room and after work pub discussions which have been integral to the life of the Department of Management Studies at Brunel since its inception in 1990. One of the key research themes in the department is the broad area of technological innovation and change both within organizations and at the sectoral and societal level. One thing that has increasingly struck us is the wide variety of social science disciplines which are concerned with this issue but how little interaction or debate there often appears to be between them. One of our objectives in putting together this edited volume has, therefore, been to provide a forum in which different perspectives on innovation, organizational change and technology can be articulated and encouraged to interact.

We sought to lay the foundations for this volume at a workshop held at Brunel in September 1995, attended by an invited audience of about 30 people. We would like to acknowledge the financial support given to the workshop which was jointly sponsored by the Department of Management Studies and the Centre for Research on Innovation, Culture and Technology (CRICT) at Brunel. In organizing the workshop and producing this volume we also need to record our thanks to a number of individuals. First, Steve Woolgar, Jon Clark, Christian Koch and Janes Wickham who chaired some of the workshop sessions and made lively and informed suggestions, both during and after the workshop, about the content of this volume. Second, to all the other participants in the workshop for their contributions; and, above all, the authors for their time and efforts in making both the workshop and this volume possible. Finally, we must thank Donna Baston for helping us organize the workshop, the series editors – in particular David Preece for his encouragment and support – and the famous 'Coopers Curry' which sustained workshop participants in a style they will long remember!

Contents

Figures

Figure 8.2 appears by permission of Oxford University Press and Figure 10.1 by permission of Cambridge University Press

Contributors

Richard Badham is professor in the BHP Institute for Steel Processing and Products, and head of the research programme on Managing Innovation and Change Across Cultures (MICAC) at Wollongong University, Australia.

David Buchanan is professor of organizational behaviour at De Montforte University, Leicester. He is author and co-author of numerous books, including *Organisational Behaviour: an Introductory Text* (Prentice-Hall, 1991) and *The Expertise of the Change Agent: Public Performance and Backstage Activity* (Prentice-Hall, 1992).

Paul Couchman is senior research fellow at the Centre for the Management of Integrated Technological and Organisational Change at Wollongong University.

Patrick Dawson is senior lecturer in organizational studies at Adelaide University, Australia. He is author of *Organizational Change: A Processual Approach* (Paul Chapman, 1994), co-author of *Quality Management: the Theory and Practice of Implementing Change* (Longman, 1995), and author of *Technology and Quality: Change in the Workplace* (ITP, forthcoming).

Keith Grint is lecturer in management studies and fellow in organizational behaviour at Templeton College, Oxford. His books include *Management: A Sociological Introduction* (Polity, 1995) and *The Sociology of Work* (Polity, 1991). He is also co-editor of *The Gender-Technology Relations* (Taylor & Francis, 1995) and co-author of *The Essence of the Machine: Work, Organisation and Technology* (Polity Press, 1996).

Martin Harris is lecturer in the management studies department at Brunel University. He has written papers on technology and organization for several journals and is writing a book on the social implications of information and communications technologies.

Stephen Hill is professor of sociology and pro-director of the London School of Economics. He is the author of *Competition and Control at Work* (Heinemann, 1981), co-author of *The Dominant Ideology Thesis* (Allen and Unwin, 1980), *Sovereign Individuals of Capitalism* (Allen and Unwin, 1986) and co-editor of *Dominant Ideologies* (Allen and Unwin, 1990). He is editor of *The British Journal of Sociology*.

Paul Jackson is lecturer in management studies at Brunel University. His doctoral thesis is entitled *Telework: Theories and Issues* (unpublished, Cambridge University, 1994). He is visiting research fellow at the Work and Organizational Research Centre, Tilburg University, Netherlands.

Ian McLoughlin is reader in management studies at Brunel University. He is co-author of *The Process of Technological Change* (Cambridge University Press, 1988), *Technological Change at Work* (Open University Press, 1988, 2nd edn. 1994) and *Enterprise Without Unions: Industrial Relations in the Non-Union Firm* (Open University Press, 1994).

Roderick Martin is professor of organizational behaviour and director of the Glasgow University Business School. He is author or co-author of nine books, including *New Technology and Industrial Relations in Fleet Street* (Oxford University Press, 1981), *Bargaining Power* (Oxford University Press, 1992) and *Managing the Unions* (Oxford University Press, 1996).

John Storey is professor of human resource management at the Open University Business School. His publications include *Cases in Human Resource and Change Management* (Blackwell, 1996), *Human Resource Management: A Critical Text* (Routledge, 1995), *Developments in the Management of Human Resources* (Blackwell, 1992) and *New Wave Manufacturing Strategies* (Paul Chapman, 1994). He is editor of the *Human Resource Management Journal*.

Leslie Willcocks is fellow in the Oxford Institute of Information Management and lecturer in management studies at Templeton College, Oxford. He is co-author of *Computerising Work* (Paradigm, 1987), *Rediscovering Public Services Management* (McGraw Hill, 1992), *Information Management* (Chapman & Hall, 1994) and *Investing in Information Systems* (Chapman & Hall, 1995). He is also editor in chief of the *Journal of Information Technology* and visiting professor in information systems at Amsterdam University.

Robin Williams is co-ordinator of socio-economic research on technology at the Research Centre for the Social Sciences, Edinburgh University. He is co-author of *Expertise and Innovation* (Oxford University Press, 1995).

Paul Willman is professor of organizational behaviour and industrial relations at the London Business School. He is author of *Technological Change, Collective Bargaining and Industrial Efficiency* (Oxford University Press, 1986) *Union Business: the Management of British Unions in the Thatcher Years* (Cambridge University Press, 1993).

Introduction: understanding innovation, organisational change and technology

Ian McLoughlin and Martin Harris

Technological innovation and technology-related organisational change have been a pivotal theme in social scientific research agendas since the mid-1970s and are a recurrent topic in policy-making and practitioner circles (see e.g. Office of Science and Technology, 1993). These issues have been a long-standing focus of interest for a wide variety of disciplines, such as innovation studies, technology management, organizational sociology, industrial relations and the sociology of technology. The object of this edited collection is to draw together key insights from the work of leading academic researchers in many of these fields. Our aim is twofold: firstly to explore new ways of understanding the relationship between technology and organizational change, particularly where the ideas of one discipline such as organizational sociology are able to interact with others, such as innovation economics or the sociology of technology. Secondly, we subscribe to the view that there is no inevitable divorce between theory and practice, and believe that such dialogues are capable of better informing organizational practice – or to put it another way, can be of relevance to users.

The brief for the contributors to this volume has not been an easy one. They have been asked to supply 'state of the art' research papers accessible to a broadly defined student audience. As such, many of the arguments contained in the individual chapters will not be immediately accessible to the novice without some orientation and priming. One of our intentions in this introductory chapter, therefore, is to provide an 'intellectual map' which, while not describing the academic terrain in all its undulations and other topographical detail, will provide enough 'sharp relief' to let the reader understand and locate particular contributions in their broader context.

We will use the first part of this introductory chapter to discuss three questions. The answers to these are necessarily varied, and they provide the intellectual and substantive starting point for the chapters which follow. These questions are:

- What is technological innovation?
- What is the nature of technological and technology-related organizational change?
- What is technology and what does it do?

WHAT IS TECHNOLOGICAL INNOVATION?

Technological innovation has been defined in a number of ways (Roy, 1986). In some usages it has been seen as almost synonymous with the term invention, or new technology-based product or production processes (e.g. Burns and Stalker, 1961). In others, following Schumpeter (1939), it is seen as a key 'milestone' in the process which begins with the invention of a new product, process or system and concludes with the diffusion of this artefact within a given population of 'users'. In the most often cited version of this view, Freeman (1982) defines 'innovation' as the point of 'first commercial application of a new process or product'. Here, a distinction is normally made between product and process innovation, the former involving incorporating new technology into new or existing products (or services), whereas the latter involves adopting new technology in the actual production of new products (or services). In practice, however, this distinction has proven increasingly difficult to draw and it probably makes more sense to regard them as opposite ends of a continuum rather than as mutually exclusive categories of innovation (Gattiker, 1990, p. 20).

Markets, innovation and expertise

Underlying this concept of technological innovation and its associated problems is the question of 'who is the mother of invention' – that is, do innovations occur as the result of a technology push or a market pull? In the popular imagination it is the former that seems to be the most convincing explanation. The growth of large-scale productive organizations has been accompanied by the advent of specialised R&D departments whose purpose is to develop new products and processes. R&D departments in this purely descriptive sense can be regarded as the literal source of innovation. However, it has also been argued that innovation owes less to the brilliance of inventors, their organization and management, and rather more to the way the market generates demands for new products and processes. For Freeman (1982) neither of these explanations is convincing and both fail to account for the view that technological capabilities and market needs may be 'matched' together within the innovation process. Thus Freeman argues that:

Innovation is essentially a two-sided or coupling activity . . . . On the one hand, it involves the recognition of a need or more precisely in economic terms, a potential market for a new product or process. On the other hand, it involves technical knowledge, which may be generally available, but may also often include new scientific and technological information, the result of original research activity. Experimental development and design, trial production and marketing involve a process of 'matching' the technical possibilities and the market. The professionalization of industrial R&D represents an institutional response to the complex problem of organizing this 'matching', but it remains a groping, searching and uncertain process. (1982)

As Freeman's last sentence implies, the notion of innovation as a coupling of innovations to changing market needs raises a number of important issues. For example, what are the relations between marketing and other functions whose activities may have a direct bearing on research, design and development (RD&D)? How can RD&D itself be most effectively managed and in particular the skills, knowledge and expertise of the professional occupations which constitute it be best developed and deployed? What kind of institutional and regulatory frameworks are most appropriate to support RD&D activities and the 'supply side' creation of technological expertise by education systems and labour markets?

The diffusion of innovations: technological trajectories and paradigms

Conventionally, innovation economists have been concerned with the rate of diffusion, that is the extent and pace at which an innovation, once proven a commercial success, is taken up by others in the market place. A whole variety of issues emerge here, ranging from relatively simple questions of measurement, to rather more complex issues of explaining why some firms, regions, or countries adopt innovations more quickly than others, through to macro-level attempts to develop predictive models of diffusion.

In the past a distinction has frequently been made between incremental and radical innovations. The former implies more or less continuous marginal changes to existing products or processes. The latter involves discontinuous events (such as the application of new ideas generated through R&D) which produce entirely new products or processes. For some, these distinctions can be linked to a product life cycle effect where radical product and process innovation is subsequently followed by incremental innovations (Abernathy and Utterback, 1978). This distinction has frequently been found wanting in practice (Clark and Staunton, 1989) and this has prompted attempts to develop a broader taxonomy of technological innovations (Pavitt, 1984).

Of particular importance here is the work by the 'neo-Schumpeterian school', who have sought to build on the work of economist Joseph Schumpeter (1939). The neo-Schumpetarian approach combines policy work on technical change in all its aspects with a highly distinctive theoretical orientation which features technology as a key variable in social and economic transformation. This includes work on natural 'technological trajectories' (Nelson and Winter, 1982; Dosi, 1982; Pavitt, 1984) and the shift to a new 'techno-economic paradigm' (Dosi, 1982; Freeman and Perez, 1988). A central feature of this approach is the explanatory status accorded to technological knowledge, and the view that the sources and directions of technical change are heavily influenced by technological 'trajectories'. Technical change unfolds along 'pathways', derived partly from the possibilities inherent in the technology itself, and partly from the technological strengths of innovating firms. Thus Nelson and Winter argue that,

> 'natural trajectories', particularly in industries where technological advance is very rapid, seem to follow advances in a way that appears somewhat 'inevitable' and certainly not fine tuned to the changing demand and cost conditions. (1982, p. 57)

The appeal of the related idea of a technological paradigm is that it provides a 'structural' account of the process through which technical innovation leads to economic development. Dosi summarizes the position thus:

> In particular there appear to be technological paradigms . . . performing a similar role to scientific paradigms. The model tries to account for both continuous changes and discontinuities in technological innovation. Continuous changes are often related to progress along a technological trajectory while discontinuities are associated with a new paradigm. (Dosi, 1982, p. 147)

According to this view economic growth will increasingly occur around a radically new micro-electronics based 'techno-economic' paradigm. The shift is enabled by a 'bandwagon' effect whereby pioneering firms initially develop new technological innovations to produce new products or incremental innovations in existing products. New firms and industries 'spin off' from these pioneers to manufacture and sell new products which are subsequently bought and adopted as process innovations by more mature firms who do not have the expertise to develop these innovations themselves.

Significantly, the nature of such changes is not just technological. The revolution in micro-electronics also implies changes in organizations, management structures and institutions. The paradigm shift in the underlying techno-economic system is closely associated with the highly influential concepts of 'flexible specialization' (Piore and Sabel, 1979) and 'lean production' (Womack *et al.*, 1990). These models relate organizational, managerial and institutional changes to changing market and technological conditions. They also link directly to a number of organizational sociological issues which are considered below.

Diffusion or innofusion?

How realistic is it to view the process of technological innovation as concluded once a product achieves its first successful commercial application? This question has been raised by James Fleck (1987), who has coined the term 'innofusion' to refer to an activity where innovation occurs during the diffusion of a product or process beyond the point of first successful adoption. This idea has particular implications for concepts such as technological trajectories and technological paradigms since it suggests that much of what occurs in these respects may owe less to the 'natural' and 'inevitable' properties said to be 'inherent' in technologies and rather more to how adopting firms assimilate and apply these capabilities. This is particularly so when innovation involves what Fleck terms 'configurational' as opposed to 'generic' technologies.

The distinction can be illustrated by considering a simple artefact such as the bicycle. This can be regarded as a generic technology in that it is a 'recognizable and more or less standard system for human-powered transport' where all possible user requirements and information about the circumstances of use are largely anticipated in the design of the system before first adoption. While individual users will fine tune or customize their cycles to suit their particular requirements and purposes, these acts amount to 'adjusting the parameters' rather than fundamentally 'altering the essential character' of the system. Configurational technologies, by contrast, do not possess generic qualities which allow them to be applied with only minor adjustments by other users. Rather, configurational technologies are largely shaped in each application by user requirements and the specific circumstances in which they are to be used, or as Fleck puts it they

> essentially comprise more or less unique assemblies of components, some standardly available, others specially developed, built up to meet the particular requirements of user organization (1993, p. 19).

Significantly, many micro-electronic information and computing technologies have turned out to have configurational rather than generic characteristics. Fleck points to the example of the industrial robot. Originally its inventor envisaged it as a generic technology which could be applied 'off the shelf' to replace human workers doing any physical manipulation task. In practice, more or less different types of robot models and configurations have emerged in user organizations specific to local requirements and circumstances. These configurations cannot be readily applied elsewhere by other users to do different tasks. These observations thus turn our attention directly to what occurs within adopting organizations, and in particular highlight the importance of choices concerning the implementation and the actual operation of new technologies.

WHAT IS THE NATURE OF TECHNOLOGICAL AND TECHNOLOGY-RELATED ORGANIZATIONAL CHANGE?

The idea that firms are primarily driven by technological and competitive imperatives to innovate and have little choice in the matter if they wish to survive has had considerable influence. In particular it has conditioned the way organizational sociologists and others have sought to understand the impacts or effects of computer-based technological change on variables such as skills, job content, work organization, employee attitudes and behaviour and organizational structure and design (see e.g. Blauner, 1964; Woodward, 1980). However, the idea of an unyielding technological and commercial imperative has increasingly been viewed as problematic, in particular since it tends to evaluate the role of such things as management and worker attitudes, existing organizational structures and cultures, industrial relations and so on, in relation to their propensity to either facilitate or impede innovation. Where these factors are seen as barriers to this all-important process remedial action is normally recommended which aims to improve either management education and training or communications with workers and unions, so as to achieve the appropriate understanding of commercial realties and technological requirements.

The trouble with this, as Wilkinson (1983) notes, is that technology is characterized:

> as a neutral input to individual production systems, the motivation behind its introduction being purely competitive, and its effects, apart from the improvement of the competitive position of the firm or nation-state, being largely incidental. (1983, p. 9)

> Moreover, technological and technology-related organizational change are assumed to be largely a matter of adaptating to the inherent and unavoidable requirements of technology and the need for commercial survival. Such 'technological determinism' has attracted various criticisms (see McLoughlin and Clark, 1994, pp. 41–2).

The first problem area concerns the 'political' nature of technological change. Technological innovations are seen to arise in a more or less neutral way out of the activities of inventors or professional research and development laboratories. However, critics argue that the form and direction of technological innovation should be seen as a product of the direct influence of social and political factors, not least the interests of the state and employers.

Second, those who believe in a technological imperative assume that managers play the role of unreflective 'messengers' whose task is to read the technological and commercial signals emanating from the firm's environment and take appropriate adaptive action – for example promoting R&D research in an area of new technology, or developing new products in response to changing market trends. However, critics argue that managers should be seen as 'creative mediators' whose decisions and choices critically influence the ways in which particular technological and market options are selected for development.

The final area of contention concerns the implicit assumption that technological innovation is inevitably of benefit to all, if not in the short term, then certainly in the long term. Employers, management, workers and unions are held to have a common interest in ensuring technological progress. However, technological innovation may be an area over which interests diverge, or where co-operation in respect of particular changes is conditional rather than given. If new technologies are designed and used to serve particular interests, and if organizations are seen, not as arenas of consensus, but rather the locus of conflict, then disagreement over particular technical changes may be seen as an inevitable and legitimate feature of organizational life, and not as the aberrant consequence of bad communications, poor management or 'Luddite' unions.

Fordism and post-fordism

Some of these points have been addressed by radical or critical organizational sociologists, in particular those influenced by Harry Braverman's (1974) work derived from the Marxist theory of the labour process theory (see, for example, Knights et al., 1985; Knights and Willmot, 1988; Thompson, 1989). For writers working in this tradition, technological innovation is shaped by the social and economic characteristics of capitalist societies – particularly by the need to generate profits or accumulate capital. One consequence of this is that management will seek to find ever more effective ways of controlling employees' behaviour and productive efficiency. According to Braverman and other labour process writers, this was achieved in the early part of the 20th century by adopting the techniques of scientific management pioneered by Frederick Winslow Taylor and Henry Ford, whose ideas continue to manifest themselves in the working assumptions of production engineers, managers, systems analysts and work study experts. Taylorism involves a radical separation of conception and execution. Those in control of organizations seek to de-skill operators' work, either by eliminating the need for direct human intervention by automation, or by using new technologies to break jobs down into fragmented tasks which require little or no conceptual ability or autonomous intervention by workers.

The extent to which work has been 'Taylorised' and subject to a 'Fordist' production paradigm of this type has been hotly disputed. Indeed, the temperature in his debate has been raised by the arguments, noted above, that new 'post-Fordist' production paradigms are emerging, based on principles such as 'flexible specialization' or 'lean production', to replace those of 'scientific management' and 'Fordism'. The Fordist paradigm, it has been claimed, has flourished in the context of particular market, technological, organizational and job/employment characteristics (see Sabel, 1982; Piore and Sabel, 1984; Wood, 1989). Mass production requires large investments in dedicated plant and equipment. For this to be profitable the markets for mass-produced products must be both large and have a stable pattern of demand which allows them to absorb high volumes of standardized products over time. The large-scale organization, utilising Taylorist methods of work design and managed through an adversarial industrial relations system, is the dominant organizational form.

There is the general agreement that Fordism (a concept based on a much broader set of factors including stable growth rates, corporatist industrial relations, welfare capitalism and mass production, and mass consumption) began to unravel from the early 1970s onwards (Harvey, 1989). The capacity of large organizations to maintain high levels of productive efficiency has been fatally undermined (Sabel and Piore, 1984; Hall and Jaques, 1989; Lash and Urry, 1987). Domestic demand for consumer goods has been saturated in the advanced industrial nations, leaving home markets unable to absorb further increases in output. Corporations must respond by seeking new markets in both developed and developing nations. Moreover, efforts to engage in global competition have failed to restore productive efficiency. Instead, the growth points of national economies – often small- and medium-sized enterprises which clustered together in particular regions – have been those which have eschewed the Fordist approach. These firms have taken advantage of flexible capabilities and characteristics of micro-electronics-based technological innovations to cut the cost of producing customized – as opposed to mass market – goods and services.

In a situation where product markets are characterized by instability and uncertainty, firms seek to generate product and process innovations which will meet the new 'fragmented' pattern of demand. The organizational forms associated with pursuing this objective are typically small-scale producers linked by tightly-knit industrial networks to each other and to larger producers which they supply. These organizations are non-hierarchical, adopt skill-based job designs, and are based on more co-operative employee relations. Further, as similar product market conditions begin to confront larger organizations, they too will seek to exploit new technological innovations, and they will adopt similar organizational forms by downsizing, replacing Taylorist work designs with team-based systems, newly 'empowered' workers and delayered managerial structures. An important consideration here is the issue of national context. According to Piore and Sabel some national economies will be more disposed to move towards this new production paradigm of 'flexible specialization' than others. For example, those with adversarial industrial relations systems will find it harder than those where the basis of co-operative employer-employee relations already exists. Thus, 'the balance of power between labour and capital' will 'have to be fought out country by country' (1984, p. 277).

A number of commentators have questioned these ideas. Pollert (1991) argues that movement towards flexible forms of work organization is a manifestation of free market ideology which will further deregulate labour markets and undermine working conditions. Hyman (1991) has argued that the concepts of Fordism and post-Fordism are too general and 'grandiose' to add anything useful to any serious analysis of late capitalism. It has also been argued that mass production, although strategically important, has never been an all-pervasive feature of capitalist societies and that much productive activity has always been undertaken under craft conditions and/or in small organizations (Smith, 1991; Tomaney, 1994; Coriat, 1991). Moreover, Taylorism is not synonymous with mass production, but can and has been extensively applied in small batch production and within small organizations. Similarly, the techniques of flexible production can be applied in mass production settings. These points suggest that the distinction between mass production and flexible specialization, compelling though it may be, is difficult to sustain both conceptually and theoretically (see Amin, 1994; Kumar, 1995, pp. 36–65).

Strategic choice and organizational politics

A common feature of Fordist and Post-Fordist models of technological and technology-related organizational change is that, despite protestations to the contrary, they retain a strong flavour of change within organizations as an essentially adaptive activity dictated by broader economic and technological factors. An alternative framework is provided by the notion of strategic choice (Child, 1972). The concept highlights the key role played by organizational politics and divergent stakeholder interests in shaping the organizational outcome of technological change where external factors are regarded not as determining, but rather as contextual referents for decision-makers. This view has influenced a broad range of contemporary research on the implications of new computing and information technologies and has stressed the need to view such change as more or less unique organizational processes rather than as an external force imposing change on organizations (see e.g. Wilkinson, 1983; Boddy and Buchanan, 1983; Clark *et al.*, 1988; Batstone *et al.*, 1988; Dawson, 1994; Preece, 1995; Hill *et al.*, this volume).

Conceptualizing technological change as a process means that it makes little sense to try and find or predict uniform effects or outcomes *a priori* of an analysis of change processes. Moreover, there is doubt about whether it is useful to see such processes as merely mediating the generalized tendencies and globalized trends presented in generic models such as Fordism and flexible specialization. The price, as critics have not been slow to argue, is that a preoccupation with process separates technical-organizational change issues from the broader 'structural' context and in consequence outcomes tend to be explained in highly localized, 'idio-syncratic' terms (Reed, 1985; Whittington, 1988; Elger, 1990). Finally, the role of technology itself as a factor influencing change also tends to be downplayed or ignored in the face of what are seen as the far more significant social and political processes shaping the organizational outcomes of change (Clark *et al.*, 1988).

The management of change

Despite these criticisms processual models of change have a number of advantages over more conventional understandings of the problem of change management. Dawson (1994, this volume) argues, for example, that management literature has in the past been dominated by 'one best way' organizational development models of change. Many of these draw on the work of Lewin (1951), who saw change management essentially as an activity of 'unfreezing' existing behaviour and attitudes which restrain change, executing the desired change programme, and then 'refreezing' by positively reinforcing desired outcomes and encouraging the internaliza-tion of appropriate attitudes and behaviour.

Although fitting quite neatly with ideas about managers' need to adapt their organizations to prevailing commercial and technological impera-tives, such prescriptions are less helpful in circumstances – such as those described in models of post-Fordism – where market and technological change may be in perpetual transition. Here attempts to 'freeze' desired outcomes in an organization may be rendered pointless. Moreover, merely modifying the approach to suit different types of contingent circumstance may still maintain an overly rational model of change management (Daw-son, 1994, pp. 13–22). Process models aim to contextualize such concerns by seeking to reveal and explain the political nature of change-management decisions, how the history of such decisions is socially constructed by those who took them, and by seeking to deconstruct the 'rationalizations' pre-sented to justify them (Dawson, 1994, p. 25).

However, in the face of such claims Buchanan (1994) argues that, while process models may improve our understanding of organizational change, they still remain weak when it comes to informing its management. The very complexity of organizational change, it seems, mitigates against detailed prescriptions which might improve managerial or other agents' capacity to intervene in shaping its outcomes. As a result the field has been open to exponents of what Buchanan and Storey (this volume) call 'listology', whose shorthand prescription, although often compelling and 'user friendly', rarely offers anything ultimately convincing and may occasionally be simply misleading to the practitioner. On the other hand, the elegant models of change constructed out of academic research leave the 'user' equally short-changed through their inaccessibility and failure to address issues of practical concern.

Nevertheless, the insights offered by a process perspective would seem to provide an opportunity for rethinking the role of the change agent and the effectiveness of change-management initiatives. If change is essentially a political process requiring the capacity to mobilize power resources, it would seem to have specific and important consequences for the kinds of expertise required by change management. It can also be argued that these observations apply to a broader constituency of organizational actors who may seek to influence particular change issues (e.g. trade unions, consultants, action researchers) (Buchanan and Boddy, 1992; Buchanan and Storey, this volume; Badham *et al.*, this volume).

WHAT IS TECHNOLOGY AND WHAT DOES IT DO?

As we have seen, organizational sociologists have criticized those who have viewed technology as 'neutral' and as having an inevitable determining impact on organizations. This criticism is shared by a number of schools of thought which have sought to reveal and explore the manner in which technology is 'socially shaped'. Moreover, by attacking the idea that the form of technologies is necessarily fixed and derived from an immutable technical logic, the social shaping approach opens up new possibilities for both the design of artefacts and systems and for the redirection of programmes of technological innovation. Just as organizational sociologists have stressed the role of choices in, and the negotiated nature of, the organizational outcomes of technological change, the social shaping perspective points to the socially contingent form of technology itself.

Social shaping approaches can be divided into two broad categories (Edge, 1995, p. 16). First, there are those which start from social context and 'work inwards' to show how this shapes technology and the direction of technological innovation. Second are those which start from technology and 'work outwards' to show the social content of a particular technological development. The latter 'social constructivist' approach can be divided between those which see social shaping as essentially a process whereby a technology becomes 'stabilized' and those which question any notion of 'stabilization' and the idea of technology having 'effects' on society.

The socio-economic shaping of technology

The first approach is the most widely represented and is exemplified in a variety of studies and research programmes (see e.g. MacKenzie and Wacjman, 1985; Williams, this volume) which have sought to identify factors which influence the form or content of technology, the direction of technological innovation and its ultimate social effects. Technology is accorded a specific causal status: the idea that technology has 'causal effects' on society is rejected, but the idea of technological influences on the shaping of technology itself is not. A precondition of much technological innovation is in fact seen to be existing technology. Indeed, it is the development and gradual evolution of existing technological know-how, rather than 'flashes of inspiration' among inventors, which is responsible for much new technology (MacKenzie and Wacjman, 1988). Similarly, in so far as new technologies are increasingly required to operate within or in the context of broader technological systems, there are constraints on how they can be designed. Indeed, Hughes (1987) argues that much innovative effort can be seen as driven by the 'reverse salients' within large-scale technological systems – that is, those parts of the system which are perceived as problematic to its overall functioning.

Obviously, the social shaping perspective does not see technological factors alone as shaping technology. Indeed economic factors such as costs are inextricably bound up with the technological lines of reasoning which identify problems such as 'reverse salients'. More generally, questions of profit and loss play a crucial role in decisions over both which and where technological innovations take place. However, as MacKenzie and Wacjman (1985, pp. 15–18) argue, the frameworks of economic calculations which guide technological innovation are themselves socially shaped and, to a highly significant extent, social factors can override economic calculation in determining particular lines of development. For example, while all societies have to come to a view over the costs and benefits of a particular technological design or choice, this judgement is highly variable, differing for example between advanced western capitalist economies, the former state socialist societies and developing societies. What is 'economically rational' about technology is informed in each of these circumstances by the social context in which decisions are made.

Even within a particular social setting, economic calculation about technological innovation is not straightforward and is open to challenge. For example, proponents of an innovation will present calculations which show the benefits of change in a positive light, opponents will highlight damaging costs, and the basis on which they do this will reflect the values, goals and norms behind the particular social interest they are seeking to advance or defend. Finally, while firms' capacity to escape profit and loss criterion is circumscribed, the state can play a particularly important role in promoting, underwriting or supporting lines of technological development which private enterprise calculates as economically unviable. Here explicitly social factors can have an enormous influence on technology and innovation. For example, the most important source of state influence is through its sponsoring of military technology. As MacKenzie and Wacjman note, war and the threat of war have 'coerced' the shape of technology. In doing so, otherwise insuperable economic barriers to technological development have often been overridden by military interest, ultimately permitting civilian technologies to develop – in areas such as nuclear power, air transport and electronics – which would otherwise have remained dormant and unrealized (1988, pp. 18–20).

Another important consideration is how gender relations impinge on our understanding of technical change. In patriarchal societies the role of women relative to men is undervalued in both domestic and work settings. In the latter sphere this means that women may be seen as a cheaper resource then men. Feminists have argued that this is one factor which shapes technology in a gendered fashion. For example, technologies may be designed to permit the replacement of skilled, high cost male workers with less skilled and lower cost female workers. Cockburn (1983), for example, has argued that this has been a major social factor shaping the design of new typesetting technology in newspaper publishing. In a similar vein, technological 'know-how' is frequently parcelled out according to a prevailing division of labour where men dominate technological and scientific occupations. It follows, some argue, that the technology that they produce is inevitably a reflection of male dominance in the labour market and society at large.

The social construction of technology

The second type of social shaping approach owes its origins to developments in the sociology of scientific knowledge (SSK). Here attention has recently been turned to the social construction of technological knowledge embodied in individual artefacts and systems (Edge, 1995). The SSK approach has been to study fields of scientific development with a view to revealing key points of ambiguity in the development of a scientific knowledge base, for example a controversy between competing theories seeking to explain an empirically observed phenomenon. The resolution of these ambiguities has a significant impact on the future development of the area of scientific knowledge concerned. For sociologists of science these 'branch points' can be understood as providing the social actors concerned with 'interpretive flexibility'. Explaining why one interpretation prevails over others is a key objective of SSK. Moreover, 'strong' versions of the SSK approach take the view that it requires impartiality as to the truth or falsity of the beliefs under scrutiny. That is, all knowledge claims must be treated 'symmetrically' where the explanation for their creation or ultimate acceptance rests not on the natural world but on social factors.

Pinch and Bjiker (1987) have applied these principles in developing their social construction of technology (SCOT) approach. They argue that technological development can be regarded as a 'closure' process during which the form of an artefact or system becomes 'stabilized' as consensus emerges among key social groups with a stake in the design. This view contrasts with the linear models of technological innovation presented by many innovation economists. These assume a rational progression through successive stages of invention, design, and first adoption. Explanations for an innovation's success or failure largely ignore the technology itself, which is treated as a 'black box' with essentially 'given' characteristics and capabilities. In Pinch and Bjiker's perspective the lid of the 'black box' is 'lifted' to show the way social factors explain why some variants of a design 'die' and others 'survive'. Thus, rather than being uni-linear, technological innovation can be regarded as 'multi-directional' and only in hindsight can it be made to look to have followed a rational sequential progression through distinct stages, or to have a 'natural' 'trajectory' (Bjiker and Law, 1992).

In reality technological innovation involves competition and conflict between the views of relevant 'social groups' who share a particular set of understandings and meanings concerning the technology, such as designers, consumers, protestors. These groups will have different views about the most appropriate design of the artefact, or even whether it is a desirable technology at all. Various technical, social, legal and moral solutions are likely to be articulated as possible ways of resolving the problem of the most appropriate form of the technology. In this context, technological artefacts can be viewed as both culturally constructed and interpreted, not only in how technology is thought of but in its design.

Metaphors, texts and technology

Others informed and influenced by the SSK perspective question the idea that technologies and systems become 'stabilized'. They argue that any notion of technology having fixed and discrete requirements, capabilities and characteristics, even if they are the product of some kind of social shaping, is erroneous. For example, Grint (1995) identifies three problems with the idea. First, the idea that antecedent circumstances such as the interests of particular social groups are built-in or embodied in technologies is ambivalent. This would seem to suggest that technologies are neutral up to the point that a social and political veneer is attached. Second, the idea that the nature of such antecedent circumstances is easily identified is problematic. In practice, identifying the interests and motives of technology's designers is itself subject to interpretive flexibility. Finally, the idea that 'stabilized' technologies can have independent effects retains the idea that it is the requirements, capabilities and characteristics of technology which have the effect, rather than the historically and culturally bound interpretations of what the effect of a particular technology is. What in effect happens, argues Grint, is that the social shaping perspective seeks to replace technical determinism in explaining the content of technology with social and political determinants whose embodiment in the technology explain the effects it has. However, in doing this 'the object of critique is *technological* determinism, not technological *determinism*' (original emphasis, 1995 p. 194).

These objections are illustrated by Grint in relation to the notion that one element of the social shaping of technology involves 'gendering', whereby male dominance in the design process and division of labour is manifested in technologies which contribute to the oppression of women, both in the domestic sphere, and more centrally for the concern of this volume, in work organizations. He suggests that if a technology has 'masculine' characteristics built into it, this presupposes a time when the technology was supposedly 'neutral' and 'gender-free'. 'When was this and what does such a technology look like?' asks Grint and 'who says it was neutral but is now masculine?' (1995 p. 193). To put it rather crudely for Grint, just because the owners, management and design staff of typesetting machinery manufacturers are predominantly male does not mean that the technologies they produce are thus 'gendered' by masculine motives and interests. Furthermore, neither can it be assumed that the resultant technology has clear and unambiguous effects such as enabling management to adopt organizations to 'feminize' and de-skill particular jobs. A further example of this line of argument is provided in relation to the effects of Business Process Re-engineering (BPR) in organizations provided by Willcocks and Grint's contribution to this volume.

What is at stake here is made a little clearer by the introduction of the challenging idea that technologies are best regarded in metaphorical terms as 'texts'. As Morgan (1986; 1992) has argued, much of organizational life – if not social life in general – can be understood in the metaphors or images which underpin the way we make sense of our experience. Much common sense and theoretical understanding of the relationship between organization and technology is predicated on a view of organizations based on the metaphor of the machine. In this view much of the management task is represented as an attempt to get the human and organizational machinery to function in a way conducive to the efficient operation of the material technology of production. However, different views or representations of the organization and technology relationship can be generated using alternative metaphors (see Jackson, this volume).

According to Woolgar, the text metaphor provides a highly potent antidote to the prevalent 'common sense' view that machines and systems have inherent technical capacities.

> The metaphor of system as text is a vivid way of stressing the 'interpretatively flexible' nature and capacity of a machine or system. In this view, machines (systems) do not have inherent capacities; rather their capacity and capability is the upshot of users' interaction with the system. In the post-modern adage, it is the reader who writes the text. Relatedly, the notion of machine/system as text encourages us to view processes of design, construction and use of systems as analogous to processes of producers writing and consumers reading text.
>
> (Woolgar, 1994 p. 205).

While encouraging us to see the nature of technologies as in their reading, Woolgar argues that this does not mean that any reading is possible. Rather, in practice only a limited number of readings can by offered, the number of which is delimited by 'the organization of the text', which suggests certain readings and denies others. The key point, as Jackson argues below, is that we are no longer concerned with what a technology 'can and can't do' but rather with the way in which such accounts are socially represented.

The utility of these rather abstract and counter-intuitive ideas is illustrated by Woolgar with reference to 'the problem of the user' in computer system design. Traditionally this problem has been viewed as one of devising appropriate methods by which system designers can 'capture' the requirements of the user and thereby design a system to meet them. In practice, 'capturing' users' requirements is highly problematic – they do not know what they want, they know but cannot articulate, they keep changing their minds, say different things to different people etc. One response to this is to try and develop more sophisticated methods of requirements analysis which, in particular, recognize the social, not just technical, dimensions of the problem. However, an alternative approach is to view the users' inability to say unambiguously what they require as being a result, not of their shortcomings or those of method, but rather the different ways in which what computer systems can and cannot do are represented to them by the various groups – hardware engineers, product engineers, project managers, salespersons, technical support, purchasing, finance and control, legal personnel etc. These groups are all architects or authors of the system 'text', and in 'writing' the text contribute to a definition of the 'reader' (user) and the parameters of their actions.

In essence, 'the whole history of a system project can be construed as a struggle to configure (that is, to define, enable and constrain) the user'. Configuring the user is problematic because the system architects' knowledge about what the user is like differs from group to group and varies over time. By means of an ethnographic study of a project to produce a new range of micro-computers, Woolgar encountered several dimensions of this struggle. Of particular symbolic importance was the computer's external case. This defined the boundary of the system and the system itself prescribed appropriate methods, provided information, sources of assistance, and warnings of the consequences of inappropriate actions, which would enable the user to operate (read) the system (text) in the 'correct' fashion.

The problem with this 'extreme' relativist approach, as critics have observed, is that the influence of broader social structure and distributions of power, even organizational structure and the roles of competing stakeholder interests are viewed as superfluous to the analysis of technology and technological change (see McLoughlin, this volume). It is as if the 'lid' of the 'technological black box' has been 'opened' but then shut firmly tight behind the analyst (Williams and Russell, 1987).

CONTRIBUTIONS TO THIS VOLUME

The individual chapters which follow have been organized into four categories. Chapters 1 and 2 are concerned with the nature of technological innovation. Chapters 3, 4 and 5 explore the role of social choice and politics in technological and technology-related organizational change. Chapters 6 and 7 deal with the issue of change management. Chapters 8, 9 and 10 are concerned with the social shaping of technology.

Choice, knowledge and markets

The study of technological innovation has long occupied a theoretical no-man's land between economics and sociology. The first two chapters of the book are concerned with analysing how economics has traditionally treated questions of innovation and seeking to find new ways to extend our understanding of this process through the application of more sociologically based ideas and concepts. In chapter 1 Harris argues that critics of the 'neo-Schumpetarians' have frequently overlooked the behavioural origins of their school in the work of Nelson and Winter (1982), and the fact that the broad sweep of neo-Schumpeterian ideas has always included an 'institutional' strand of analysis. The chapter begins by considering the part played by technological knowledge and firm-specific trajectories within the neo-Schumpeterian approach. Leading members of the school have emphasized the role of 'institutional' factors in 'macro' level accounts of technical change and economic growth. However, the trajectory view of technological change is an inherently determinist one, and it is apparent that questions of power, political process and strategic choice have been marginalized within 'micro' level investigations of the innovating firm. These theoretical issues reflect the 'conceptual divide' which separates innovation theory from organizational sociology. However, in a further twist Harris argues that there exists an equally significant division over 'technological content' and 'social process' issues within the neo-Schumpeterian school. The problem is not a substantive one of bringing 'political process' and 'technological content' aspects together, but an essentially conceptual one of explaining the nature and extent of managerial choice and social action. The chapter concludes by arguing that the perception of a single divide obscures and oversimplifies the range of positions held within innovation theory and organizational sociology. Further conceptual development will depend on a willingness to overcome the intellectual barriers which isolate one school of thought from another.

In chapter 2 Paul Willman responds to this challenge by seeking to provide new purchase on a key issue for innovation economics by introducing ideas from organizational sociology. Willman's focus is firms' ability to benefit exclusively from their own innovative activity. For many economists such features are problematic since they appear to constrain the transfer to competitors through the market mechanism of information about how a product or process works. From a purely sociological perspective such organizational capabilities are intrinsically interesting because they point to idiosyncratic features of organizations, not least in circumstances where firms find it difficult to appropriate all, or any, benefits from their innovative activity. This problem of internal appropriability points to the particular competencies that firms possess – the routines, expertise, know-how, formal and tacit knowledge – that have been accumulated and routinized over time, and critically the manner in which this knowledge base is organized and managed. Internal appropriability may be highly problematic where tacit knowledge accumulates – say on the shop floor – but is inaccessible to the owners of firms because those who possess it have no incentive or motivation to share it. The success of Far Eastern firms can, conversely, be attributed to providing such incentives and motivation to its workforce, thus promoting the full appropriation of innovation's benefits, that is the firm's ability to take advantage of a given technology, or elements of technological knowledge. He argues that firms protect innovation benefits by bundling together technical and business knowledge. The chapter shows the ways in which sharing economic rents may generate conflicts. The paper closes with some observations on the organizational strategies available for managing appropriability.

Flexibility, re-engineering and collaboration

Chapters 3 and 4 examine two of the most influential organizational models of technical change to emerge since the mid 1980s. Chapter 5 turns attention to the increasingly important phenomenon of inter-organizational collaboration between system designers and system adopters.

The background to Chapter 3 is provided by the debate between Fordists and post-Fordists introduced above. Most analyses within the debate ignore or obscure the role of managerial choice. The chapter by Hill *et al.*, seeks to redress this by considering managerial choices in five companies employing advanced manufacturing technology. Case study evidence is used to show that product innovation, process technology and changes in organizational design (in both managerial structures and work organization) are not linked together in the ways advocated by proponents of the new 'post-Fordist' paradigm. Rather, it was found that companies choose both to respond more flexibly to their product markets and to limit the range of products manufactured through value engineering and other forms of rationalization. Moreover, traditional issues of productivity and costs, which tend to be overlooked in the new paradigm, co-exist with the recent concern with flexibility and continue to exert a strong influence on managerial choice. New technology has not resolved the old dilemma of efficiency versus flexibility or productivity versus innovation. The paper concludes by discounting the possibility that 'societal effects' (manifested in the pressure on British managers to demand exceptionally high rates of return when they allocate internal funds for investment in new capital equipment) may account for these findings. These findings suggest processes and outcomes which are very different from those assumed by the new technological paradigm.

In Chapter 4 Willcocks and Grint focus on the business process re-engineering (BPR) phenomenon. This represents the latest in a series of managerial 'recipes' which advocate the use of technical-organizational changes. BPR is closely associated with information technology, which often features as the main 'driver' for transforming organizations. The implementation of new systems is often used to symbolize a radical break with previous organizational practices and the advent of a 'radically new, discontinuous future'. The authors link BPR to the idea that well established practices may be subjected to a process of 'deracination' whereby existing organizational norms and traditions are uprooted. The expression 'don't automate, obliterate' effectively captures the rhetorical force of the prescriptions offered by proponents of BPR. However, although BPR is widely discussed in practitioner circles, examples of effective implementation are scarce. Willcocks and Grint attribute this to the multi-disciplinary nature of the required changes which embrace divergent organizational practices and functions. Large-scale radical changes of the sort carried out within BPR programmes, by their very nature, involve risks and uncertainties, which are added to by the technological dimension within many projects. Willcocks and Grint observe that, despite this complexity, BPR practitioners have called for 'organizational politics' to be 'cast aside'. However, BPR is itself an inherently political process which involves projecting 'utopian' visions, managing competing human and organizational interests and portraying information technology as a 'thing' to which organizational processes have to be 're-engineered'. Thus, while the goals of BPR are portrayed as 'depoliticizing' the organization, the means of achieving this are explicitly political.

The politics of the change process is also emphasised by Patrick Dawson in Chapter 5. He notes that the complexity of much technological innovation and the problems of dealing with the human and organizational dimensions have prompted an increase in collaborative work between firms and in allegiance with government-supported agencies. One important area of such collaboration is between system designers and system adopters. Frequently the former task is accomplished in isolation from the context in which adoption occurs. As a result, technical constraints can be built into a system which limits the room for manoeuvre when human and organizational concerns come to the fore during implementation in an adopting organization. However, such collaborative work serves to highlight further the political dimensions of change where projects both extend across organizational boundaries and embrace new constituencies of organizational interest group. In such circumstances conventional 'Lewinian' 'unfreeze/freeze' models of change have little to offer. Dawson illustrates his argument with reference to two detailed case studies of long-term collaboration between the Australian Commonwealth Scientific and Industrial Research Organisation (CSIRO) and two industrial partners – General Motors Holden and Boeing – to develop new software for cellular manufacturing installations. In each collaboration the substance and context of change generated a series of political issues, the resolution of which were the determinants of the speed, direction and outcomes of the projects.

The practice of change management

The authors in Chapters 6 and 7 are concerned with whether the complexities identified by the process approach, in particular the ubiquity of politics, the non-sequential nature of change and the influence of context, necessarily mean that little of practical import can be said to 'the user' concerning the management of, or intervention in, change.

Buchanan and Storey confront this problem head on in Chapter 6. They suggest that to move beyond the construction of ever more complex models of the change process will require a shift of academic attention from analysing the multi-faceted and multi-variate nature of the 'field' on which the change process takes place. Instead, more attention will have to be devoted to the role of the 'players' themselves in actually bringing about change. Their chapter focuses on the skills required by 'change agents', those actors who present themselves as the 'drivers' of change. In itself this focus is not new. Much attention is played in the technology management literature, for example, to the role of 'product/change champions' in steer-ing technological innovations along a linear sequential path of change through the application of project management and planning techniques. However, Buchanan and Storey present a much more complex model of agency which challenges the conventional view of change management. Rather than focus on individual actors roles they argue for a more pluralistic concept of change agency. This focuses on the plurality of organizational actors involved, including not only those trying to drive change but those resisting or agnostic towards it; the plurality of types of change driver, ranging from those who initiate change, through those who co-ordinate and facilitate, to the final owners; the plurality of change phases from initiation, through implementation to routine operation; and the plurality of change roles performed at different points such as 'vision-ing', 'analysing', 'team-building', 'implementing', 'fixing' and 'auditing'. The skills of change agency revolve around being able to take and knowing when to switch these roles. As such, change management can best be regarded as an 'orchestrated performance' rather than a 'carefully planned and managed process'.

The following chapter by Badham *et al.* provides a different kind of insight into change management from the perspective of the action researcher. The authors here are concerned with the management of 'vul-nerable' 'socio-technical' projects such as the introduction of team-based cellular manufacturing. The vulnerability of such projects derives from the complexity and radical nature of the technical and organizational changes involved. Such projects cut across horizontal and vertical boundaries in the organization and impinge on the interests of stakeholders, presenting both threats and opportunities. Such projects are highly susceptible to organizational and micro-political disturbances. Their management requires at least two distinct capacities on the part of the change agents. First, they need to have a good understanding of the organizational and human dynamics of the technological change entailed – especially in what the authors call the 'configurational activity' involved in adapting generic models of new production techniques to local operating and environmental conditions at national, sectoral, company and workplace levels. Second, they require a self-awareness of their role as 'configura-tional intrapreneurs' shaping both the technical and social outcomes of change. Much of this activity is political, involving such activities as enrolling and re-enrolling support for the project, building alliances, overcoming resistance and 'selling' the idea, progress and achievements of change. Aspects of this configurational activity are illustrated with reference to a second set of Australian experiences derived from the 'SMART' manufacturing techniques project conducted in three organiza-tions in the early 1990s by action researchers from Wollongong University. The authors conclude by fleshing out their configurational process model and suggesting this as a basis for developing more effective tools and techniques for managing vulnerable change projects.

Social shaping, representation and interpretive flexibility

The final three chapters are concerned with the social shaping of technology. In chapter 8 Robin Williams explores the implications of the social shaping school for technology and work organizations. In contrast to instrumental views, which see technology as being readily adapted to organizational goals, Williams' analysis is concerned with the tensions and contradictions in the mutual shaping of technology and work organization. As such he is critical, as are many of the other authors in this volume, of 'universalistic' conceptions of technology and its effects within organizations that are central to concepts such as 'technological trajectories' and 'technological paradigms'. Neither, however, does he put forward a view that technologies can be readily shaped within their adopting context to suit local conditions and contingencies. Rather there are a range of potential contradictions and disjunctures between technological capabilities and organizational requirements, where neither 'what the technology can do' and 'what the user wants' is self evident or clear cut. Instead we have a subtle process of mutual shaping which occurs both within and beyond the adopting organization over time. Aspects of this analysis are explored in accounts of the development of three types of technology: computer-controlled machine tools, computer-aided production management (CAPM) systems, and 'inter-organizational network' systems based around the electronic interchange of data to allow such things as automatic billing and invoicing. Williams' final observations alert us to a shift in the process by which technology and work organizations are mutually shaped. Increasingly, the capacity to 'configure' technologies locally is providing the user with more options to customize and personalize technologies and systems and to shape the way technology affects their own work.

In Chapter 9 Paul Jackson adopts a more radical constructivist perspective to explore the importance of IT-related innovation and new forms of organization often referred to in concepts such as 'teleworking', 'networked organizations' and 'virtual organizations'. He argues that these concepts – and related notions such as the 'digital economy', 'information age' and 'post-industrial society' – are based on a new metaphor through which organizations can be understood and constituted. This 'information system' metaphor differs from the more mechanistic metaphors underpinning our understanding of organizations in the past. Rather, it draws on certain features of advanced information systems – most significantly the ability to manipulate and communicate data – to challenge how we understand the physical and temporal dimensions of organizations, and the nature of work 'within' them. Jackson examines three analytical dimensions, each of which provide the basis for particular 'representations' of information technology: first, the representation of IT as a space-transcending technology; second the role of IT in providing representation for work tasks to be mediated electronically; and thirdly the representation of organizational time and space in certain IT-related concepts. Jackson's point is that it is not the technology itself which brings forth these ways of representing what it can and cannot do. Rather, these are the product of social and cultural processes and it is perfectly possible for alternative representations to be 'imaginized'. Indeed, the challenge for organizational practitioners and policy makers is to seek out new forms of representation in order to better inform innovative organizational practice. At the same time, Jackson alerts us to the way in which existing distributions of material and political power are likely to skew future 'images' of 'virtual' organizations and the 'information society' in certain directions.

Finally, in Chapter 10 McLoughlin takes issue with both organizational sociologists who over-stress social choice at the expense of technological influences and those of a constructivist persuasion who seek to eliminate any distinction between the 'technical' and the 'social'. McLoughlin argues that there has been a tendency in much recent research by organizational sociologists to emit the 'technology baby' with the 'determinist bathwater'. As a result the technical conditions enabling and constraining organizational decisions are not fully explored or explained, although often noted at least implicitly in the findings of empirical studies. He re-states the argument of Clark *et al.* (1988) that a specific attempt to provide a conceptual basis for understanding the 'effects' of a given technology or system has its merits in fleshing out the strategic choice/processual approach. The extent to which the constructivist perspective can add to this project is less clear cut. The relative arguments are explored through a rehearsal of the debate between Kling and Woolgar/Grint concerning whether technical artefacts have fixed and immutable capacities. For Kling, whereas the way these artefacts are used is a matter of social context and choice, what they can be used for is a function of certain inherent technical capacities. For Woolgar/Grint, what artefacts can and cannot do is entirely a social argument. They have no inherent, fixed technical capacities. McLoughlin accepts that the notion of 'interpretive flexibility' has considerable analytical utility. However, there are material limits to the representational options that are available to organizational actors. He draws on Orlikowski's (1992) notion of technology as both an objective reality and as a socially constructed product to underpin this conclusion.

Postscript

There is much debate in organizational sociology concerning the incommensurability or otherwise of different paradigms and the extent to which different theoretical approaches either have or should be 'closed'. A similar debate has not been waged in relation to the study of innovation, organizational change and technology. Our premise in commissioning this volume has been that different theoretical traditions have examined these issues largely in isolation. In our view this has not been a healthy state of affairs and many opportunities for creative theoretical and empirical work, as well as the identification of new insights for the practitioner, may have been missed. None of the contributions in this volume seek to make any kind of case for a synthesis of the approaches of innovation economists, organizational sociology and the sociology of technology. Indeed, given the variety of positions within each of these broad traditions the task of synthesis within each would be highly problematic. Our aspiration is more modest, but nonetheless potentially fruitful: to encourage 'cross-border' co-operation where there are areas of common interest and sufficient common ground to warrant it. Many of the contributions to this volume offer positive pointers along these lines and map out the basis on which future research agendas might usefully be constructed.

References

Abernathy, W.J. and Utterback, J. (1978) Patterns of industrial innovation, in *Technology Review*, June–July, pp. 40–47.

Amin, A. (ed.) (1994) *A Post-Fordist Reader*, Blackwell, Oxford.

Batstone, E., Gourlay, S., Levie, H. and Moore, R. (1988) *New Technology and The Process of Labour Regulation*, Clarendon Press, Oxford.

Bjiker, W.E. and Law, J. (eds.) (1992) *Shaping Technology/Building Society: studies in socio-technical change*, MIT Press, Cambridge, Massachusetts.

Blauner, R. (1964) *Alienation and Freedom*, University of Chicago Press, Illinois.

Boddy, D. and Buchanan, D.A. (1983) *Organisations in the Computer Age: Technological Imperatives and Strategic Choice*, Gower, Aldershot.

Braverman, H. (1974) *Labour and Monopoly Capital: The Degradation of Work in the Twentieth Century*, Monthly Review Press, New York.

Buchanan, D.A. (1994) *Theories of Change*, Business School research series paper, Loughborough University.

Burns, T. and Stalker, G. (1961) *The Management of Innovation*, 2nd edn, Tavistock, London.

Child, J. (1972) Organisation structure, environment and performance: the role of strategic choice, in *Sociology*, 6 (1), pp. 1–22.

Clark, J., McLoughlin, I.P., Rose, H. and King, J. (1988) *The Process of Technological Change: new technology and social choice in the workplace*, Cambridge University Press.

Clark, P. and Staunton, N. (1989) *Innovation in Technology and Organisation*, Routledge, London.

Cockburn, C. (1983) *Brothers: Male Dominance and Technological Change*, Pluto Press, London.

Coriat, B. (1991) Technical Flexibility and Mass Production, in *Industrial change and Regional Development* (eds G. Benko, and M. Dunford) Belhaven, London.

Dawson, P. (1994) *Organizational Change: A Processual Perspective*, Paul Chapman, London.

Dosi, G. (1982) Technological paradigms and technological trajectories, in *Research Policy*, 11 (3).

Edge, D., (1995) The social shaping of technology, in *Information Technology and Society* (eds N. Heap, R. Thomas, G. Einon, R. Mason and H. Mackay), Sage, London, pp. 14–32.

Elger, T. (1990) Technical innovation and work re-organisation in British manufacturing in the 1980s: continuity, intensification or transformation? in *Work, Employment and Society*, special issue, pp. 67–101.

Fleck, J. (1987) *Innofusion or Diffusation: The nature of technological development in robotics*, Department of Business Studies working paper 87/9 Edinburgh, University.

Fleck, J. (1993) Configurations: crystallising contingency, in *International Journal of Human Factors in Manufacturing*, 3 (1), pp. 15–36.

Freeman, C. (1986) The diffusion of innovations – microelectronics technology, in *Product Design and Technological Innovation* (eds R. Roy and D. Wield), Open University Press, Milton Keynes, pp. 193–200.

Freeman, C., Clark, J. and Soete, L. (1982) *Unemployment and Technical Innovation*, Frances Pinter, London.

Freeman, C. and Perez, C. (1988) Structural crises of adjustment, business cycles and investment behaviour, in *Technical Change and Economic Theory* (eds G. Dosi, C. Freeman, R. Nelson, G. Silverberg, and L. Soete), Pinter, London, pp. 38–66.

Gattiker, U.E. (1990) *Technology Management in Organisations*, Sage, London.

Grint, K. (1995) *Management: A Sociological Introduction*, Polity Press, Cambridge.

Harvey, D. (1989) *The condition of Postmodernity*, Blackwell, Oxford.

Hughes, T.P. (1987) The evolution of large technological systems, in *The Social Construction of Technological Systems: new directions in the sociology of history and technology* (eds W.E. Bijker, T.P. Hughes, and T.J. Pinch), MIT Press, Cambridge, Massachusetts, pp. 51–82.

Hyman, R. (1991) *Plus ça change?* The theory of production and the production of theory, in *Farewell to Flexibility*, (ed. A. Pollert), Blackwell, Oxford.

Jaques, M. and Hall, S. (eds) (1989) *New Times*, Lawrence and Wishart, London.

Knights, D. and Wilmott, H. (eds) (1988) *New Technology and the Labour Process*, Macmillan, London.

Knights, D., Wilmott, H. and Collinson, D. (1985) *Job Redesign: Critical Perspectives on the Labour Process*, Gower, Aldershot.

Kumar, K. (1995) *From Post-Industrial to Post-Modern Society*, Blackwell, Oxford.

Lash, S. and Urry, J. (1987) *The End of Organised Capitalism*, Polity Press, Cambridge.

Lewin, K. (1951) *Field theory in Social Science*, Harper & Row, New York.

MacKenzie, D. and Wajcman, J. (1985) Introductory essay, in *The Social Shaping of Technology* (eds D. MacKenzie, and J. Wajcman), Open University Press, Milton Keynes, pp. 2–25.

McLoughlin, I. and Clark, J., (1994) *Technological Change at Work*, 2nd edn, Open University Press, Buckingham.

Morgan, G. (1986) *Images of Organisation*, Sage, London.

Nelson, R. and Winter, S. (1982) *An Evolutionary Theory of Economic Change*, Harvard University Press, Boston.

Orlikowski, W.J., (1992) The duality of technology: rethinking the concept of technology in organisations, in *Organisational Science*, 3 (3), pp. 398–427.

Pavitt, K. (1984) Sectoral patterns of technical change: towards a taxonomy and a theory, in *Research Policy*, 13, pp. 83–94.

Pinch, T.J. and Bijker, W.B. (1987) The social construction of facts and artifacts: or how the sociology of science and the sociology of technology might benefit each other, in *The Social Construction of Technological Systems: new directions in the sociology of history and technology* (eds W.E. Bijker, T.P. Hughes, T.J. Pinch), MIT Press, Cambridge, Massachusetts, pp. 17–50.

Piore, M.J. and Sabel, C.F. (1984) *The Second Industrial Divide: Possibilities for prosperity*, Basic Books, New York.

Pollert, A. (1991) The orthodoxy of flexibility, in *Farewell to Flexibility?* (ed. A. Pollert), Blackwell, Oxford, pp. 3–31.

Preece, D. (1995) *Organisations and Technical Change: Strategy, Objectives and Involvement*, Routledge, London.

Office of Science and Technology (1993) *Realising Our Potential*, HMSO, London.

Reed, M. (1985) *Redirections in Organizational Analysis*, Tavistock, London.

Roy, R. (1986) Meanings of design and innovation, in *Product Design and Technological Innovation*, (eds R. Roy and D. Wield), Open University Press, Milton Keynes, pp. 2–7.

Sabel, C. F. (1982) *Work and Politics: the Division of Labor in Industry*, Cambridge University Press.

Schumpeter, J. (1939) *Business Cycles*, McGraw-Hill, New York.

Smith, C. (1989) Flexible specialisation, automation and mass production, in *Work, Employment and Society*, 3 (2), pp. 203–20.

Smith, C. (1991) From 1960s automation to flexible specialization: a *déja vu* of technological panaceas, in *Farewell to Flexibility*, (ed. A. Pollert), Pinter, London.

Thompson, P. (1989) *The Nature of Work*, 2nd edn, Macmillan, London.

Tomaney, J. (1994) A New Paradigm of Work Organization and Technology? in *A Post-Fordist Reader* (ed. A. Amin), Blackwell, Oxford.

Whittington, R. (1988) Environmental Structure and Theories of Strategic Choice, in *Journal of Management Studies*, vol. 25, no. 6, pp. 521–36.

Wilkinson, B. (1983) *The Shop Floor Politics of New Technology*, Heinemann, London.

Williams, R. and Russell, S. (1987) Opening the black box and closing it behind you: on microsociology in the social analysis of technology, PICT working paper 3, Edinburgh University.

Williams, R. and Edge, D. (1992) *Social shaping reviewed: research concepts and findings in the UK*, PICT working paper series, Edinburgh University.

Womack, J.P., Jones, D.T. and Roos, D. (1990) *The Machine That Changed the World*, Maxwell MacMillan International, Oxford.

Wood, S. (ed.) (1989) *The Transformation of Work?*, Unwin Hyman, London.

Woodward, J. (1980) *Industrial Organisation: Theory and Practice*, 2nd edn, Oxford University Press.

Woolgar, S. (1994), Rethinking requirements analysis: some implications of recent research into producer-consumer relationships in IT development, in *Requirements Engineering: social and technical issues*, (eds M. Jirotka and J.A. Goguen), Academic Press, New York.

Chapter 1

Technological knowledge, strategic choice and the neo-Schumpeterian school

Martin Harris

INTRODUCTION

Innovation theorists and industrial sociologists have long been divided on the nature and sources of technological change, and there has been particularly sharp disagreement about how technical change occurs as a process within organizations. The conceptual divide which separates sociological accounts of technical change from innovation theory derives from the two approaches being rooted in quite separate intellectual traditions. Many sociological accounts of technological change focus on organizational choice and the 'political' nature of the processes observed. The neo-Schumpeterian school, by contrast, has developed analyses based on large-scale statistical aggregation. This school also makes extensive use of metaphors from the natural sciences. Despite these differences, some have argued that innovation theory and industrial sociology may well be converging on a view of the innovating firm which puts firm strategy, technology and organizational learning at the centre of the analysis (Pavitt, 1990; Coombs *et al.*, 1992). It is one thing, however, to suggest a common research focus on the innovating firm and quite another to explore the theoretical 'no-man's land' which divides perspectives whose assumptions about the very nature of the phenomena observed may be fundamentally different. An important part of the theoretical debate turns on the ways in which determinist (or 'structural') accounts of technical change are counterposed with accounts which emphasize the part played by human agency, organizational process, and social choice. The theoretical 'state of the art' is greatly complicated, moreover, by the fact that this divide separates various positions and stances *within* the two schools.

The first part of this chapter introduces a number of key concepts which form the basis for the neo-Schumpeterian school. The second part examines the theoretical underpinnings of the natural technological trajectories concept (Dosi, 1982; Pavitt, 1984) and relates this to the broader corpus of neo-Schumpeterian work (Freeman and Perez, 1988; Dosi *et al.*, 1988; Pavitt, 1987, 1990). This part of the critique shows that social and behavioural aspects feature centrally in Nelson and Winter's treatment of the innovating firm. It is argued, further, that leading members of the school give institutional factors a key explanatory role in macro level accounts of technical change and economic growth. However, the institutional strand of analysis coexists with the overtly determinist natural technological trajectories concept.

Part three explores an attempt by one of the most prolific and influential members of the neo-Schumpeterian school to incorporate technological content and social process accounts of technological change in a theory of organizational learning (Pavitt, 1986a, 1986b, 1987, 1989, 1990). A critical review of these developments reveals that questions of power, political process and strategic choice continue to be marginalized within micro level investigations of the innovating firm.

The chapter relates a range of substantive innovation issues to the conceptual divide which separates innovation theory from industrial sociology. However, it can be argued that there exists an equally significant division over technological content and social process aspects within the neo-Schumpeterian school. The chapter concludes by arguing that both innovation theory and sociological treatments of these issues can productively be augmented by more cogent theorizations of strategic action and social choice.

THE NEO-SCHUMPETERIAN SCHOOL: CONCEPTUAL FOUNDATIONS

The neo-Schumpeterian school of innovation theory (Schumpeter, 1950) is associated with the debate on 'demand pull' and 'technology push' explanations for the technological revolutions since the late 18th century. The conceptual breadth of the neo-Schumpeterian project is exemplified by the work of the economic historian and innovation theorist Nathanial Rosenberg (1982), whose research has consistently illuminated work carried out at the Science Policy Research Unit (SPRU). Other leading contributors include Freeman (1990), Dosi (1982), Pavitt (1984), Mowery and Rosenberg (1979) and Perez, (1983). A common theme is the argument that the successive waves of technical change which have underpinned economic growth cannot be explained by the workings of markets and the speculative activities of investors.

A central feature of the neo-Schumpeterian project is the explanatory status accorded to technological knowledge, and the view that the sources and directions of technical change are heavily influenced by technological 'trajectories' (Nelson and Winter 1982; Dosi, 1982; Pavitt, 1984). Technical change unfolds along 'pathways', which derive partly from the possibilities inherent in the technology itself, and partly from the technological strengths of innovating firms.[1]

Nelson and Winter's work on the 'evolutionary' theory of the innovating firm (1982) showed that technological knowledge has two interconnected properties: it is specific in application and cumulative in development. This view of technological change is rooted in an explicitly behavioural theory of the firm. Nelson and Winter draw on March and Simon's concept of bounded rationality (1958) and they reject the profit-maximizing imperatives of neo-classical economics. The innovating firm is characterized by technological changes which derive from routines, rules of thumb, and heuristics. Firms do not 'search' for innovations in a general pool or stock of knowledge, all of which is equally assimilable by them. The innovating firm is seen as a repository of cumulative knowledge about particular products and processes.

A significant part of the neo-Schumpeterian project is concerned with the part played by technology in stimulating long-run social and economic change. This work puts institutional factors at the centre of the analysis (Freeman, 1990; Perez, 1983, Rosenberg, 1982). However, the broader institutional strand of analysis has coexisted with the overtly mechanistic and deterministic technological trajectories concept (Dosi, 1982). The technological trajectories concept forms part of the theoretical underpinning for the view that microelectronics will pervade every economic sector and form the basis for a new techno-economic paradigm (Freeman and Perez, 1988; Freeman et al., 1993). As noted in the introduction to this volume, the shift to the new paradigm signals a complete break with the past, the decline of the old industrial centre economies, and new sources of economic growth[2, 3].

THE TRAJECTORY CONCEPT, NATURALISM AND SOCIO-INSTITUTIONAL FACTORS.

The technological trajectories concept is a central feature of Neo-Schumpeterian projects. The concept was originally derived from 'technology push' explanations of technological change. Thus Pavitt argues that:

> Explanations of the sources and rate of technological change based entirely on economic signals and institutional constraints have limited explanatory power. For example they neglect accumulated mechanical and production engineering skills in explaining international variations in the adoption of robots. Or they are tempted to explain the advent of flexible automation as a rapid response in the 1970s to the requirements of slow and volatile economic growth, and to neglect the contribution of the semiconductor, and of twenty years of accumulated experiment in learning in CAD, NCM and robots.
>
> (Pavitt, 1986a, p.51)

Technological knowledge and selection processes are at the heart of this analysis. Sociologists have long argued that the focus on the technological content of innovation obscures the investigation of organizational process. Trajectory analyses (see for example Dosi, 1982) make little or no mention of contending stakeholders or institutional barriers to change. Managerial choices are concerned mainly with the purely technical aspects of production, and changes in the organization of production are subordinated to an immanent logic of technological development. In the earliest formulations, (e.g. Pavitt, 1984) the treatment of the technical change process has a strongly teleological, or predictive flavour. The implication is that an end state can be predetermined from a series of factors which define a starting point. Technological change is seen to unfold along quasi-natural lines of development. However, in Pavitt (1990) (reviewed in the next section) the technical change process receives a less structural treatment and becomes much more dependent on managerial learning and strategic choice.

The issue of naturalism in trajectory analyses is discussed by MacKenzie (1990), who points out that the notion of a trajectory is important in two main respects.

> First, technological change does show persistent patterns: for example the increasing mechanisation of manual operations, the growing miniaturisation of microelectronic components and the increasing speed of computer calculations. Second, it is clear that neither the formulation of R+D projects nor their evaluation can proceed in an unconstrained way . . . it makes theoretical and empirical sense to assume that the result of today's searches is both a successful new technology and the natural starting place for the searches of tomorrow.
>
> (1990, p.8)[4]

For MacKenzie the problem with the notion of a trajectory lies rather with:

> 'the particular connotation of the mechanical metaphor. That connotation is that when technological change is initially set on a given path (for example by the selection of a given 'paradigm') its development is then determined, in some unexplicated sense, by technical forces alone. The connotation is strengthened by the attachment of the adjective 'natural'. As Dosi puts it: Once a path has been selected and established it shows a momentum of its own . . . which contributes to define the directions towards which the problem solving activity moves: those are what Nelson and Winter define as 'natural trajectories' of technological progress.
>
> (1990, p.9)[5]

The naturalistic assumptions on which trajectory concept is based are thus difficult to reconcile with those analyses which regard social choice as central to the understanding of the technical change process. However, the neo-Schumpeterian school is by no means confined to the trajectory concept, and it is necessary at this point to take a somewhat broader view of the various ways in which social choice features in the broad sweep of neo-Schumpeterian ideas. The question of socio-institutional process and social choice receives explicit treatment in Dosi (1982), Perez (1983) and in Freeman (1990). In arguing 'The Case For Technological Determinism' Freeman associates the microelectronic revolution with the emergence of a new 'techno-economic paradigm'. Jon Elster (1983) is cited to the effect that

> the new paradigm emerges not from rational choice nor from cumulative small modifications, but from new combinations of radical innovations.
>
> (1990, p.5)

The advantages offered by these new technological systems are such that their adoption

> becomes a necessity in any economy exposed to competitive economic, social, political and military pressures. These pressures are such that it is very hard to be non-conformist once the new paradigm has crystallised.
>
> (1990, p.16)

The title of the article gives the impression that Freeman is advancing a structurally determined, historically inexorable view of scientific and technical advance. This is consistent with the trajectory approach and with the notion that technology might contain the seeds of its own *telos*, or logic of development.

However, political choice far from being marginalized or disregarded, is accorded key significance, despite the advent of the new 'techno-economic paradigm'. This is illustrated in Freeman's discussion of Perez (1983). Perez argues that the new techno-economic paradigm involves a new 'best practice' set of rules and customs for engineers and designers, entrepreneurs and managers which differ in many important respects from the previously prevailing paradigm. According to Freeman:

> The development of the new paradigm, based on product, process and organisational innovations offers tremendous scope for employment generating investment and productivity gains. However, these are conditional on institutional adaptation and structural change. This in turn entails changes in the organisational structure of firms, skill mix and management.
>
> (1990, p.15)

The focus on structural adaptation is reminiscent of the population ecology school of organizational change (Aldrich, 1979; Hannan and Friedman, 1977) – but the political contingency re-asserts itself towards the end of the paper. The strength of the new paradigm notwithstanding:

economies, firms and regions will prosper depending on the 'goodness of fit' between their activities and the characteristics of the new technologies, and there is scope for a variety of social and economic solutions in achieving this good match. The present period is characterised by the continued search for satisfactory solutions. The outcome depends on the lucidity, strength and bargaining force of the conflicting groups involved.

(1990, p.17)

In this way Freeman and Perez acknowledge the relevance of political processes for our understanding innovation at the broader socio-institutional level. A pervasive concern with politics and institutions is also apparent in Dosi *et al.*, (1988).

Social choice and the trajectory concept

As noted above, the idea of a natural technological trajectory, developed by Nelson and Winter (1982), Dosi (1982) and Pavitt (1984), has featured as something of a leitmotif for the neo-Schumpeterian school. Nelson and Winter's original analysis of trajectories and selection processes allowed a variety of commentators to highlight the key issue of firm-specific technological knowledge, thus avoiding the constraining influence of narrowly defined 'demand pull' explanations. The trajectory idea has since become synonymous with dynamic, and apparently self-sustaining, patterns of technological change. However, one can question whether configurations of technological knowledge really do 'evolve' over time. There are several analyses which argue that trajectories are extrapolated from the actions of innovators 'after the event' (Clark and Staunton, 1989)[6], and that the unfolding of 'configurational technologies' is heavily influenced by both managerial expectations and existing institutional and social structures (Fleck, 1987; MacKenzie, 1990; Harris and Howells, 1994).

Whatever the merits and demerits of the trajectory concept, the discussion of Freeman and Perez indicates that social choice is an essential feature of the wider neo-Schumpetarian project. Technological knowledge is seen to have its own historically specific character, and particular choices about which pathways are selected are embedded in the workings of institutions. It is important to note that Freeman (1990) and Perez (1983) are concerned with technological change and its relation to social and institutional structures broadly defined. Analysis of the part played by social and political choice *within* the innovating firm does not feature in this work. The question of firm-specific knowledge, organizational learning and the 'strategic' management of innovation features in the work of Pavitt (1986, 1990), and it is to this that we now turn.

STRATEGIC MANAGEMENT, POLITICS AND LEARNING IN THE INNOVATING FIRM

The contributions by Pavitt (1986, 1990) represent a noteworthy attempt to develop a 'strategic' view of innovation and organizational learning. Pavitt (1986) indicates the importance of the strategic dimension for the study of technical change, and he endorses Nelson and Winter's (1982) view of the innovating firm as a repository of technological knowledge. Uncertainties are reduced in ways which reflect the accumulated experience of the past, and firm-specific knowledge is combined in judgements about the future in the formulation of strategy.

The 1990 contribution incorporates a critique of 'political process' and 'technological content' approaches to technological change. The process school (exemplified by the work of commentators such as Child, 1972 and Pettigrew, 1973 and 1985) emphasizes actors' constructions of context and views organizational processes in 'political' terms. The content school is concerned with technological trajectories, and the effect of core activities and firm size on innovation.

According to Pavitt, the process view makes a valid contribution to research in this field, but tends to reduce our understanding of innovation to the study of political infighting and the interplay of factional interests. Pavitt outlines a new research agenda, calling for social scientists and innovation theorists to collaborate on empirical investigation and theory-building. The content view:

> neglects the context within which, and the processes whereby, technological strategies are generated, chosen and implemented. . . . Given that technology strategy involves many functions and professions, as well as major uncertainties, its formation and implementation are bound to be choice territory for the advocacy, battles and negotiation that analysts in the process school of strategy give such great importance.
>
> (1990, p.86)

However, the main thrust of this argument is directed at the political process approach:

> Previous research shows that technology strategy cannot be described solely in terms of political negotiation between hostile professional and functional tribes.
>
> (1990, p.87)

Pavitt uses two arguments to support his attack on the political process theory of organizational change. First,

> in the market system the ability to satisfy users needs better than the alternatives on offer is the ultimate measure of success and profitability,

and consequently the allocation of power and prestige within the firm.

(1990, p.87)

Second, the work of Dodgson (1989) is used to posit an alternative to the political process view of innovation, based on the notion of organizational learning. This, it is argued, provides a more convincing account of technical change than the concern with advocacy and functional in-fighting:

> innovation research has come to robust conclusions about the factors associated with successful innovations . . . in addition to the quality of the technical work, these include strong horizontal linkages among functional departments, with outside users, and with other sources of relevant technical expertise; and a responsible manager with experience of all the functional activities involved.

(1990, p.87)

> Either by conscious choice or by trial and error, successful innovating firms are more likely to evolve routines or rules of thumb which reflect these ingredients. Given the high uncertainties involved trial and error is inevitable in the development and implementation of innovation.

(1990, p.87)

> In addition, the ability to learn from experience whether internally (learning by doing) or from suppliers, customers and competitors (learning by using, learning by failing, reverse engineering) is of major importance in the management of innovation.

(1990, p.87)

Dodgson (1989) is quoted to the effect that

> learning from experience, thus defined, actually dissolves the distinction in the strategy debate between content, process, and contexts . . . because processes of learning about the context help to define the content of a strategy, the implementation of which in turn helps to define the nature and directions of subsequent learning processes and changes in context.

(1990, p.87)

The core argument is that:

> research has to go beyond purely political relations between functional and professional groups, to include learning from experience, and communication within and among the firms' functional elements.

(1990, p.88)

PAVITT'S THEORIZATION OF STRATEGIC CHOICE IN THE INNOVATING FIRM: A CRITICAL EVALUATION

Pavitt's (1990) contribution to the debate on strategic choice and technical change exhibits a number of distinctive strengths. His analysis demonstrates a commendable breadth and a militant disregard for disciplinary boundaries; the objective constraints on technology strategy are noted, but the 'tacit knowledge' aspect is developed at the expense of the harder, more structurally determined position elaborated in the 'Chips and Trajectories' paper. (Pavitt, 1986a)

The shift to a more 'strategic' viewpoint means that innovation becomes more dependent on the choices of those in control of the firm, and the viewpoint of contending stakeholders is acknowledged. Pavitt calls on scholars from economics, management studies, innovation theory, and sociology to develop new research agenda.

The theoretical framework for considering the 'strategic' management of innovation is provided by the adapting concepts of organizational learning, particularly those developed by Argyris and Schon (1978) and Rosenberg (1982). Pavitt includes the finance and R+D functions in his discussion of 'politics'. However, the full implications of this plurality are not followed through. Pavitt's attack on the political process perspective derives from the incorporation of work by Dodgson, which promulgates a unitarist view of the firm based on a biological metaphor (Dodgson, 1989, p. 1–23). One consequence of this is that the analysis fails to take account of the ways in which different managerial activities occur at different levels within the organization. The organizational learning processes described by Dodgson take place at the operational level. However, it can be demonstrated that many of the crucial choices and selection processes take place at the strategic level. These choices have an 'agenda-setting' influence on managerial initiatives at the operational level (Boddy and Buchanan, 1986; Hill, Harris and Martin, this volume). The organizational learning concept does little to capture this broader context of resource allocation activities and strategic decision making.

Pavitt criticizes the process approach for its tendency to reduce the study of technological change to the study of 'politics' and factional infighting, and he appears to have excluded the political dimension, preferring a functionalist theory of organizational learning which equates innovation with selection, adaptation and search processes. This takes no account of Child's (1972) work on strategic choice, a concept whose development was closely bound up with the need for a theory of the firm which was capable of transcending the determinist and reductionist aspects of functionalism[7].

Subsequent studies showed that the adoption and implementation of new production technologies is likely to involve a range of organizational actors at different levels (Child, 1972, 1984; Boddy and Buchanan, 1983 and 1986; Child et al., 1987; Child and Smith, 1987; Child et al., 1986; Wilkinson, 1983; McLouglin and Clark, 1995). Engineers, accountants and various categories of management may have markedly different objectives and thus conflict and goal divergence may be present from the earlier planning stages through the implementation phase to routine operation and monitoring. This work suggests that there is little to be gained by separating 'political process' and 'technological content' analyses of the innovation process. Organizational interests, technological knowledge, managerial expectations and occupational priorities all need to be considered by research on technical-organizational change.

CONCLUSION: POWER, KNOWLEDGE AND THE NEO-SCHUMPETERIANS

This chapter began by considering the part played by technological knowledge and firm-specific trajectories within the neo-Schumpeterian school. Leading members of the school have emphasized the role of institutional factors in macro level accounts of technical change and economic growth. However, the trajectory view of technological change is an inherently determinist one, and it is apparent that questions of power, political process and strategic choice have been marginalized in micro level investigations of the innovating firm. This tendency is reflected in the strict separation of political and learning aspects in Pavitt's consideration of strategic management and innovation. This is at odds with a large body of sociological work carried out since the early 1980s, and it fails to provide a viable account of managerial agency and social action. These oppositions form the basis for part of the conceptual divide which separates innovation theory from industrial sociology.

Nevertheless, it can be argued that a significant division over 'technological content' and 'social process' aspects exists *within* the neo-Schumpeterian school. This division has not been widely recognized, but it has been remarked on by Boyer (1988) who acknowledges the tendency for the macro-level analysis of technological paradigms, employment and economic growth to 'relapse into technological determinism' (Boyer, 1988, p. 67). It may be argued that the problem derives from the methodological issue of adapting the tools developed for macro-level analyses of technological paradigms to more finely grained change processes observed at the level of the firm (Coombs et al., 1992)[8]. However, these issues do not pose insurmountable difficulties for Nelson and Winter (1982), whose analysis of the innovating firm retains its status as the key formative influence on neo-Schumpeterian work at the micro level. Technology is represented as knowledge about products and processes rather than an independent variable with a life of its own. The emphasis on institutionalized firm-specific knowledge (MacKenzie, 1990; Willman, this volume) offers potentially fruitful links with sociological work on technical-organizational change.

Nelson and Winter's account of technological change borrows directly from March and Simon's (1958) work on the cognitive limits to rationality. The view that choices about innovation may be in large part shaped by cognitive limits is easily squared with the view that the innovation process is influenced by political factors within the organization. There is no good reason, on this view, to suppose that the 'power' and 'knowledge' elements of the problem should remain isolated within neo-Schumpeterian explanations of technical change. The significant problem is not a substantive one of bringing political process and technological content aspects together, but an essentially conceptual problem of explaining the nature and extent of managerial choice and social action. It may be appropriate, at this point, to return to a consideration of Child's (1972) formulation of strategic choice[7]. Explaining technical change by agency rather than structure highlights the key role played by organizational interests. Technical and organizational change are enabled by processes of interpretation and negotiation. External pressures for change are regarded not as determining givens, but as contextual referents which are used by stakeholders who hold particular viewpoints and perspectives. However, industrial sociology has its own conceptual difficulties and 'divides' (Burell and Morgan, 1979; Reed, 1985; Whittington, 1988; Harris, 1992) and two final qualifying points can be made. The action process approach has been criticized for its tendency to emphasize process to the point where technical-organizational change becomes separated from broader 'structural' issues. This has resulted in a tendency for outcomes to be explained in purely local 'idiosyncratic' terms[9]. A second, related point is that the action process approach should be regarded, not as the last word in the explanation of technical change, but as an intellectual departure point which may lead to further development. Recent work on 'situated practices' (Reed, 1985), organizational rationalities (Brunsson, 1982; Bryman, 1984) and 'strategy as discourse' (Knights and Morgan, 1991) offer constructive ways forward.

This chapter began by noting the existence of a 'conceptual no-man's land' which divides innovation theory from the sociological study of technological change. However, it is apparent that this does not do justice to the complexity of the terrain explored in this volume. The perception of a single divide oversimplifies and creates a distorted view of the range of positions held by various members within the two schools. Further development is certain to depend on a continued willingness to overcome rigidities and question the intellectual barriers which isolate one school of thought from another.

Notes

[1] The trajectory idea has also been applied to the intersectoral sources and channels of technological change (Pavitt, 1986a, 1986b; Pavitt et al., 1989).

[2] The view that we are experiencing an historically significant paradigm shift in the underlying techno-economic structure is part of a broader tendency to see the advent of microelectronics-based technologies in 'apocalyptic' terms (Kumar, 1995). Significantly, Christopher Freeman borrows directly from Sabel and Piore's work on Fordism, Post-Fordism and the 'second industrial divide' (Freeman et al., 1993, p. 11).

[3] Boyer (1988) illustrates the link between neo-Schumpeterian innovation theory and the structurally determinist Regulation school (Aglietta, 1979). Boyer argues that

> . . . technological determinism . . . has turned out to be a salient feature of the present recovery of neo-Schumpeterian ideas. He argues that 'a major challenge is to see if one can distinguish between two dynamics – one concerning institutional forms and the other the technological system – and then to investigate their *ex post* compatability.

[4] Child (1987) makes substantially the same point when he argues that the notion of organizational conservatism is an essential part of any theory of technology and organization. MacKenzie calls for work on the ways in which 'ethno-accountancy' impinges on product innovations. There are already a number of studies which investigate the working assumptions and organizational interests which influence the evaluation of new production technologies before their implementation (see for example Senker, 1984, Currie, 1989, Harris, 1996). Here again, the need is to examine the precise ways in which political factors and firm-specific technological knowledge influence the evaluation and implementation of new technologies.

[5] MacKenzie does not take the view that technological change can proceed in isolation from the properties of the physical world. On the contrary, he argues that these are central to our understanding of how technological change occurs. However, he does present evidence which demonstrates the ways in which technologies are socially shaped at their inception. He uses a range of technological examples, (QUERTY keyboards, microchips and supercomputers) to demonstrate the ways in which managerial expectations had a key bearing on the development of these technologies.

Rosenberg (1982) also shows the significance of expectations at US Steel where it was observed that:

> Expectations of continued improvement in a new technology may . . . lead to postponement of an innovation, to a slowing down in its rate of diffusion, or to an adoption in a modified form to permit greater future flexibility.
>
> (Rosenberg, 1982, p. 114)

[6] Clark and Staunton (1989) argue that 'trajectories' are extrapolated from the actions of innovators 'after the event'. This work supports Mackenzie's argument about the role of institutions and expectations in our understanding of the technical change process. The unfolding of 'generic technologies' is heavily influenced by existing institutional and social structures.

[7] 'Strategic' considerations of market expansion and diversification can be seen as more significant influences on growth and profitability than the 'adaptive' behaviour which are seen to determine particular decisions about structure. The

functionalist emphasis on system maintenance and external constraint is replaced by a 'political process' view which treats external constraints as open to interpretation and manipulation. Managerial agency is placed at the centre of the analysis, and the 'action process' perspective which emerged in the sociology of organizations (see Silverman 1970) can be seen as part of a wider critique of positivism. This emphasis on organizational interests had a very marked influence on subsequent work on technological change. Much of this work treats 'political' contingencies and organizational process as synonymous. (see for example Wilkinson, 1983; Boddy and Buchanan, 1983, 1986; Pettigrew, 1985)

[8] Coombs *et al.* (1992) argue that analysis common 'objects of study' like firm strategy and technology - however they argue that this is a 'temporary convergence' because the tools of analysis remain different.

[9] Reed (1985) and Whittington (1987) have argued that managerial agency is as much bound by process as it ever was by structure in these accounts of organizational change. It has also been argued that the the changes associated with the microelectronic revolution need to be situated in a broader socio-historical setting than has been acheived to date (Kumar, 1995).

References

Aglietta, M. (1979) *A Theory of Capitalist Regulation: The US Experience*, Verso, London.

Aldrich, H. E. (1979) *Organizations and Environments*, Prentice Hall, Englewood Cliffs, New Jersey.

Argyris, C. and Schon, D. (1978) *Organizational Learning*, Addison-Wesley, London.

Boddy, D. and Buchanan D.A. (1983) *Organizations in the Computer Age*, Gower, Aldershot.

Boddy, D. and Buchanan, D.A. (1986) *Managing new Technology*, Gower, Oxford.

Boyer, R. (1988) Technical Change and the Theory of Regulation, in *Technical change and Economic Theory* (eds G. Dosi, C. Freeman, R. Nelson, G. Silverberg, and L. Soete), Pinter, London.

Brunsonn, N. (1982) The irrationality of action and action irrationality: decisions, ideologies and organizatinal actions, in *Journal of Management Studies* 19 (1), pp. 29–44

Bryman, A. (1984) Organization studies and the concept of rationality, in *Journal of Management Studies* 21 (4), pp. 391–408

Burrell, G. and Morgan, G. (1979) *Sociological Paradigms and Organizational Analysis*, Heineman, London.

Child, J. (1972) Organizational structure, environment and performance – the role of strategic choice, in *Sociology*, 6 (1–22)

Child, J. (1984) New technology and developments in management organization, in *Omega*, vol. 12, no. 3, pp. 211–23

Child, J., Loveridge, R., Harvey, J. and Spencer, A. (1986) Microelectronics and the quality of employment in Services, in *New Technology and the Future of Work and Skill*, (ed. P. Marstrand), Francis Pinter, London.

Child, J., Ganter, H.D. and Kieser, A. (1987) Technological innovation and organizational conservatism, in *Technology as Organizational Innovation*, (eds J. Pennings and A. Buitendam), Ballinger, Cambridge, Massachusetts.

Child, J. and Smith, C. (1987) The context and process of organizational transformation – Cadbury Limited in its sector, in *Journal of Management Studies* (24) 6.

Clark, P. and Staunton, N. (1989) *Innovation in Technology and Organization*, Routledge, London.

Coombs, R., Saviotti, P. and Walsh, V. (1992) Technology and the firm: the convergence of economic and sociological approaches? in *Technological Change and Company Strategies* (eds R. Coombs, P. Saviotti and V. Walsh), Academic Press, London.

Currie, W.L. (1989) The art of justifying new technology to top management, in *Omega*, vol. 17, no. 5.

Dodgson, M. (1989) Introduction: technology in a strategic perspective, in *Technology Strategy and the Firm: Management and Public Policy* (ed. M. Dodgson), Longman, London.

Dosi, G. (1982) Technological paradigms and technological trajectories, in *Research Policy*, 11 (3).

Dosi, G., Freeman, C., Nelson, R., Silverberg, G. and Soete, L. (eds) (1988) *Technical change and Economic Theory*, Pinter, London.

Fleck, J. (1987) *Innofusion or Diffusation: The nature of technological development in robotics*, Department of Business Studies working paper 87/9, Edinburgh University.

Freeman, C. (1990) The case for technological determinism, in *Information Technology: Social Issues. A Reader*, (eds R. Finnegan, G. Salaman and K. Thompson), Hodder and Stoughton, London.

Freeman, C. and Perez, C. (1988) Structural crises of adjustment: business cycles and investment behaviour, in *Technical Change and Economic Theory* (eds G. Dosi, C. Freeman, R. Nelson, G. Silverberg and L. Soete), Pinter, London.

Freeman, C., Sharp, M. and Walker, W. (1993) *Technology and the Future of Europe: Global Competition and the Environment in the 1990s*, Pinter, London.

Harris, M. (1992) *Strategic Choice and the Sources of Technological Change*, unpublished Phd thesis, London University.

Harris, M. and Howells, J. (1994) *Power and knowledge in the theory and analysis of technical change: A critical review of the Neo-Schumpeterian School*, paper presented to the EASTT Conference, Budapest, August.

Harris, M. (1996) Organizational politics, strategic change and the evaluation of new production technology – the case of CAD, in *Journal of Information Technology*, 11, 1.

Knights, D. and Morgan, G. (1991) Corporate strategy, organizations and subjectivity: a critique, in *Organization Studies* 12/2.

Kumar, K. (1995) *From Post-Industrial to Post-Modern Society*, Blackwell, Oxford.

MacKenzie, D. (1990) *Economic and Social Explanation of Technical Change*, paper presented to conference on Firm Strategy and Technical Change, UMIST, 27–28 September.

McLoughlin, I. and Clark, J. (1995) *Technological Change at Work*, Open University Press, Milton Keynes.

March, J.G. and Simon, H.A. (1958) *Organizations*, John Wiley, London.

Mowery, D. and Rosenberg, N. (1979) The influence of market demand upon innovation: a critical review of some recent empirical studies, in *Research Policy*, 8, pp. 102–53.

Nelson, R. and Winter, S. (1982) *An Economic Theory of Technical Change*, Harvard University Press, Cambridge, Massachusetts.

Pavitt, K. (1984) Sectoral Patterns of technical change: towards a taxonomy and a theory, in *Research Policy*, 13, pp. 83–94.

Pavitt, K. (1986a) Chips and trajectories: how does the semiconductor influence the sources and directions of technical change? in *Technology and the Human Prospect* (ed. R. MacLeod), Francis Pinter, London.

Pavitt, K. (1986b) Technology, innovation, and strategic management, in *Strategic Management Research* (eds J. McGee and H. Thomas), John Wiley, London.

Pavitt, K. (1987) Commentary on Chapter 3 in *The management of strategic change* (ed. A. M. Pettigrew), Blackwell, Oxford, pp. 123–127.

Pavitt, K., Robson, M. and Townsend, J. (1989) Accumulation, diversification and organization of technological activities in UK companies 1945–83, in *Technology strategy and the firm: Management and Public Policy* (ed. M. Dodgson), Longman, London.

Pavitt, K. (1990) Strategic Management in the innovating firm, in *Frontiers of Management* (ed. R. Mansfield), Routledge, London.

Pennings, J. and Buitendam, A. (eds) (1987) *The Implementation of New Technology*, Balinger, Cambridge, Massachusetts.

Perez, C. (1983) Structural change and assimilation of new technologies in the economic and social systems, in *Futures* 15, pp. 357–75.

Pettigrew, A.M. (1973) *The Politics of Organizational Decision Making*, Tavistock, London.

Pettigrew, A.M. (1985) *The Awakening Giant*, Blackwell, Oxford.

Reed, M. (1985) *Redirections in Organizational Analysis*, Tavistock, London.

Rosenberg, N. (1982) *Inside the Black Box: Technology and Economics*, Cambridge University Press.

Schumpeter, J.A. (1950) *Capitalism, Socialism and Democracy*, Harper and Row, New York.

Senker, P. (1984) Implications of CAD/CAM for management, in *Omega*, vol. 12, no 3, pp. 225–31

Silverman, D. (1970) *The Theory of Organizations*, Heineman, London.

Whipp, R. and Clark, P.A. (1986) *Innovation and the Auto Industry: Product, Process and Work Organization*, Francis Pinter, London.

Whittington, R., (1988) Environmental Structure and Theories of Strategic Choice, in Journal of Management Studies, vol. 25, no. 6, pp. 521–36

Wilkinson, B. (1983) *The Shopfloor Politics of New Technology*, Heineman, London.

Chapter 2

Appropriability of technology and internal organization

Paul Willman

In business, a combination of research, and (more important) develop-ment, testing, production engineering and operating experience accumulates knowledge on the many critical operating variables of an artifact, and result in knowledge that is not only specific but partly tacit (uncodifiable) and therefore difficult and costly to reproduce.

(Pavitt, 1991a, p. 111)

INTRODUCTION

The statement that knowledge about the performance of a product or, in particular, a process is in some way embedded within specific firms and is, in consequence, costly to transfer is not difficult for organizational sociologists to digest. It sits relatively easily alongside intellectual predispositions emphasizing the idiosyncratic nature of organizations, the difficulties involved in organizational learning and the problems involved in identifying and capturing diffuse, tacit knowledge. On the contrary, the obverse – that information flows easily between firms – appears counter-intuitive. Yet appropriability of the benefits of innovation by the firm is seen as a problem by many economists, who see markets as costless means of information transfer and often assume that knowledge is primarily embodied in products and processes that may be easily copied by competitors.

Digestion is, however, not necessarily followed by the regurgitation of any theoretical basis for this position. Economists have a theoretical basis for their arguments that spillovers occur, but sociologists cannot counter with a justification for inappropriability as a natural state of affairs. In subsequent sections, I shall explore some of the issues involved, particu-larly from a sociological viewpoint. However, it is appropriate to begin with a statement of some of the key differences between economic and sociological approaches.

SOCIOLOGY AND APPROPRIABILITY

In attempting to understand the relationship between the organization of the firm, its innovative capacity and its commercial success, one is tempted to cross the boundary between organizational sociology and economics. Despite a convergence of concerns, manifested in the increasing interest among sociologists in rational choice and that of some economists with internal organizational form, there remain differences in core assumptions both about the nature of the phenomena under investigation and about the methods one might use to analyse them.

The analysis of technological change is beset with such problems. As Elster (1983) has noted, there have been two main approaches to the analysis of such change. The first, naturally favoured by economists, conceives of technological change as involving rational goal-directed activity, seeking the best option within a given innovation set. The second emphasizes the incremental, cumulative and historically-influenced nature of change in discussing evolutionary technological trajectories. Sociologists have been drawn to it, as have economists of the evolutionary school, such as Nelson and Winter (1982). The former approach has tended to sustain certain generalizations about change, perhaps at the expense of operating with rather rigid, counter-intuitive assumptions about the processes involved. Sociologists following the latter have tended to an idiographic approach, in some cases going so far as to argue that generalizations about either the process of technological change or its outcomes are impossible for theoretical reasons and that indeterminacy in outcomes is a consequence of the variable, socially created nature of the process of innovation itself. This view tends towards an almost anthropological perspective (for example, Barley, 1986). Few predictive statements are possible.

A core issue concerns the definition of the term 'technology'. For economists, 'technologies' are often considered as pieces of hardware, for example, robots, CNC machines or Bessemer converters. The diffusion of a 'technology', so defined, across a sector can then be relatively easily studied and then modelled as a series of epidemic curves (Stoneman, 1983; Davies, 1977; for a review, Karshenas and Stoneman, 1995). These hardware items are conceptualized in part as embodied process or product knowledge and their adoption, finance permitting, is not treated as inherently problematic. Two assumptions are prevalent. The first is that it is more costly to produce new knowledge than to transfer it. Several devices of varying effectiveness exist to restrict or delay information transfer (Levin et al., 1987), but the firm's appropriation of its own innovative benefits activity's is problematic in the face of attempts by competitors to imitate it. The second, following from the identification of technology as hardware, is that process and product technologies are seen as items adopted by firms with measurable consequences for productivity and costs.

Sociologists, by contrast, have tended to a woollier, more 'Schumpeterian' definition of technology in which the development and application of a technology is seen to be embedded in organizational practices. The operation of a particular technology is seen to be context-specific. There may be 'generic' technologies applied within a firm, but as Clark *et al.* (1988) put it, an 'engineering system' surrounding a particular technological application allows sufficient design freedom to those concerned with implementation to permit any such application to develop highly idiosyncratic features on the basis of which tacit, non-transferable skills develop. The status of 'technology' as an independent variable is compromised where it is allowed that any particular application is in some way a consequence of organizational shaping. If one goes further, to regard 'technologies' entirely as social constructs, embedded in highly idiosyncratic contexts, one may not allow for independent status at all (see McLoughlin, this volume).

This view may be supported indirectly by the shortcomings on some empirical work. Where organizational sociologists have begun with simple definitions of technology similar to those accepted by many economists, they have experienced considerable difficulty in sustaining generalizations about the impact of technology. Features of interest to organizational sociologists, such as organizational structure, job content, or the nature and extent of resistance to change do not appear to vary systematically with the adoption of CAD, or robotics, or information technology. Sociological work which has begun with such definitions of technology has been disappointingly non-cumulative (Willman, 1986). There is, in any event, an earlier but more impressive literature on the relationship between technology and organization which attempts to classifiy processes by certain common parameters relevant to organizational functioning rather than nominal type (for a review, see Gerwin, 1981). As a consequence of these differences, the study of appropriability, i.e. the ability of the firm to benefit from its own innovative activity, proceeds from different starting points. However, logically, it also has a rather different destination. Differences in conceptions about technology are reinforced by different approaches to the organization of the firm.

Economic approaches concern themselves with appropriation by competitors, because they operate with a conception of the firm which encourages concentration on only one type of appropriability problem. Firms are regarded as points in market space; little or no attention is paid to internal structure. Learning curve effects within firms which may differ according to structure are treated as conceptually distinct from the process or product technologies to which they might relate. The problem of appropriability is defined in relation to imitation by competitors. The idea that there may be a problem of appropriability internal to the firm, i.e. that the firm itself cannot appropriate the benefits of innovative activity internal to it, is under-emphasized.

Although commercial performance has not always concerned sociological researchers, their natural intellectual predisposition is to regard external appropriability as less of a problem than internal appropriability; the latter issue concerns the firm's ability to secure the benefits of the process and product knowledge latent in the organization in pursuit of commercial success. Central questions concern the location of innovative activity or knowledge within the firm, the possibility of poor internal information transfer and inter-personal or collective conflict, all of which may affect the extent of the benefit deriving from use of technology or indeed the extent to which any technological insight might be used at all.

It is only a short step from the acknowledgement of technological idiosyncrasies to the idea of related, equally idiosyncratic technological competences. As Pavitt notes:

> economists and other social scientists will benefit enormously in both the accuracy and the impact of their analyses if they drop their conceptualization of science and technology as activities producing easily transmissible and applicable 'information' and recognise them instead as search processes and skills embodied in individuals and institutions.
>
> (1991b, p. 118)

However, we must also treat the nature of 'embodiment' as problematic, particularly 'embodiment' within institutions. I shall return to this below.

To summarize, economists tend to focus on technology as a generic, independent variable. The key problem concerns the avoidance of external spillovers. Sociologists tend to treat technology as idiosyncratic and socially produced; the key problem concerns the extent of internal spillovers. While some relatively unorthodox economists, from Penrose (1959) to evolutionary economists such as Nelson and Winter (1982), treat the firm as a point for knowledge accumulation, they do not explicitly link this to organizational processes (Nonaka and Takeuchi, 1995). The next section discusses such a link.

INNOVATION, KNOWLEDGE AND EXPERTISE

Pavitt remarks:

> large innovating firms in the 20th century have shown resilience and longevity, in spite of successive waves of radical innovations that have called into question their established skills and procedures. . . . Such institutional continuity in the face of technological discontinuity cannot be explained simply by the rise and fall of either talented individual entrepreneurs or of groups with specific technical skills. The continuing ability to absorb and mobilise new skills and opportunities has to be explained on other terms.
>
> (1991a, pp. 41–2)

He identifies four properties of innovative activities in large firms. They are firm-specific and cumulative, highly differentiated, and highly uncertain in outcome; organizationally, they involve continuous and intensive collaboration between functionally and professionally specialized groups. Much emphasis is placed on firm-specific competences 'that take time or are costly to initiate' and key features of innovative firm competences are, first, the ability to combine technical competencies into effective innovation and, second, the generation of effective organizational learning.

Pavitt's observations are inductive, based on UK data. They raise several issues for organizational research. The first is that the emphasis is on organizational knowledge rather than structure; the latter has tended to preoccupy those concerned with the organization analysis of technological change. The second is that the existence of institutional continuity renders 'entrepreneurial' or 'intrepreneurial' explanations and prescriptions – at face value – inadequate. Although it remains unanalysed, the implication is that the organization itself, rather than individuals who pass through it, retains and generates innovative capacity, even though at any time particular individuals who propagate or encourage learning may be identified.

Procedures for incremental adaption to changing circumstances become part of the organization's rule structure. The appropriate questions concern, first, the necessary conditions for establishing of such innovative routines and, second, their durability in the face of various types of change over time. A third issue concerns appropriability. Firms will not see benefit in extending their knowledge base unless there is the prospect of a short- or long-term return, but what are the organizational factors which underpin appropriability? Organizational research has tended to focus on initiation and implementation, but not appropriation. In what follows, I focus first on the knowledge-base and the process of learning and second on appropriability issues.

The general idea that firms possess a body of idiosyncratic competencies has been approached from several directions. Nelson and Winter's formulation is one of the most influential, and it relates such competencies directly to the existence of routines, in that:

> the routinisation of activity in an organization constitutes the most important form of storage of the organization's specific operational knowledge.
>
> (1982, p. 99)

Organizations, in this formulation, possess repertoires of routines consisting of all routines used and retained from the past and such a repertoire constitutes an asset of considerable value. However, it is not easily transferable since it exists beyond the reach of any set of individuals performing the routine at a given time and, indeed, is in some sense embedded in organizational processes. This is a rather difficult area, since the contention that organizations, as opposed simply to the individuals within them, know and learn implies some independent existence for the organization *per se*. However, the idea that the sum of organizational knowledge might be greater than that of the individuals within it is less difficult to accept if we assume that individual knowledge is additive (for an example, see Nonaka and Takeuchi, 1995). This is Nelson and Winter's assumption. Nevertheless, it is worth remembering at this point, since we shall return to it later, that, as Hedberg notes:

> Organisations do quite frequently know *less* than their members.
>
> (1981, emphasis added)

However, Nelson and Winter do not spend much time 'unbundling' routines. Two specific matters are of interest. Within any given successful innovative routine, to what extent is the basis of success technological rather then lying in a broader business knowledge, such as that concerning deployment of associated assets? Second, how much of the overall knowledge involved is tacit rather than explicit? Both dimensions may affect the extent to which the firm can appropriate the benefits of innovation. An innovation based on generic, formalized scientific knowledge is likely *ceteris paribus* to be harder to protect from competitors. One based on a bundle of tacit business knowledge is *ceteris paribus* likely to be harder for competitors to imitate but perhaps for the same reasons harder for the firm to appropriate, particularly if controlled by some strategic, non-ownership group. I shall discuss each in turn.

Expertise and know-how

I define the knowledge base of a firm as the sum total of information within the firm relevant to the conduct of its business. It will be greater, in most cases, than the sum of individual knowledge bases because such knowledge is a social and organizational construct not appropriable by individuals; however, it may not be available *in toto* to those managing the firm. The effective knowledge base will, however, be less than the sum total of information within the firm, some of which will be commercially irrelevant and some relating to redundant or divergent definitions of business need.

The knowledge base of an organization will relate to markets, employees, government activities and a range of other items which have no immediate bearing on technological change (Teece, 1992). It will, to a greater or lesser degree, consist of technical expertise *per se*, but the importance of technology for competitive success is likely to be highly variable across sectors. From this perspective, the key issue for the firm concerns the protection, deployment and extension of the knowledge base contained within it. Firms may be differentially capable of locating and appropriating their own knowledge bases, and this differential capability will influence their innovative capacity.

There is a clear distinction to be made between the knowledge base of an organization and the technological expertise it possesses (see Dyerson and Roper, 1990). Expertise, rooted in scientific or engineering competence, is, in this conception, part of the knowledge base. In high technology firms, it is likely to be an important part. Within the firm, there will also be various forms of technical expertise, relating to different product and process technologies, current and perhaps prospective. The relationship between expertise and know-how which deploys the knowledge base is, however, problematic. In some firms, expertise is the core of know-how. What might be termed 'technology push' firms driven by R&D may generally fall into this category. However, in many firms technical expertise is a necessary but not a sufficient condition for competitive success. An understanding of the centrality of technical expertise to business know-how is essential (Kay 1993, Kay and Willman 1993).

The issue here is similar to Daft's (1982) notion of the 'dominant innovation issue' facing the firm. It is possible that management within the firm will misinterpret a market or administrative problem as requiring a technological solution. Put another way, the innovation in know-how or in the deployment of know-how necessary to solve a given business problem might not require technological expertise. Although, as Damanpour *et al.* (1989) have illustrated, non-technological innovations may influence the capacity of the firm to effect and, presumably, appropriate technological change, the issue concerns the effective use, rather than the rate of development of, technological innovation.

Technological expertise itself will consist of a range from generally applicable expertise, valuable within an industry or sector, through to highly project-specific expertise which may not be transferable even within the firm. Dodgson (1991) indicates, in his analysis of Celltech, that these different categories of knowledge may be distinguished and purposively enhanced by firms. Scientists are encouraged to develop expertise across a variety of projects both for professional interest and for firm-specific interests in expanding the knowledge base. Firms may generate and distribute technical information to enhance their reputation and to attract good scientists (Nelson, 1990, p. 204). Expertise will generally be rooted in an externally-focused scientific community in which information is, in principle, freely available; I shall return to this point below.

Formal and tacit knowledge

Analysts concerned with innovation and, more generally, organizational learning have discussed the distinction between formal and tacit knowledge extensively and it needs little repetition here (see Pavitt, 1991a; Dodgson,

1993, Nonaka and Takeuchi, 1995). Tacit knowledge is contextualized, personal and hard to communicate. Formal or explicit knowledge is systematically communicable and intersubjectively testable. The distinction goes back to Polanyi, who remarks 'we can know more than we can tell' (1966, p. 4). Recalling Hedberg (1986), we might ask, 'under what circumstances will employees know more than the organization can tell?'; but to answer this, we need to revisit the distinction.

The origins of the distinction are essentially cognitive; tacit knowledge is that set which is easier to show than to say. However, the divide is porous since tacit knowledge can become explicit through organizational practice – what Nonaka and Takeuchi call 'externalization' (1995, pp. 56–70) and it can develop on the basis of explicit knowledge ('internalization', essentially learning by doing).

In analysing appropriability, one needs to go further. Some tacit knowledge may be necessarily so, in that the costs of externalization may be prohibitive or the translation is, for some reason, qualitatively imperfect. I distinguish this from the subset which may be seen as contingently tacit, dependent either on deficiencies in organizational processes for externalization or, more intractably, on conflicts of interests over rent-sharing.

To illustrate, assume two firms, A and B, identical in all respects except the balance between formal and tacit knowledge. The imbalance arises because (a) firm A has a clear and effective externalization policy, involving documentation of all local work innovations, but firm B does not; and (b) firm A offers rent-sharing opportunities to employees generating local work innovations, firm B does not and suffers from opportunistic behaviour on the part of a strategic group controlling local work innovations but retaining the benefits.

Firm A will appropriate a greater proportion of its tacit knowledge base than firm B. The difference is organizationally produced and therefore contingent, although in the use of a standard Williamsonian approach here I make no parallel assumptions about remediability. Indeed, contingency (b), which is largely ignored by the popular managerial literature on learning and tacit knowledge, is intractable. It follows that I view the problem of internal appropriability not simply as a question of organizational learning but also as a question of contract and work organization; both internal to the organization and externally, the market for tacit knowledge is more a labour market than a product market. I shall return to this below.

The relationship between explicit and tacit knowledge on the one hand and technical expertise and business knowledge on the other is contingent. Figure 2.1, which illustrates, indicates that all combinations are feasible. I turn now to the managerial issues involved.

	Technical expertise	Business know-how
Formal knowledge	Document software applications	Process mapping; market analyis
Tacit knowledge	Learning by doing, Kaizen	Local market/ customer behavior

Figure 2.1 The 'bundling' of technical and business knowledge

MANAGING THE KNOWLEDGE BASE

I define 'know-how' as application of the knowledge base to particular problems. A correct appreciation of the relationship between a particular technology and business needs is thus important. By this definition, any firm operating with some success will deploy know-how in pursuit of competitive advantage. This statement does not imply either that the body of know-how within the firm is codified and programmatic or that there is consensus within the firm about the best way to pursue competitive advantage. On the one hand, much know-how may be tacit and localized within particular functions of the firm. On the other, there may be competing definitions, or at least substantial differences of emphasis, between functions in discussions about what constitutes know-how. Both may affect the reception and performance of any new technology adopted by the firm.

Generation of know-how involves understanding the relationship between technical expertise and competitive advantage. It requires integration of functions, in particular user involvement in and commitment to technological change. In many businesses considering new technology, the preliminary requirement of understanding the core knowledge base of the business is absent. In such circumstances, the firm exercises little influence over how much new technological applications may improve or destroy competence.

In Tushman and Anderson's (1986, pp. 439–65) original formulation, competence enhancement or destruction were conceptualized as necessary consequences of an incoming technology. However, where generic technologies such as information technology are concerned, the organization may, through its management or mis-management of the innovative process, act to enhance or destroy the already existing knowledge base. The firm's

knowledge of the incoming technology and definition of the strategic importance of expertise related to it may thus be an intervening variable. The pre-
existing level of understanding of the technical expertise involved – as well
as the firm's understanding of its own knowledge base – will be important.

Enhancement of the knowledge base may involve research of various
forms but is likely, following the Nelson and Winter argument, to follow
from practice – learning by doing. Enhancement may involve drawing in
technical expertise or non-technical knowledge from outside; however, it
may also involve selective inclusion of groups within the firm in the
process of innovation. Over time, the locus of both expertise and know-
how may shift and, in order to capture a greater proportion of the available
knowledge base, senior managers may have to share information with
certain strategic groups. In doing so, they run the risk that employees
will leave, taking know-how to competitors. In failing to do so, the firm
may forgo competitive advantage.

Two examples of this shift in locus of innovation may be offered here:
both relate to the changing balance between process and product innovations in life-cycle models of innovation. In the Abernathy-Utterback
model, based in Abernathy's work in the car industry, the balance shifts
from product to process innovation over time (Abernathy, 1978; Abernathy
and Utterback, 1982). With the rising commercial importance of radical
and incremental process innovation, it is plausible to suggest that the locus
of innovation shifts from the manufacturer's own design facility to process
equipment suppliers in the one hand and the shop floor on the other. Recent
work on the auto industry would suggest that this is the case (Jurgens *et al.*,
1989, Womack *et al.*, 1990, 1991). A second example comes from financial
services. Barras (1990) has suggested a reversed cycle in which information technology based process innovations became the basis for subsequent
product innovations. The relationship between marketing and information
technology becomes a key axis for product development and delivery.

Within any firm, there may be groups of employees possessing know-
how which is neither available to the firm, because employees keep the
information to themselves, nor exportable elsewhere, because of its tacit
and idiosyncratic nature. There may be tensions between the generation
and enhancement of the knowledge base on the one hand, which may imply
extension of involvement in process or product redesign, and appropriability on the other. If there are different definitions, say between functions,
about what constitutes the appropriate knowledge base, these tensions may
break out into covert or overt conflict, involving information retention,
competing objectives and a failure to co-ordinate actions. To manage the
knowledge base successfully and in the long term through sequences of
technological change, the firm must firstly identify, locate and capture the
pre-existing knowledge base, secondly understand how successive

changes can relate to it in a competence-enhancing way, and thirdly, appropriate the returns to innovation.

INTERNAL AND EXTERNAL APPROPRIABILITY

From the economists' point of view, the problematic nature of appropriating the benefits of innovative activity by the firm weakens incentives to engage in it. There are public policy issues raised by this but, from the point of view of the firm, the essential objective is to restrict diffusion of new knowledge in order to profit from innovation (Geroski, 1995). In its simplest form, the economic approach does not consider organizational issues, regarding firms as points between which information may flow and markets as relatively costless means of transfer. In practice, there are a number of obstacles to simple transfer of knowledge which arise from differences in organizational capability. For example, the survey by Levin *et al.* (1987) established that, for many firms, independent R&D was seen to be the most effective means of learning about rival technology. Without such independently established competence, the firm cannot easily imitate a rival's innovation.

This observation may be taken rather further. The base assumption about the relative costs of knowledge production and dissemination rests on the idea that a discrete bundle of information may be transferred from one innovation point to another imitative one. Levin *et al.*'s (1987) findings simply introduce the condition that the receiving point be competent: it is basically competence as parallel expertise. As Cohen and Levinthal (1990) note, what they term the 'absorptive capacity' of a firm depends on expertise but also on certain features of the organization itself: while the expertise may be leaked, stolen or traded, the absorptive capacity itself cannot. As they put it:

> an organization's absorptive capacity does not simply depend on the organization's direct interface with the external environment. It also depends on transfers of knowledge across and within subunits that may be quite removed from the original point of entry.
>
> (1990, p. 128)

The focus is thus on the internal distribution of expertise and the mechanisms available for transferring it. In an earlier paper (1989, p. 570), Cohen and Levinthal describe the firm's absorptive capacity as its 'stock of prior knowledge'.

One may extend this view of absorptive capacity to embrace the differential ability of firms to use and develop their own know-how. From Cohen and Levinthal's (1989) analysis, absorptive capacity relates to external appropriability; firms which lack it cannot monitor competitors' developments. However, it may also relate to internal appropriability. Put simply, not only may the ability to benefit from external spillovers be predicated on internal organization but the ability of the firm, in Hedberg's terms, to know as much as its members, may be an organizational issue. These issues are clearly related, in at least two ways. Firms which capture their own know-how will be better placed to absorb competitor's advances. On the other hand, internal appropriability problems may become external if employees possessing know-how go to, or become, competitors.

There is a continuing debate within organizational sociology concerning the organizational features which might sustain successful innovation, but many authors, following Burns and Stalker (1961), emphasize the importance of informality, autonomy and teamwork at least in the creative phase of innovation. As Feldman (1989) has noted, there may be considerable conflict between autonomy and firm objectives; autonomy may be indicative of mis-communication, divergent goals and interest conflict as much as being the underpinning of creativity. In the terminology used here, autonomy may be the basis for internal appropriability problems.

Popular writing often dissociates innovative success from bureaucracy, yet institutional economists often discuss innovation in relation to routines. Teece *et al.* (1991, pp. 26–7) have helpfully distinguished between 'static routines', which 'embody the capacity to replicate previously performed tasks' and 'dynamic routines' which are 'directed at establishing new competences'. They also remark – indicating the rather specialized usage of the term in institutional economics – that routines cannot be fully captured in codified form. The notion of a routine does not, therefore, correspond to the notion of a bureaucratic procedure, which has low tacit content. Nor does it correspond to the idea of a skill set, since routines are regarded as in some sense supra-individual and coded. However, it is implicit in the notion of an innovative routine, through the base assumption that it is appropriable by the firm rather than the individual, that it does not co-exist with the types of bureaucratic procedures conventionally assumed to foster alienation among employees.

In an important sense, internal appropriability differs from external. The issue externally is the use of information by the firm or by its competitors. Internally, a third option exists. Because much technically relevant information, particularly concerning processes, is tacit and idiosyncratic, it may remain unappropriated by the firm and of little use to competitors.

FIRM-SPECIFIC KNOWLEDGE AND APPROPRIABILITY

In conclusion, I would like to explore further the relationship between internal and external appropriability. Owners of the firm will seek to maximize internal spillovers and minimize or control external ones[1]. What then are the organizational options? The place to begin is with the structure of the internal knowledge base.

To simplify matters, let me make two assumptions. The first is that we may hold the external environment – what Teece (1986) terms the 'appropriability regime' i.e. factors to do with technology, regulation, and market structure – constant for the moment. The second is that commercial success requires constant interplay between externally available sources of information and the internal knowledge base, i.e. isolation is not a feasible strategy.

The defensibility of the firm's knowledge base depends on the extent to which it avoids reliance on formal generic knowledge, since such knowledge cannot be uniquely appropriated to sustain competitive advantage. Generic technologies, such as information technology, may be bundled with non-technological competences in a protectable way, but it is the nature of these latter competences or other co-specialized assets, rather than the technology, which constitutes the advantage (Kay, 1993). In defending innovations from competitors, firms may need to protect knowledge in ways which prevent maximum benefits accruing from internal spillovers. Paradoxically, the solution of the external appropriability problem may generate the internal one.

Figure 2.2 attempts to illustrate. In attempting to apply a generic technology embodying formal knowledge to a business problem, the exemplar firm moves from A to B. i.e. from formal generic knowledge to tacit,

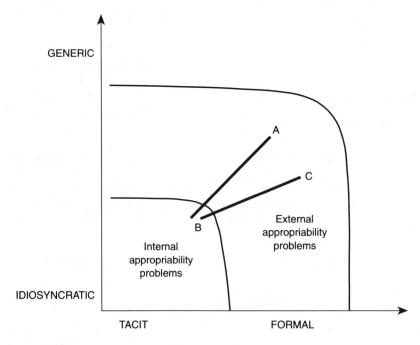

Figure 2.2 Skills and appropriability

idiosyncratic know-how. The issue then is to enable the tacit knowledge so generated to be captured and developed for subsequent, more general use within the firm. The firm thus moves back from B to C, reopening the external appropriability problem[2].

A key question is the relationship between those at the point (or points) in the organization where tacit knowledge accumulates and those who own or control the firm. From a rational self-interest viewpoint, those who retain tacit knowledge at position B will yield it only to the extent that they share in the additional rent which its formalization permits. Since the knowledge to be internally traded has no immediate external markets until formalized, the game approximates a prisoners' dilemma[3]. Serious problems arise where the accumulation of tacit knowledge occurs among employees who have traditionally neither perceived rent sharing, nor that they possess tacit skills.

I suggest that something like this has happened in the UK car industry in the period from 1945 to, approximately, 1982 (Lewchuk, 1987; Tolliday and Zeitlin, 1986; Willman and Winch, 1985). In the absence of any formal policy of 'externalization' and in the context of full employment in the 1950s and 1960s, tacit knowledge developed among assembly line workers whose collective organization both insulated them from work study techniques and provided the basis for control over work methods and the rate of local work innovations. In the terms of Figure 2.2, the move from A to B involved the accumulation of bargaining power. The move from B to C, beginning in the early 1980s, involved the reassertion of managerial control and the introduction of a variety of externalizing techniques.

The example indicates some correlation between arguments based on appropriability and those based on other approaches. The appropriability argument characterizes the development of Fordist production methods as the institutionalization of a division of labour which generates no transferable know-how on the assembly line and concentrates explicit knowledge at the apex of the firm. Under Fordism, tacit skills are discouraged as providing the basis for conflicts over rents. One might see the demise of these systems in the face of what Jurgens *et al.* (1989) have called 'Toyotism' as manifesting the competitive superiority of a production system capturing tacit knowledge – firm A *versus* firm B in the example above.

Figure 2.3 attempts to consider further the relationship between, on the one hand, the balance between internal and external spillovers and, on the other, the extent to which rent-sharing exists. Consider first the right hand boxes. In box B both the firm and the individual employee have high sunk costs. This is a Williamsonian transaction in which both parties lose by ending the contract and gain by fulfilling it in a 'consummate' rather than 'perfunctory' manner. In box C, the pay-off structure is such that a prisoners' dilemma arises and both parties confess: an equilibrium is established based on low information transfer and high transaction costs.

High transaction costs are a feature also of Box D, where no incentive exists on either side to move away from a spot contracting mode. In Box A, which might characterize a scientist in a biotechnology firm or a financial professional in any business, the potential for external spillovers is high. Two broad approaches may be taken by the firm to control spillover risk. The first, which focuses on the terms of the contract, involves rules on information disclosure and external contact together with devices such as

	Generic	Idiosyncratic
	A	**B**
Present (high value to business)	Low exit costs without restrictive convenants High external spillover risk	Enter and stay, high trust system High internal spillovers Low external spillovers
	D	**C**
Absent (low value to business)	High turnover, regime, with high transaction costs Low exit costs Low internal and external spillovers	Low trust, Taylorist regime Low internal spillovers Low external spillover risk Strategic bargaining by employees

Rent Sharing

Figure 2.3 Types of 'know-how'

restrictive covenants to raise exit costs. The second focuses on job design and is in effect an attempt to migrate the individual into Box B. It involves bundling generic with idiosyncratic skills to raise the incentive to remain. Although Figure 2.3 is a static simplification, it indicates the problems which may arise for the business where the idiosyncratic perceived low-value know-how in Box C become important, and the objective, through exercises in involvement and empowerment, is to move to Box B, in effect from a low-trust to a high-trust regime.

It is perhaps worth noting that the suggestion that rent-sharing with possessors of tacit knowledge has efficiency consequences is convergent with that of economists studying principal-agent relationships under conditions of information asymmetry. Minkler, for example, notes:

> the problem of asymmetric knowledge can be mitigated with profit sharing or some output sharing rule that gives the knowledgeable agent the incentive to utilize his knowledge.
>
> (1993, p. 20)

SUMMARY AND CONCLUSIONS

Incentives to innovate are conventionally seen to depend on the ability to appropriate the benefits of innovation, but the study of appropriability has been seriously distorted by a failure to come to terms with the internal appropriability problem. This is essentially an economic problem, but its analysis requires the tools of organizational sociology. With such tools, it emerges that the achievement of the economic objective attributed to the innovating firm, that is the maximization of internal spillovers and the minimization of unplanned external ones, is problematic because it is relatively easy to describe situations where trade-offs can emerge.

The central assumption, that firms may recognize and administer their knowledge bases differentially with different efficiency and performance consequences, leads to a focus on the determinants of internal spillovers. I have isolated two sets of determinants. The first lie in the organization of work, in particular the extent to which it generates information asymmetries; these are particularly difficult for the ownership of the firm to manage where they centre on transferable knowledge. The second lie in the contractual structure which generates incentives to reduce contingently tacit knowledge. In particular, the introduction of rent sharing arrangements may lock in components of the knowledge base; these are particularly important where there are low exit costs.

The argument has a number of interesting implications which will be explored in further work. Two are alluded to in the text. Differences in internal appropriability may shed insight on the study of the competitive advantage of organizations. I have remarked that the success of Toyotism over Fordism may be construed in relation to differential appropriability properties. The opportunity exists to study the differential efficiency or innovation properties of a number of work flow systems in this respect. The second concerns the long-term differences in innovative success sustained by large firms, discussed by Pavitt. Perhaps these differences are embedded in enduring features of the work organization and contractual structure of the businesses concerned. The terminology here is deliberately Granovetter's (1985) rather than Williamson's (1995); if these are the roots, they are unlikely to be remediable in the short to medium term. Low R&D, or low rates of innovation may reflect disincentives rooted in the organization, rather than fears about imitation by competitors.

Notes

[1] Cross-boundary management of knowledge flows, rather than their eradication, is probably the normal condition. Cohen and Levinthal's argument would support it and two-way management is essential to the success of technology-based joint ventures of strategic alliances (Teece, 1992).

[2] For example, a retailing organization may seek to automate the customer interface and may develop software to do so which builds on the accumulated tacit knowledge of customer behaviour possessed by staff. The issue is: why should they divulge? Subsequently, the software is documented (externalization) to facilitate further development and wider use within the firm. The issue now, since the know-how is likely to leak out, is: should it be obfuscated, copyrighted or licensed?

[3] The argument, incidentally, shows the limitations to the effectiveness of restrictive covenants; they address external appropriability problems only.

References

Abernathy, W.J. (1978) *The Productivity Dilemma: Roadblock to Innovation on the Auto Industry*, John Hopkins, Baltimore.

Abernathy, W.J. and Utterback, J.M. (1982) Patterns of industrial innovation, in *Readings in the Management of Innovation* (eds M. Tushman and W. Moore), Pitman, London.

Barley, S. (1986) Technology as an occasion for structuring, in *Administrative Science Quarterly*, vol. 5, no. 4 pp. 31.

Barras, R. (1990) Interactive innovation in financial and business services, in *Research Policy* 19, p. 215–37.

Burns, T. and Stalker, G.M. (1961) *The Management of Innovation*, Tavistock, London.

Clark, J., McLoughlin, I., Rose, H. and King, J. (1988) *The Process of Technological Change; New Technology and Social Choice at the Workplace*, Cambridge University Press.

Cohen, W. and Levinthal, D. (1989) Innovation and learning; the two faces of R&D, in *Economic Journal*, 95, pp. 569–96.

Cohen, W. and Levinthal, D. (1990) Absorptive capacity; a new perspective on learning and innovation, in *Administrative Science Quarterly*, 35, pp. 128–52.

Daft, R. (1982) Bureaucratic versus non-bureaucratic structure and the process of innovation and change, in *Research in the Sociology of Organizations* (ed. S. Bacharach), JAI, Greenwich, pp. 129–66.

Damanpour, F., Szabat, K.A. and Evan, W.M. (1989) The relationship between types of innovation and organizational performance, in *Journal of Management Studies*, 26 (6) pp. 587–601.

Davies, S. (1977) *The Diffusion of Process Innovations*, Cambridge University Press.

Dodgson, M. (1991) Technology learning, technology strategy and competitive pressures. *British Journal of Management*, vol. 2, 2, pp. 133–49.

Dodgson, M. (1993) Organisational learning; a review of some literatures, in *Organisational Studies*, 14, pp. 375–94.

Dyersen, R. and Roper, M. (1990) When expertise becomes know-how. *Business Review*, 2 (2) pp. 55–73.

Elster, J. (1983) *Explaining Technical Change*, Cambridge University Press.

Feldman, S.P., (1989) The Broken Wheel; the inseparability of autonomy and control in innovation within organizations, in *Journal of Management Studies*, 26 (2) pp. 82–101.

Geroski, P. (1995) Markets for technology; knowledge, innovation and appropriability, in *Handbook of the Economics of Innovation and Technical Change* (ed. P. Stoneman), Blackwell, Oxford, pp. 90–132.

Gerwin, D. (1981) Relationships between structure and technology, in *Handbook of Organisational Design* (eds P.C. Nystrom and W.H. Starbuck), vol. 2, Oxford University Press.

Granovetter, M. (1985) Economic action and social structure: the problem of embeddedness, in *American Journal of Sociology*, 91, 3, pp. 481–511.

Hedberg, B. (1986) How organisations learn and unlearn, in *Handbook of Organisational Design* (eds P. Nystrom and W.H. Starbuck), *op. cit* vol. 1, pp. 3–27, vol. 11, Oxford University Press.

Jurgens, U., Malsch, T. and Dohse, K. (1989) *Moderne Zeiten in der Automobilzulieferindustrie*, Springer, Berlin.

Karenshas, M. and Stoneman, P. (1995) A flexible model of technological diffusion incorporating economic factors with an application to the spread of colour TV ownership in the UK, in *Journal of Forecasting*, 111 (7), pp. 577–602.

Kay, J. (1993) *Foundations of Business Success*, Oxford University Press.

Kay, J. and Willman P. (1993) Managing technological innovation: architecture, trust and organizational relationships in the firm, in *New technologies and the firm: innovation and competition* (ed P. Swann), Routledge, London.

Levin, R., Klevorick A., Nelson, R. and Winter, S. (1987) Appropriating the returns from industrial R&D, *Brookings papers in Economic Activity*, 3, pp. 783–820.

Lewchuck, W. (1987) *American Technology and the British Vehicle Industry*, Cambridge University Press.

Minkler, A.P. (1993) Knowledge and internal organisation, in *Journal of Economic Behaviour and Organisation*, 21, pp. 17–30.

Nelson, R. (1990) 'Capitalism as an Engine of Progress', *Research Policy*, vol. 19, No. 3 pp. 193–214.

Nelson, R. and Winter, S. (1982) *An Evolutionary Theory of Economic Change*, Harvard University Press, Boston.

Nonaka, I. and Takeuchi, H. (1995) *The Knowledge-Creating Company*, Oxford University Press.

Pavitt, K. (1991a) Key characteristics of the large innovating firm, in *British Journal of Management*, vol. 2, No. 1 pp. 41–50.

Pavitt, K. (1991b) What makes basic research economically useful?, in *Research Policy*, vol. 20, No. 3 pp. 109–19.

Penrose, E.T. (1959) *The Theory of the Growth of the Firm*, Blackwell, Oxford.

Polanyi, M. (1966) *The Tacit Dimension*, Routledge, London.

Stoneman, P. (1983) *The Economics of Technological Change*, Oxford University Press.

Teece, D.J. (1986) Profiting from technological innovation, in *Research Policy*, 15, No. 4 pp. 285–305.

Teece, D.J. (1992) Competition, cooperation and innovation, in *Journal of Economic Behaviour and Organization*, vol. 18, no. 1, pp. 1–25.

Teece, D.J., Pisano, G. and Shuen, A. (1991) Dynamic capabilities and strategic management, School of Business, Berkeley, California, mimeo.

Tolliday S. and Zeitlin J. (eds) (1986) *Between Fordism and Flexibility*, Polity Press, Oxford.

Tushman, M. and Anderson, M. (1986) Technological discontinuities and organizational environments, in *Administrative Science Quarterly*, vol. 31, no. 3, pp. 439–66.

Willman, P. (1986) *Technological Change Collective Bargaining and Industrial Efficiency*, Oxford University Press.

Willman, P. and Winch, G. (1985) *Innovation and Management Control*, Cambridge University Press.

Womack, J.P., Jones, D.T. and Roos, D. (1990) *The Machine that Changed the World*, HarperCollins, New York.

Williamson O.E. (1985) *The Economic Institutions of Capitalism*, Free Press, New York.

Chapter 3

Flexible technologies, markets and the firm: strategic choices and FMS

Stephen Hill, Martin Harris and Roderick Martin

INTRODUCTION

This chapter arises out of research into the management of technological innovation which investigated relationships between product innovation, process innovation and company organization.[1] The chapter is based on a study of five companies in the mechanical engineering industry: two manufacturers of diesel engines and three manufacturers of capital goods. The problem addressed here is the adequacy of the treatment of managerial strategy and the relationships among product, process and organizational innovation, in the 'new technological paradigm' which has developed since the mid-1980s.

The chapter is in five sections. The first reviews the literature that constitutes the new technological paradigm. It identifies a number of analytical difficulties and problems of confounding evidence. It highlights the issue of strategic managerial choice. The second identifies the contexts that inform choice in the mechanical engineering companies (the classical location of the new paradigm). These include product markets and the requirement for product innovation, and the profit expectations of the corporation. The third examines managerial decisions about organizational design and new process technologies. The fourth focuses specifically on implementing flexible manufacturing systems (FMS). The final section relates the evidence from the companies to the issues identified in the first section. Since our findings and conclusions depart from the prevailing view, we then consider whether this variation might be explained by peculiarities of the British situation.

We argue that a new technological paradigm does not simply follow from new technologies or changing markets, but depends on the choices made by senior managers. Moreover, managerial choice is still based on the traditional criteria of managerial capitalism, notably profitability. Within this framework management has to balance the demands of innovation in products, technical processes and organization against the need to minimize costs: the requirement now is for more adaptability and flexibility, but more cheaply. This balancing act is reflected in three sets of choices that are implied by the new paradigm. These choices cover the appropriate response to product markets, the role of organizational as distinct from technological change, and decisions about the introduction of FMS and its mode of implementation. But most accounts do not adequately analyse the choices made by managers, while they wrongly assume that the dilemma of efficiency and productivity versus flexibility and innovation has substantially been resolved. Nor can the failure of the paradigm be explained by British exceptionalism.

THE NEW TECHNOLOGICAL PARADIGM

Jones (1990) has synthesized a range of views regarding the organizational implications of new manufacturing technology. He documents a consensus at the end of the 1980s, that a new technological paradigm had emerged in advanced industrial economies. This has apparently resolved the traditional incompatibility between efficiency and stable forms of productivity growth, on the one hand, and continuing innovation on the other.[2] Considering the operational level, the solution to the dilemma of efficiency and productivity versus innovation lies in combining flexible (programmable) production technologies with flexible work organizations. The new model combines product innovation with these operational changes. The linkages between the three elements – *product innovation, flexible automation, work reorganization* – form a tight nexus.

Flexible specialization, formulated initially by Piore and Sabel (1984) and developed by Sabel (1989; 1991) is a key element of the paradigm at the centre of debates about the changing relationship between organization and technology. Flexible specialization can be seen as

> an operations and product market strategy which involves a portfolio of distinct products aimed at market niches, specialist customers and quality-seeking consumers. Production runs tend to be short and done by versatile production machinery which is frequently reset by skilled production staff who work on a co-operative high trust basis with design and technical staff and even customers. These types of organizational relationships enable the enterprise to shift rapidly from one type of product to another.
>
> (Jones, 1990, p. 295)

Flexible specialization is consistent with the 'new production concept' approach of Kern and Schumann (1987) and neo-Schumpeterian innovation theory. Members of this latter school argue that production is being reorganized around an entirely new 'techno-economic paradigm' based on micro-electronics (Perez, 1983; Dosi *et al.*, 1988; Freeman *et al.*, 1993; Freeman and Perez, 1994).

Haywood and Bessant (1990) add *organizational change* – the redesign of organizational structures and managerial roles above the point of production – to the nexus of product innovation, flexible automation and work reorganization.[3] They maintain that the full benefits of flexible automation are realized when accompanied by organizational change. In their view, the integrated character of the latest process technologies, such as FMS, is incompatible with the segmentation of traditional organizational structures. In particular, functional boundaries need to be relaxed to create a single system without artificial breaks, and the depth of managerial hierarchies reduced and vertical integration increased, in order to use new technology effectively. The nexus is not tight, because organizational change introduced independently of technology still delivers many of the benefits. However, they suggest that there is a particular affinity, in effect a functional fit, between integrated organizations and integrated technologies. The neo-Schumpeterians point to the same functional fit of new process technologies with work reorganization and organizational redesign (Freeman *et al.*, 1993). In this account, changes in the technical sphere require corresponding adjustments to the institutional context.[4]

Bessant (1993) has tightened the linkage between new technology and organizational design. He reaffirms that integrated flexible technologies require new organizational forms if they are to function properly. He now suggests that the characteristics of process technology determine the space within which managerial choices regarding organizational design take place. Clark (1993, p. 213), developing this latter view, argues for the revival of the idea of technological determinism, albeit in what he calls a 'soft' form, to indicate that process technology has its own influence on organizational structure.

Advocates of the new technological paradigm ascribe several characteristics to the flexible work organization that enables the full potential of flexible technology to be realized. Employees have greater job autonomy and discretion in performing their tasks and the introduction of team-based production further enhances the area of autonomous decision-making. Employees have multiple competences (polyvalency) and can perform a wider range of tasks, and in many cases polyvalency involves raising skill levels and companies put more effort into training. However, Jones (1990); McLoughlin (1990); Badham (1991) and McLoughlin and Clark (1994) believe that the potential benefits of advanced manufacturing technologies may be lost, because managers resist autonomy, discretion and retraining, and therefore neglect the human factor. US evidence shows that neo-Taylorist forms of work organization are widely retained notwithstanding the potential for organizational change, while the UK reveals a pattern of diversity rather than a single line of development (Jones, 1990). Jones argues that British managers are willing to sacrifice the clear advantages of the new paradigm, because they doubt 'whether fully flexible operating

STANDARDIZED PRODUCTS

standard products

cost efficiencies

long production runs

→

SEGMENTED MARKETS

product variety and innovation

quality/performance improvements

short production runs

→

FLEXIBLE PRODUCTION TECHNOLOGIES

'costless' switching and logistics enable rapid product line changes

→

NEW FORMS OF ORGANIZATION

1. Work organization

multiskilling/polyvalency responsible autonomy

2. Management organization

less horizontal and vertical segmentation

more integration

Figure 3.1 New technological paradigm

capacity is compatible with secure strategic control from the top' (1990, pp. 293–4).

The new technological paradigm is both descriptive and prescriptive: it describes what is and what should be. However, it has long been clear that advanced manufacturing technologies, including FMS, often fail to deliver all the benefits attributed to them (Bessant, 1983; Voss, 1986; Fleck, 1987). These include the classical benefits of reduced costs and greater productivity, which are always expected to flow from technological progress. They also include the new benefits of economies of scope, i.e. the ability to switch cost effectively from one product to another, which resolve the efficiency versus innovation dilemma and are central to the new technological paradigm. Furthermore, various investigations of FMS in Germany, Denmark and the UK suggest that introducing flexible manufacturing systems into firms that are already flexibly specialized (i.e. firms that produce a diversity of products in small batches, use stand-alone computer numerically controlled machinery [CNC] operated by skilled labour and have responsible autonomy and flexible work organization) has been associated often with a *reduction* in product diversity, process flexibility and the use of employees' skills (Lay, 1990; Kristensen, 1990; Corbett, 1990). These findings have not been considered by advocates of the new paradigm and the doubts they raise have been smothered by the weight of the dominant orthodoxy. It looks as if firms may choose to use FMS to achieve scale economies and thus increase their batch sizes and reduce product diversity (Slack, 1990; Lay, 1990). Our interpretation of the findings is that managers may deliberately turn their backs on the economies of scope that supposedly typify flexible manufacturing systems and opt for productivity over flexibility and efficiency over innovation.

The new technological paradigm has key areas of analytical blindness, in addition to these empirical shortcomings. First, there is a deterministic, or at least a functionalist, bias to the discussion that plays down the relevance of managerial strategy and fails to give prominence to managerial choice. This affects the analysis of how companies respond to product markets, their stance on process technologies and how they choose to organize themselves. The prime mover of change, product innovation, is taken for granted. It is assumed that contemporary product markets require companies to innovate along certain lines: following a high value-added strategy of greater product specialization and niche marketing; more rapid product changes; higher quality products; products incorporating more knowledge. In turn, innovative products are thought to require new and flexible process technologies based on micro-electronics. It is then further assumed that these flexible processes need a particular style of flexible organization if they are to work effectively. This includes flexible work organization in every version of the new paradigm, and in some versions flexible managerial organization follows as well. In the more deterministic accounts, new process technology in fact directly influences both areas of organizational design. A consequence of this bias is that managerial choices, about how they will respond to product markets and which technical and organizational arrangements they will adopt, are not dealt with satisfactorily.[5]

Secondly, the reciprocal interaction of process and product innovation is ignored. The necessity of adopting automated process technology to make new products is taken for granted, yet there is no consideration of the possibility that, in a tightly linked nexus of relationships, advanced process technologies may set technical or economic limits on product innovation. But the evidence that flexibly specialized firms may reduce product diversification with the introduction of FMS or other integrated technologies indicates that managers may indeed perceive constraints on product innovation arising out of the process technology.

Third, the economics of new process technologies within capitalist market economies are not treated adequately. Coriat (1991) suggests that, from the viewpoint of economic theory, it is likely that flexible automation will come to be associated with economies of scale and the benefits of long production runs. Tomaney (1994) has also argued that management will continue to regard high rates of utilization and high volumes as central to the operation of flexible manufacturing systems. This suggests that the sharp discontinuity of the new technological paradigm is overstated.

New technology and 'strategic' managerial choice

Separate from the discussion of the new technological paradigm, and in many cases predating it, is the literature on managerial choice. This focuses on organizational processes and the strategic choices surrounding technology and organization. Technology adoption and implementation need to be understood in relation to decision-making junctures, which occur in a design, selection, implementation and routinization sequence. The introduction of new technology involves a range of organizational actors at different levels (Boddy and Buchanan, 1983; McLoughlin and Clark, 1994). These may have markedly different objectives, and so conflict and goal divergence exist from the earliest planning stages, through the implementation phase to routine operation and monitoring (Boddy and Buchanan, 1983, 1986). Nonetheless, the process of selection and justification has a strong 'agenda-setting' influence on the subsequent introduction of the technology (Boddy and Buchanan, 1983, 1986; Wilkinson, 1983; Child, 1984; McLoughlin and Clark, 1994). Such analyses accord a key role to organizational interests and to the 'negotiated' character of the technical change process.

This literature illuminates the components of managerial activity in process innovation (i.e. the adoption and implementation of production technologies). However, much of this work is not centrally concerned with the really 'strategic' product market environment and so product innovation gets little attention. Equally, the factors which link product market pressures to managerial choices about new process technologies and work organization are also largely ignored.[6]

THE CONTEXT INFORMING STRATEGIC CHOICE

The companies

The companies discussed here fall into two groups according to their product market and production characteristics. The three companies in group 1 supply capital goods to diversified markets, resulting in wide product ranges and relatively low production volumes for any one product. Automation occurs on manufacturing operations in the form of flexible manufacturing cells for common families of parts, while final assembly is done by hand. A flexible cell comprises two or more computer controlled machines, served by automated part loaders ('robots') and linked by automated transfer equipment, the whole system being managed by a central computer. These firms had been flexibly specialized in terms of market posture and craft-based production (using a mixture of manual and CNC machines) before integrated flexible automation was introduced. The companies produce pumps (Pump Co.), construction and mining equipment (Drill Co.), and generating plant (Generator Co.).

Group 2 comprises two manufacturers of diesel engines which, in response to changing product market requirements, had moved from a broadly Fordist stance – selling comparatively standardized engines, produced in large batches on specialized machines and using considerable numbers of semi-skilled workers – towards more differentiated and specialized products, sold in smaller numbers and manufactured using more flexible production systems. Diesel 1 had extensive and integrated automation in a completely modernized plant assembling a new product range. Diesel 2 had introduced islands of automation into an existing process. The group 2 firms would thus appear to provide good examples of the new technological paradigm in operation.

Managerial perceptions of product markets and innovation

Senior managers identified response to product markets as the central issue facing all five companies. In every case managers said that the rate of market change was accelerating, while in four companies they saw their markets differentiating and fragmenting as well. Product innovation was therefore crucial if companies were to continue to meet customers' expectations and survive. Innovation could take place at three levels:

longer-term development of new products (which might involve basic research and development); the redesign and development of existing products required by customization or new market niches; improved design for manufacture with the view to making products easier to produce, thereby reducing time and costs and improving product quality and speed of response to customers.

The product market for Generator Co. had changed over ten years from massive bespoke sales to the oil and gas industry, where performance, reliability and long-term supplier relationships mattered more than price, to a much wider range of customers across the spectrum of oil and gas extraction, manufacturing and service industries. This new market was characterized by much smaller individual sales, including single generator sets, customer requirements for more models across a wider range of capacities and with considerable customization of ancillaries. In ten years, its range of gas turbines had increased from two to six and its typical batch had declined from over ten to between two and three. (Batch sizes on certain families of parts, such as turbine blades, were much larger.) With 23,000 parts in the current MRP catalogue and a further 51,000 that could be demanded as spares for older models, this was a classic low volume, flexibly specialized operation. There had also been increased technical and price competition. The market therefore required continual product innovation, including basic R&D (involving new design concepts, materials and control systems) to increase efficiency and performance, together with extensive design and development effort to introduce new models, update existing models and customize ancillaries. The company also prioritized design for manufacture in product development, in order to cut production times and costs and supply customers more rapidly.

The market for pumps grew rapidly and differentiated significantly as industrial applications of vacuum, previously a technology used mainly in scientific research, became more commonplace during the 1980s. Pump Co. changed from being a manufacturer of scientific equipment to a producer of capital goods used in industrial processes and supplied around 2,000 discrete products. The main competitive pressures were technology, quality and price, and to develop products for new industrial markets where the possibilities of vacuum-based processes were just becoming appreciated. The company led in a particular pump technology, which it had pioneered, and in control systems. Product innovation, in order to further develop its technological breakthrough, create new products for new markets and improve the manufacturability of the product range, was central to its competitive strategy.

Drill Co. operated in a market for standard industrial products that could be bought off the shelf from a wide range of manufacturers. Differentiation was not a major feature but market change was seen as significant, the result of new sensitivities to environmental, health and safety issues. Competitive pressures focused on reliability and durability, price, noise reduction and improved ergonomics and safety. Of all the cases examined here, this company's product market made the fewest demands on product innovation.

Diesels 1 and 2 sold in the same product market. In place of fairly standard products customers now expect a much higher degree of customization. Standard engine blocks can be configured into a variety of different base engines depending on the internal components. Diesel 1, for example, had two standard engine blocks and 23 different cylinder heads in its medium-horsepower range. These base engines are given further variety when the ancillaries and trim are added, leading to 2,500 variants deriving from the two medium-horsepower engine blocks. In addition, there is a demand for better performance (more horsepower per dollar), fuel economy and emission reduction. Price competition remains important (the major concern of customers is the total cost of ownership, which comprises purchase price plus reliability and servicing costs). Product innovation is clearly important in this environment. Innovation requires both longer-term research and development and the ability to redesign and develop in response to immediate customer requirements. As with Generator Co. and Pump Co., design for manufacture has become an important consideration in developing products in both companies.

Profitability and the issue of costs

Competing successfully in the product marketplace was insufficient on its own. Such success had to be accompanied by adequate levels of profitability, as defined by the board of directors in the light of shareholders' expectations. This was, moreover, against a background of rising aspirations among the generality of owners in the early 1990s (Hutton, 1995, pp. 132–69). While profitable, three of these companies failed to reach the levels specified by the boards of their parent companies. Thus increasing the rate of return was very high on the agendas of their senior managers. Equally, maintaining present levels of profit preoccupied managers in the other two companies.

The control of costs was therefore most significant. Cost reduction made a significant contribution to successfully competing in product markets and to achieving the profit targets laid down from above. The distinction often made in the 1980s, following Porter (1980), between business strategies based on product differentiation and quality versus strategies based on price leadership, indicated that companies might charge a price premium for differentiated and high quality products, thus ensuring profitability while avoiding the ruthless cost reduction required to compete on price. The new technological paradigm has assumed that producing high-added-value, high-quality products for niche markets provides some protection from

price competition. However, senior managers' perceptions of their product
markets indicate that price competition remains important even in niche
markets and leaves no great space for premium prices, while top managers'
profitability requirements add a further twist to the screw pushing down
costs.

STRATEGIC MANAGEMENT CHOICES

Senior managers saw acting effectively and swiftly in the context of change
and differentiation in product markets as one of the crucial issues from
which much else followed. The other was to achieve the financial returns
expected by their owners. Thus profitability and costs shared priority with
adaptability and flexibility in senior managers' perceptions of their environments. We now analyse how they responded.

Organizational capabilities

Both responsiveness, defined as being adaptable and flexible and sustaining
product innovation, and cost reduction, were seen to be issues of *organizational* rather than process technological capability in the first instance.
Companies had assessed their organizational capabilities and found them
lacking: they were cumbersome, expensive and thus not fully effective.
The strategic choice was to redesign the organization and change the ways
managers worked. Within the organizational sphere, managerial organization had priority over the workplace. Over the previous decade, all the
companies had moved towards more decentralized organizational structures, greater delegation and new mechanisms of integration. Some had
also delayered and removed levels of management. Effective product
innovation was to be facilitated by finding new ways of linking research
and development staff with the rest of the organization, and by maintaining
spending on R&D. The linkages between the marketing, product development and manufacturing functions had received particular attention. This
was necessary to ensure that product innovation was properly informed by
market opportunities, came to the market speedily and was designed for
ease and economy of manufacture.

Organizational redesign was intended both to decentralize decision making and to provide better integration than the functionally organized and
deep hierarchies that had existed before. Companies created cost and profit
centres, business units that controlled some of their own managerial
resources, and even span off certain areas into independent companies.
The product development functions in two companies were established as
independent businesses that interacted with their parent companies on a
supplier-customer basis (and were obliged to seek third party work). In the
other cases, parts of the function were taken out of the centre and allocated

to the business units which manufactured and marketed their designs. Thus the integration of product development with marketing and manufacturing was achieved, either via organizational change that substituted market relations for hierarchy or via new internal organizational arrangements.

Redesign was expected to benefit responsiveness and costs in several ways. First, it would focus managerial activity more on product market requirements. This is why those responsible for dealing with customers were given a lead role in determining the direction of product innovation. Second, it would lower the point of decision-making and establish new incentives for less senior managers, both increasing the organization's speed of response and putting budgetary pressure on units to control costs. Third, bureaucratic and functional sectionalism would be reduced and the organization would function more as a single system. Fourth, managerial overhead costs would be contained or reduced. Advocates of organizational redesign in the management literature hold out the promise that greater responsiveness and lower costs go hand in hand, their claim being that leaner and 'fitter' firms are also cheaper (e.g. Kanter, 1991).

A second thrust, additional to structural redesign, was to change managerial behaviour towards more interdisciplinary teamworking. This was intended both to improve the quality of decision-making and as an aid to integration. In Diesel 1, Generator Co. and Pump Co. this was a consequence of formally adopting total quality management (TQM), which places considerable weight on managing processes that cross functions and departments (Hill, 1991). Elsewhere there was also a movement towards the routine use of project teams. Interdisciplinary teams were particularly noticeable in areas such as product development and manufacturability. Finally, a faster and more effective response was thought to require new supplier relations, and there was a general movement towards longer-term and relational contracting with a smaller number of suppliers.

Process technologies

While subordinate to other priorities, the importance given to process innovation nevertheless varied across this sample. The senior managements of Diesel 1 and Pump Co. had explicit strategies of developing flexible automation to improve their response to product market change, and of being at the cutting edge of process technology. The other companies placed much less emphasis on process innovation as part of their strategy. Generator Co.'s policy had become one of spreading investment for incremental improvements over a wide range of activity rather than concentrating it into a few very expensive islands of automation. Diesel 2 had a tradition of spending as little as possible on fixed assets, refurbishing and upgrading plant rather than buying new, and avoiding being in the technological vanguard when it did invest in new machinery. Drill Co. invested heavily in new plant, but mainly in stand-alone CNC machinery apart from a single automated flexible cell.

The primary determinants of investment in manufacturing facilities were capacity constraints and cost reduction. Companies mainly bought new plant when demand for a product or component exceeded their capacity to manufacture it, or when new machinery offered major cost savings over their existing plant. Quality issues were also significant but subsidiary, in that they might form part of the financial justification but were insufficient on their own. Flexible automation became an issue once it was decided that some investment had to be made. Flexible automation is normally more expensive than dedicated machinery and paying the premium was justified on two grounds. It balanced production among a mix of products, which ensured greater machine utilization than would result from machines dedicated to different products. Therefore flexible automation could deliver a better return on investment despite the extra cost. It also reduced the risk of obsolescence when products changed during the useful life of the machinery. Pump Co. and Diesel 1, for example, assumed a machine life of eight years for investment purposes but a product life of four or less. In comparison with cheaper, stand-alone universal machines, which were also highly flexible, flexible automation was seen to be financially advantageous at higher production volumes, provided the capacity remained fully utilized.[7] These empirical observations support the analysis of Coriat (1991) that the expense of flexible automation puts greater pressure on firms to run plant at maximum capacity, in order to achieve the desired rates of return on capital invested. As will be shown, this also favours economies of scale over economies of scope.

Investment in new technology reduces staffing levels for a given level of output. This simple and well-known fact was taken for granted by managers when considering equipment purchases, whatever the impetus for the proposed investment. Every justification of new equipment routinely detailed the anticipated savings of direct labour hours, as part of the case that the investment would be profitable and deliver a certain return on assets. The emphasis on increased productivity/reduced costs and return on investment was part of a managerial culture that gave weight to the financial justifications of new technology. Previous research has questioned the part played by financial justifications in process innovation (Senker, 1984; Kaplan, 1986; Currie, 1989): proposals tend to contain an element of built-in 'slack' and technologies are seldom monitored with respect to the outcomes anticipated in the original justification. In every company considered here, however, the actual outcomes of investments were monitored and independently audited against the original justification, and this more stringent evaluation of the performance of equipment was part of a general tightening of controls designed to lower costs in all the companies. (Harris, 1996, corroborates this.) In the present study, engineering managers reported that they still preferred to put some slack into the original justi-fications if they could, deliberately underestimating the potential benefits of the equipment to ensure that they would pass the post-implementation audits more easily. The effect of understating the achievable rate of return on investment was to set an extra hurdle that reduced the likelihood of marginally profitable investments proceeding.

IMPLEMENTING FMS

Restricted flexibility

The capital goods firms in group 1 were already flexibly specialized before adopting flexible automation. However, the introduction of the latest technologies in these firms was associated with a reduction in the scope of production, rather than automation being deployed to maintain the previous variability, let alone increase its scope. Reduced scope took three forms: products were simplified, the range of parts was reduced and families of similar parts were dedicated to different cells. Flexible automation was in fact deployed to raise batch sizes and produce higher volumes, thus intro-ducing economies of scale into small batch production.

The explanation for this is primarily financial: the need to maximize return on investment. When new plant was bought to overcome capacity constraints on particular operations, it was because the volume of a specific family of parts justified the investment. In these circumstances it is hardly surprising that automated technology should be used relatively inflexibly, because scale economies are part of its projected rate of return. However, manufacturing managers in the three firms still chose to restrict the scope of flexible automation, in order to increase the rate of return by scale economies, even when this sort of capacity constraint was not an issue. Reduced scope through product simplification is one aspect of design for manufacturability. Simplification reduces the total number of operations, thereby cutting machining time, tooling requirements and, in many cases, the number of different machines an item passes through. It may also reduce the range of components required. In addition, using flexible auto-mation for a limited range of items that make up a family of parts means that tooling can be simpler, programming and proving costs lower, and the logistics of supplying parts and tools simplified. It should be noted that these forms of scope reduction are rarely technically required by the application of FMS to machining operations: in principle, complexity can be automated and variability retained or even increased. Moreover, it is obvious that a similar scope reduction might equally improve the cost effectiveness of non-FMS production. However, the managers were clear that what made them pursue reduced scope vigorously and systematically was the requirement to achieve prescribed rates of return on what, in comparison with previous investments, were very expensive pieces of new machinery.

The two diesel engine manufacturers used the flexible automation of assembly to move towards flexible specialization, that is to the smaller batches and greater variability associated with economies of scope. However, they came up against a number of obstacles when product variability exceeded certain limits. There were technological limits to the amount of variation that was possible. For example, the automated assembly system at Diesel 1 could not recognize the number of different cylinder heads that the company proposed to use in order to meet customer requirements. The plant had been designed for seven different heads, was currently operating with 23, but could not cope with the 32 that the marketing function wanted. There were economic limits as well, notably that the system's speed was determined by the most complicated product. Thus manual assembly was retained on certain engines in both companies (the most flexible technology is, of course, working by hand).

The issues of economic limits and managerial strategy can be elaborated in the contrast between the two diesel engine companies. The new facility at Diesel 1 was designed for fairly high volumes with moderate variability and limited specifications, along with a small customer base. Compared with the old product range built in the previous plant, the new engine range was intended to be more customized and the plant more flexible, but these differences were intended to be matters of degree.[8] In the event, the customer base expanded massively, there were relatively few bulk sales and the marketing function was willing to accept considerable customization. Manufacturing managers complained that marketing's willingness to accept virtually any order made manufacturing less efficient, by creating logistical problems and slowing the manual aspects of assembly, and they also doubted that the company could fully recover the extra costs involved in the design, procurement and manufacturing processes. Because the plant was running below full capacity and the new product range was still not established in the market, senior management supported marketing. But they too were concerned that excessive variety was eroding profit margins. Variability was less in Diesel 2, partly because large customers accounted for more of the output and partly because the company refused to customize in small volumes. Moreover, with more manual assembly, Diesel 2 found extreme complexity easier to handle.

Other commentators have suggested that engineers are frustrated in their efforts to introduce new technology by 'accounting lag' (Kaplan, 1986; Harris, 1996) or 'organizational conservatism' (Child et al., 1987). Comprehensive and effective investment in new process technologies is thought to be inhibited by accounting conventions or by the resistance of senior managers. We found, to the contrary, that senior engineers were themselves centrally concerned with economies of scale and utilization rates, and thus appeared to share the same agenda as the rest of the senior management team.

Operating outcomes

The central importance of financial control was evident in the monitoring of performance. We investigated how the outcomes of automation in operation matched those anticipated in the decision to purchase flexible manufacturing systems. Drill Co. and Pump Co. reported that their flexible cells performed as anticipated within a few months of commissioning on every criteria, including product mix, quantity of output, uptime, staffing and levels of maintenance. Elsewhere the results were not completely positive.

Downtime, maintenance and staffing remained greater than anticipated in both the diesel companies' automated assembly operations and in the flexible manufacturing cells at Generator Co. and at a machining plant of Diesel 1. Moreover, one of the three automated islands in Diesel 2 was unable to handle the full range of components it had been designed to assemble. (Diesel 1, however, found that its fully automated assembly plant was able to handle a far wider product mix that originally planned.) With the exception of the restricted product mix at Diesel 2 and chronic unreliability of one of the two flexible cells at Generator Co., both of which had proved insoluble over a five-year period, the performance of the other pieces of flexible automation was improving. These investments were still failing to meet certain targets, however, 18 months to three years after they were commissioned.

A common factor was that the sophistication and complexity of the automation, particularly on the scale of the two assembly operations, outstripped the technical capabilities of managers, staff and operators and their ability to learn. This showed through in unreliability, the fact that companies found it particularly difficult to solve software problems, and the amount of time taken to diagnose the causes of unreliability (whether hardware, software or the interaction of the two). Significantly, the suppliers also found it difficult to keep their installations running for the planned amount of uptime, and using a supplier's backup service did not necessarily resolve the problems.

These findings highlight the difficulties companies may face in assimilating new technology. They dispel any notion that the adoption of highly complex process technologies can be seen as a panacea for manufacturers. (Blumberg and Gerwin, 1994, highlight the difficulties in managing the complexity associated with advanced manufacturing technologies.) Our findings also support the view that process innovation tests the technical and organizational capabilities of firms, and involves a cumulative process of organizational learning (Fleck, 1987; Scarbrough and Corbett, 1992; Pavitt, 1994).

Work organization and the human factor

The amount of work reorganization at the point of production varied. Moreover, in most cases it was not obviously related to new technology.

Diesel 1 had the most radical and clear-cut work reorganization. Corporate strategy since the mid–1980s had been to improve the quality of working life (QWL) by removing tedium and fostering teamwork, and these objectives were designed into the new plant from its conception. The plant was run by a self-supervising team that reported directly to the manufacturing manager of the facility. This team was responsible for assigning its own work tasks, ensuring the delivery of materials, and controlling and improving quality. All operators were trained to perform every task and were paid by their level of training. Work reorganization was not specific to the new technology, although it was more advanced, because corporate strategy was to improve QWL everywhere. Thus teamworking was developed in older technology facilities and operator control of quality was part of a company-wide move to TQM. Multi-skilled maintenance had been introduced across the company many years previously and the company had an active policy of training craftspeople to upgrade their skills.[9]

Diesel 2 had negotiated with its trade unions a high degree of functional flexibility for all semi-skilled and maintenance staff in the early 1980s, several years before the first piece of automation. Operators can be required to do all semi-skilled tasks including minor maintenance. Self-inspection for quality was added later. Multi-skilled maintenance was negotiated at the same time and backed up by a six-month, full-time training package in the extra skills. All these changes were unrelated to new technology. The subsequent introduction of automation therefore made few differences to skills or organization among the semi-skilled staff. However, maintenance was reorganized after the first two islands of automation were up and running, in order to provide each with its own dedicated maintenance team which would develop and retain knowledge of its particular idiosyncrasies.

The flexible manufacturing cells were introduced into companies that already employed skilled labour and were experienced users of computer controlled machines (stand-alone machines which were not combined into automated systems). Generator Co. had a tradition of craft work and responsible autonomy on its stand-alone CNC machinery, notably a degree of operator input into programme editing and inspection, which it retained under flexible automation. There were now fewer occasions requiring operator reprogramming, however, given the use of flexible automation to produce a narrow range of parts in relatively high volumes. The company had reorganized the shopfloor on team lines about a year before our investigation (a team being an organizational unit and not a natural technological cell). Teams were introduced in the old technology areas as well as the new. They were part of an organizational initiative, a straightforward hierarchical delayering combined with certain TQM concepts, that substituted teamleaders (who were selected by management and paid a small additional wage) for several grades of supervision and the separate quality inspectors. Individual financial incentives were replaced by a plant-wide bonus scheme. The new teams, and in particular their leaders, were expected to become more involved in production scheduling, tool management and logistics. A flexibility agreement negotiated with the trade union allowed management to move staff between machines and transferred minor machine maintenance to machine operators. Manufacturing managers saw teams and flexibility primarily as solutions to the problems of the older technologies outside the FMS cells. They facilitated the balancing of production and increased machine utilization and labour productivity: without buying another machine or hiring another employee, the effective capacity of the plant was raised by 17 per cent.

Flexible automation at Pump Co. built on a similar tradition of responsible autonomy in the use of computer-controlled machinery, at least in the new technology plant. Managers designed the way the new cells operated with teamworking, flexible work assignments and job enlargement (including tool management, production scheduling, minor maintenance and planned maintenance, and the continuation of programme editing) in mind. The introduction of automation was accompanied by several months' training. Nevertheless, the opportunities for reprogramming were limited in number, because the cells were used for large batch production. They were also limited in their scope, because graduate technicians were used for most software tasks and operators were involved only on simple jobs where it was not worth using a more qualified person. Similarly, job enlargement to cover maintenance was constrained by a pre-existing and separate CNC maintenance team, which handled all but the minor tasks. The employment status of operators was changed from hourly paid to 'staff', a direct result of trade union refusal to agree to the new working practices if the people affected remained on the hourly paid grade (the unions put no obstacles in the way of the status change).

A different policy operated in a second plant of the same company. This was a small batch works employing a number of craftsmen on traditional manual technologies, where managers looked to new machinery to deskill craftwork. When stand-alone CNCs were introduced, the shop floor was discouraged from editing programmes and CNC was intended to transfer responsibility for production to the engineering function. Management's explanation of the different treatment of the two plants related to the different industrial relations cultures: the plant used for new technology was said to have a tradition of labour-management co-operation, whereas the other had always been more adversarial. Therefore responsible autonomy could work in the first because employees could be trusted, but not in the second.

DISCUSSION

Innovation, technology and organization

This chapter has focused on the context of the introduction of flexible automation, on strategic managerial readings of this context and the choices that they have made in response to these, and on the actual uses of this flexible technology. Three contextual features were of particular significance. First, the product market, particularly the requirements for product innovation, speed of response and price, had a significant bearing on senior management choices. Second, the profit expectations of the parent companies' top management reinforced the need for efficiency, costs and productivity alongside responsiveness. Third was the organizational context, because senior managers prioritized the need to increase their organizational capability in order to respond to product markets and maintain profitability.

The central issue for senior managers was to respond effectively (i.e. appropriately and speedily) to changing product markets. This is consistent with the ideas of flexible specialization. However, managerial readings of product markets focused on the need to combine responsiveness or innovation with cost reduction, a dimension that has not yet been sufficiently discussed in the literature. Despite the weight now given to non-price factors such as change, differentiation and quality, markets have not lost their sensitivity to price. Nor have owners become less sensitive to profits. Hence managers felt they had to remain competitive on both innovation and costs.

Both flexible response and cost reduction were pursued primarily by means of organizational change, because managers saw reorganization as the more effective way to balance these objectives. The middle and upper layers of the firm were the primary locations, and effective product innovation the primary target. Work reorganization at the point of production had a lower priority. Change was designed to create more decentralized organizational structures, more delegation and new mechanisms of integration. Restructuring included redesign to improve integration of the product development, marketing and manufacturing functions, the removal of management layers, and the redesign of business processes. Managerial teamworking and cross functional management were promoted as behavioural changes that companies expected of their managers. This squares with the view in the management literature that companies react to new environmental conditions primarily by organizational means such as restructuring (Kanter, 1991).

Our evidence shows a definite link between product innovation and organizational change, because the desire to increase responsiveness to product markets (one aspect of which is product innovation) was one determinant of restructuring. But, contrary to the model in Figure 3.1, organizational change was not at all closely related to new process technology.

Balancing efficiency and productivity with innovation, or cost reduction with responsiveness, was also an issue at the operational level. Companies tackled the balancing problem directly and at source, by means of product redesign, design for manufacture and value engineering. This was seen to be more useful than, and to take priority over, the application downstream of flexible process technology to unrationalized products. Regarding new process technology, we have argued that, within limits, FMS assisted the resolution of the dilemma among the diesel companies, but made the problem worse for the capital goods companies.

The new technological paradigm suggests that switching between products on flexibly automated manufacturing systems is virtually costless, allowing companies to produce economically for ever more differentiated markets. Senior managers here, however, saw a trade-off between control of costs and product variability beyond certain limits. It was apparent that their concern with costs and excessive variability had an 'agenda setting' influence on both manufacturing policy and technological choices. These agenda setting factors influenced the nature and extent of the choices considered.

The way flexible process technology is used by companies to compete in product markets therefore appears to be more complex than has previously been suggested. Thus relationships between product markets and process technology may well differ from the orthodox view. Our firms in fact divide in two. On the one hand, the use of flexible automation by the already flexibly specialized, capital goods firms to achieve scale economies involves a major campaign to reduce diversity, via product redesign, design for manufacture and value engineering. Reducing diversity allows companies to move in the direction of volume production, while retaining a substantial measure of product differentiation and the capability to handle change as a hedge against further shifts in product markets. On the other hand, the use of flexible automation among what were previously volume producers of diesel engines is intended to facilitate greater product diversity and a move away from volume production and the associated scale economies. This latter use supports the proponents of a new technological paradigm. However, all firms find that there are economic and technical limits which render flexible automation viable only within a specific range of variability. When this range is exceeded, companies consider whether to use one of the even more flexible technologies (e.g. hand work), or to simplify products to fit automation. In the latter case, process technology is a definite limitation on product innovation.

Work organization shows the flexibility, relative autonomy, polyvalency and, in some cases, the enhancement of skill described in the new technological paradigm. But the linkage with process automation is not at all obvious. Managerial accounts of how these forms of work organization developed include pre-existing craft traditions, earlier movements towards labour flexibility, the introduction of modern quality management, and a commitment to better quality of working life. Work reorganization may occasionally follow from the introduction of new technologies (e.g. the reorganization of maintenance at Diesel 2 around the individual islands), but often there appears to be no direct linkage. Again we find little support for the arguments of adherents to the new technological paradigm. Influence may work the other way in that firms which already have flexible work organizations, or are considering introducing them, may be the ones that later introduce flexible automation. (This would, of course, reverse the temporal and causal sequence assumed by the new paradigm, but the data do not allow us to explore this possibility.) It is clear, however, that, as with reorganization at the managerial level, there are other forces leading down the road of workplace reorganization which now have a widespread impact on managers. These include Human Resource Management and TQM, influential managerial philosophies that affect jobs and workplace organization in the same direction as the new technological paradigm. The contemporary movement to delayer and destaff management is also likely to increase the responsibilities of front line employees, while the ubiquitous cost cutting and destaffing within the workplace lead the same way.

The new technological paradigm deals with the relationship between responsiveness/innovation and efficiency/productivity, and claims that more flexibility is compatible with unchanged, or even improved, costs and productivity. The literature in fact concentrates more on flexibility and seems to assume that economy and efficiency require less analysis.[10] However, senior managers were concerned with both flexible response and costs, since both are components of profitability. Profitability can be achieved by raising prices if products have unique features that customers are willing to pay for, but competitors will be expected to catch up quickly and it is difficult to sustain this competitive advantage (Ghemawat, 1986; Kay, 1995, pp. 101–12). Costs are more easily influenced by managers and cost reductions may have more permanent effects on profitability.

British exceptionalism?

Hutton (1995, pp. 132–68) argues that British managers experience financial pressures which are both greater than in other industrialized capitalist economies and have become more intense recently. In comparison with Japan and mainland Europe, the levels of profitability that shareholders have required in Britain have always been extremely high. They have also been somewhat higher than those in the USA. Moreover, for reasons to do with the ways in which British capital markets operate, the cost of raising external capital for investment is also expensive (Hutton, 1995, pp. 151–2).

These factors mean that British companies have to demand abnormally high rates of return from internal funds invested in new capital equipment, and these rates have further increased since the mid-1980s. It is to be expected that this financial regime will significantly influence the decision whether or not to buy new machinery and, once installed, the way it will be used in order to cover its cost. In fact all the companies investigated here required their new investments to create sufficient surplus to recover their costs within two or three years (the 'payback' time). By international standards this is a stringent demand and, moreover, about half the average payback time of British companies in the 1960s. This explains the need to generate high returns from fixed assets which was so influential in the perceptions of these managers.

There may be an issue of 'societal' effects here. That is, the British use of flexible automation may reflect factors which are specific to Britain, while automation may be used differently in other societies. The financial regime is an obvious candidate for a societal influence. This might also help to account for the greater emphasis placed on economy and efficiency here relative to the other literature. Another effect suggested in the analysis of Jones (1990) and Lane (1988) is that managerial culture in Britain (and North America) prioritizes tight control over labour and so managers are less likely to organize jobs and workplaces in the ways favoured by the new technological paradigm. It is held that capitalism in mainland Europe, notably in Germany, is less dominated by the need to maximize returns on investment. It also incorporates systems of employment relations and industrial cultures that predispose managers to create workplace organizations that fit exactly the new technological paradigm.

Our evidence in fact gives no positive support to an argument for British exceptionalism. The five companies included two subsidiaries of North American corporations and subsidiaries of Anglo-French, Scandinavian and British companies. Despite this variety of national origins among their parent companies, there were no differences in the expected rates of returns among these subsidiaries and no signs that national origins had any effect on the financial regimes affecting managers. In fact, they all conformed to the 'British' standard. Work organization also failed to show societal effects and mainly conformed to the new model, despite the managers of the subsidiaries being British except in the Scandinavian company. There was little sign of the concern about control loss that supposedly characterizes British and North American managerial cultures.

Britain and America are sometimes seen as similar and as constituting a distinctive Anglo-American model of capitalism. If so, the effective mix of national backgrounds among these firms is narrowed to include three examples of the Anglo-American model, a single example of the continental European model and a hybrid. This makes discussing the role of national differences among this group of firms more problematic. Still, it remains the case that the expected rates of return for the Scandinavian and Anglo-French companies conform to the British model. Moreover, managers of the Anglo-French company complained that it had become more difficult rather than easier to invest, following the merger a few years previously of the British and French components and the greater influence of French top managers and procedures.

Given the small numbers involved, these findings may not dent the view that in general there are societal effects, but they do show that the approach is not useful for understanding these particular companies. However, there is stronger evidence that societal effects may be low, insofar as implementing flexible automation is concerned. The surveys cited earlier show that many flexibly specialized firms in continental Europe, including German manufacturers, use flexible automation to reduce scope and increase scale in the same way as the British. Furthermore, in about half the German companies that have adopted flexible automation, the new technology has also been accompanied by a narrower job content for operators and their deskilling (Lay, 1990; Fix-Stertz et al., 1990). Paradoxically, while many German companies follow what is alleged to be a typically Anglo-American practice, this was in general unimportant among the firms investigated here.

Britain displays, perhaps in a heightened form, tendencies that one might expect to operate in all capitalist economies. First, the need to control costs in order to contain prices derives from product markets as well as from owners and financial regimes. If markets are competitive, the cost dynamic will affect everyone. Second, companies owned by shareholders have to make surpluses to remit as dividends and to cover the costs of external debt, and this profitability requirement will influence how expensive investments are deployed and what level of costs will be tolerated. Expectations of a lower rate of profit would give managers more room to manoeuvre, but they will never be free of the constraint to deliver a required rate of return.

CONCLUSION

We have foregrounded managerial choices about product innovation, process technology and organizational design (at managerial and workplace levels). Our evidence is that the sharp discontinuity of the new paradigm is overstated. The relationship between flexible process technologies and work organization, managerial organization and product innovation, whether with each separately or in combination, is neither simple nor direct. Nor is it consistent across companies. The only consistent tendency across the sample is for managerial organization to take priority over technology. Companies do seek to respond more flexibly to their product markets, and flexibility does include meeting customer requirements for more differentiated products and higher rates of product innovation. Here the new paradigm is quite correct. However, our evidence that companies then seek to limit the flexibility of their market response does not fit the model. The contradiction becomes even more marked with a paradox that emerges from this chapter, that it is 'flexible' technology itself that sets the major technical and economic limits on product variation.

Our focus on how senior managers 'read' their environments for the purposes of strategic decision-making, and the choices that follow from these interpretations, shows the salience of a set of issues which has been neglected recently. This is the co-existence of the traditional concern with costs and productivity with the newer concern for flexibility. It is still necessary to strike a balance and trade flexibility for efficiency. The priority given to such a traditional concern may be greater in Britain than elsewhere but, at least in the five companies examined here, appears to be independent of the nationality of ownership.

Notes

We wish to thank Stephen Wood for his comments on an earlier draft of this chapter.

[1] This was funded by the ESRC, award number R000231478. The study covered companies in the food, drink and tobacco industry and various sectors within mechanical engineering in 1991/92. The research involved case study research in twenty companies and a large-scale postal survey of each sector. The data collection process comprised interviews with the senior manager of each function at the operating company level, with middle and other senior managers in engineering, manufacturing and technology, and with supervisors and operatives. There were also extended periods of observation. This chapter reports findings from the five companies that used advanced manufacturing systems in our mechanical engineering sample.

[2] Following the analysis of Abernathy (1977) and Clark et al., (1985).

[3] To avoid unecessary confusion, we use the term 'work organization' to denote aspects of organization which occur at the point of production. The term 'organization' refers to managerial roles and structures which occur above the point of production.

[4] Sabel (1991) also discusses managerial and structural reorganization above the workplace level as part of flexible specialization but, unlike the authors just cited, he now treats this quite independently of technology.

[5] Jones (1990) explains the observed deviations from the predictions of the model in relation to national variations in managerial style. This recognizes the issues of managerial strategy and choice, but treats them in a rudimentary and stereotypical fashion. In his more recent work, Sabel (1991) considers volume production in the automobile industry and notes how old and new technological paradigms are often hybridized, so elements of each occur together. He explains hybrids as managerial strategies to 'hedge' the risks of choosing the pure form of either. His recognition of choice is welcome, but we would wish to see a more elaborated analysis of how choices are made in a wider range of industrial settings.

[6] Studies which have investigated these links include Whipp and Clark (1986) and Child and Smith (1987).

[7] Corroboration of this was found in another firm in the engineering sample, a

company renowned for its design and development skills and as a precision manufacturer. This continued to invest in stand-alone CNC machinery rather than flexible automation, because it had insufficient volume of any family of parts to justify automation.

[8] The flexible manufacturing system was designed around this assessment of the company's product market stance. Had the full extent of product variation been anticipated, manufacturing managers said they would have chosen less automation and more manual assembly.

[9] Managers, however, regarded maintenance in the new plant as being a problem and they questioned the use of upgraded craftsmen to deal with the new demands of FMS. They suggested that a qualitatively different level of skill was required.

[10] Coriat (1991) and Tomaney (1994) are exceptions.

References

Abernathy, J. (1977) *The Productivity Dilemma*, John Hopkins, Baltimore, Maryland.

Amin, A. (ed.) (1994) *A Post-Fordist Reader*, Blackwell, Oxford.

Badham, R. (1991) *CAD/CAM and Human Centred Design*, in STA working paper series, Wollongong University.

Bessant, J. (1983) Management and manufacturing innovation: the case of information technlogy, in *Information Technology In Manufacturing Processes*, (ed. G. Winch), London, Rossendale.

Bessant, J. (1993) Towards factory 2000: designing organizations for computer-integrated technologies, in *Human Resource Management and Technical Change*, (ed. J. Clark), Sage, London.

Blumberg M. and Gerwin D. (1994) Coping with advanced manufacturing technology, in *Implementing New Technologies*, (eds E. Rhodes, and D. Wield), Blackwell, Oxford.

Boddy, D. and Buchanan, D.A. (1983) *Organizations in the Computer Age*, Gower, Aldershot.

Boddy, D. and Buchanan, D.A. (1986) *Managing New Technology*, Blackwell, Oxford.

Child, J. (1972) Organizational structure, environment and performance – the role of strategic choice, in *Sociology*, no. 6, pp. 1–22.

Child, J. (1984) New technology and developments in management organization, in *Omega*, vol. 12, no. 3, pp. 211–23

Child, J., Ganter, H.D. and Kieser, A. (1987) Technological innovation and organizational conservatism, in *New Technology as Organizational Innovation*, (eds J. Pennings and A. Buitendam), Ballinger, Cambridge, Massachusetts.

Child, J. and Smith, C. (1987) The context and process of organizational transformation – Cadbury Limited in its sector, in *Journal of Management Studies*, vol. 24, no. 6, pp. 565–99.

Clark, J. (ed.) (1993) *Human Resource Management and Technical Change*, Sage, London.

Clark, K.B., Hayes, R.H. and Lorenz, C. (1985) *The Uneasy Alliance: Managing the Productivity-Innovation Dilemma*, Harvard Business School Press, Boston, Massachusetts.

Corbett, J.M. (1990) Design for human-machine interfaces, in *New Technology and Manufacturing Management*, (eds M. Warner, W. Wobbe and P. Brodner), John Wiley, Chichester.

Coriat, B. (1991) Technical flexibility and mass production, in *Industrial Change and Regional Development*, (eds G. Benko and M. Dunford), Belhaven, London.

Currie, W.L. (1989) The art of justifying new technology to top management, in *Omega*, vol. 17, no 5.

Dosi, G., Freeman, C., Nelson, R., Silverberg G. and Soete, L. (eds) (1988) *Technical Change and Economic Theory*, Pinter, London.

Fix-Sterz, J., Lay, G., Schultz-Wild, R. and Wengel, J. (1990) Flexible manufacturing systems and cells in the FRG, in *New Technology and Manufacturing Management*, (eds M. Warner, W. Wobbe and P. Brodner), John Wiley, Chichester.

Fleck, J. (1987) *Innofusion or Diffusation: The nature of technological development in robotics*, in Department of Business Studies working paper 87/9, University of Edinburgh.

Freeman, C. and Perez, C. (1994) Structural crises of adjustment, business cycles and investment behaviour, in *Implementing New Technologies*, (eds E. Rhodes and D. Wield), Blackwell, Oxford.

Freeman, C., Sharp, M. and Walker, W. (1993) *Technology and the Future of Europe: Global Competition and the Environment in the 1990s*, Pinter, London.

Ghemawat, P. (1986) Sustainable advantage, in *Harvard Business Review*, May–June, pp. 69–74.

Harris, M. (1996) Organizational politics, strategic change and the evaluation of new production technology – the case of CAD, in *Journal of Information Technology*, 11, 1, pp. 51–8.

Harvey, D. (1989) *The Condition of Post Modernity*, Blackwell, Oxford.

Haywood, B. and Bessant, J. (1990) Organization and integration of production systems, in *New Technology and Manufacturing Management*, (eds M. Warner, W. Wobbe and P. Brodner), John Wiley, Chichester.

Hill, S. (1991) How do you manage a flexible firm? The Total Quality Model, in *Work, Employment and Society*, 5, 3, pp. 397–415.

Hutton, W. (1995) *The State We're In.*, Cape, London.

Jaques, M. and Hall, S. (eds) (1989) *New Times*, Lawrence and Wishart, London.

Jones, B. (1990) New production technology and work roles: a paradox of flexibility versus strategic control? in *The Strategic Management of Technological Innovation.*, (eds R. Loveridge and M. Pitt), John Wiley, Chichester.

Kanter, R. (1991) The future of bureaucracy and hierarchy in organization theory, in *Social Theory for a Changing Society*, (eds P. Bourdieu and J. Coleman), Westview, Boulder, Colorado.

Kaplan, R.S. (1986) Accounting lag: the obsolescence of cost accounting systems, in *The Uneasy Alliance: Managing the Productivity-Innovation Dilemma*, (eds K. Clark, R. Hayes and C. Lorenz), Harvard Business School Press, Boston, Massachusetts.

Kay, J. (1995) *The Foundations of Corporate Success,* Oxford University Press.

Kern, H. and Schumann, M. (1987) Limits to the division of labour: new production and employment concepts in West Germany, in *Economic and Industrial Democracy*, 8, 2, pp. 151–70.

Kristensen, P.H. (1990) Technical projects and organizational changes: flexible specialization in Denmark, in *New Technology and Manufacturing Management*, (eds M. Warner, W. Wobbe and P. Brodner), John Wiley, Chichester.

Lane, C. (1988) Industrial change in Europe: the pursuit of flexible specialization in Britain and West Germany, in *Work, Employment and Society*, 2, pp. 141–68.

Lay, G. (1990) Strategic options for CIM integration, in *New Technology and Manufacturing Management*, (eds M. Warner, W. Wobbe and P. Brodner), John Wiley, Chichester.

McLoughlin, I. and Clark, J. (1994) *Technological Change at Work*, Open University Press, Milton Keynes.

McLoughlin, I. (1990) Management, work organization and CAD – towards flexible automation? in *Work, Employment and Society*, 4, 2, pp. 189–216.

Oliver, N. and Wilkinson, B. (1988) *The Japanization of British Industry*, Blackwell, Oxford.

Pavitt, K. (1994) What we know about the strategic management of technology, in *Implementing New Technologies*, (eds E. Rhodes and D. Wield), Blackwell, Oxford.

Perez, C. (1983) Structural change and the assimilation of new technologies in the social and economic system, in *Futures*, 15, pp. 357–75.

Piore, M.J. and Sabel, C. (1984) *The Second Industrial Divide: Prospects for Prosperity*, Basic Books, New York.

Porter, M. E. (1980) *Competitive Strategy*, Free Press, New York.

Sabel, C. (1989) Flexible specialization and the re-emergence of regional economies, in *Reversing Industrial Decline? Industrial Structure and Policy in Britain and her Competitors*, (eds P. Hirst and J. Zeitlin), Berg, Oxford.

Sabel, C. (1991) Moebius-strip organizations and open labour markets: some consequences of the reintegration of conception and execution in a volatile economy, in *Social Theory for a Changing Society*, (eds P. Bourdieu and J. Coleman), Westview, Boulder, Colorado.

Scarbrough, H. and Corbett, M. (1992) *Technology and Organization*, Routledge, London.

Senker, P. (1984) Implications of CAD/CAM for Management, in *Omega*, vol. 12, no. 3, pp. 225–31.

Slack, N. (1990) Flexibility as managers see it, in *New Technology and Manufacturing Management*, (eds M. Warner, W. Wobbe and P. Brodner), John Wiley, Chichester.

Smith, C. (1991) From 1960s automation to flexible specialization: a déjà vu of technological panceas, in *Farewell to Flexibility*, (ed. A. Pollert), Blackwell, Oxford.

Tomaney, J. (1994) A new paradigm of work organization and technology? in *A Post-Fordist Reader*, (ed. A. Amin), Blackwell, Oxford.

Voss, C.A. (1986) Implementing manufacturing technology: a manufacturing strategy approach, in *Managing Advanced Manufacturing Technologies*, (ed. C.A. Voss), IFS, Kempston.

Whipp, R. and Clark, P.A. (1986) *Innovation and the Auto Industry. Product, Process and Work Organization*, Francis Pinter, London.

Wilkinson, B. (1983) *The Shopfloor Politics of New Technology*, Heinemann, London.

Chapter 4

Re-inventing the organization? Towards a critique of business process re-engineering

Leslie Willcocks and Keith Grint

INTRODUCTION

Startling claims are made both for the radical, discontinuous change for organizations represented by business process re-engineering (BPR), and for the transformational impacts on business performance it can, and needs to, achieve. In practice, the claims are as immodest as the reliable data is difficult to find. There is evidence that many projects seem to disappoint. Hammer and Champy (1993a) estimated a 50–70 per cent failure rate for radical breakthrough, high risk projects, though Hammer later points out that BPR 'has no natural failure rate' (Hammer and Stanton, 1994). However, several US empirical studies have found re-engineering projects consistently falling short of their expected benefits (Hall *et al.*, 1993; Moad, 1993); recently some of the leading consultancies involved have begun to suggest that it is not a total solution after all but 'a component to a solution' (Cafasso, 1993; McHugh *et al.*, 1995). In the United Kingdom case research found dramatic improvements in some companies, but documents these examples as few and far between (Bartram, 1992; Harvey, 1995; Willcocks and Currie, 1996).

Outside the burgeoning prescriptive literature, a range of work has already pointed to a number of difficulties with the claims, approaches and implementation practices labelled BPR. Hammer and Stanton (1994) suggest that problems have stemmed mainly from not doing 'real' re-engineering, and not being radical enough, while Champy (1995) suggests that disappointments stem from failure to 're-engineer' management first. Against such obvious boundary maintenance, some have pointed to a revisionist alternative, avoiding the high risk, radical approach (Craig and Yetton, 1994; Davenport and Stoddard, 1994). The extent to which BPR efforts fail has been related to poor linkage between BPR and business strategy, and lack of effective organizational processes for strategy formulation (Galliers, 1994; Watson, 1994). The multi-disciplinary holism at the heart of BPR has raised doubts about whether there are robust methodologies and tools available to facilitate the outcomes required from BPR activities (Earl and Khan, 1994; Klein, 1994). In particular, methodologies have often been found partial, reflecting their disciplinary base and handling some aspects of what should be a holistic approach better than others, particularly, as is frequently the case, where information technology (IT) is involved (Markus and Robey, 1995; O'Hara and Watson, 1995; Willcocks and Smith, 1995). Previous research has shown that adding IT to a major change project increases risk. Notably, additional technical issues and technocratic perspectives all too frequently lead to human, social and political issues becoming marginalized (Davenport, 1994; Walsham, 1993; Willcocks and Margetts, 1994). Indeed, what emerges from the BPR literature itself is how often failure is related, among other reasons, to mismanagement of human, social and political issues and processes (for examples only, see Buday, 1992; Heygate, 1994; Moad, 1993; Thackray, 1993. For a critique see Willmott, 1995).

If these preliminary criticisms can be made of BPR at the level of practice, one may also point out some of the more obvious limitations of the contextual analyses and justifications of BPR commonly presented in management literature. Here the theoretical perspectives of and findings from a series of pre-1990 studies on organizational and technical innovation are conveniently by-passed in order to arrive at the theme of necessary transformation for business survival through radical IT-enabled BPR. Thus, for example, the rich empirical work by Clark and colleagues (Clark, 1987; Clark and Starkey, 1988; Whipp and Clark, 1986) on innovation design, dynamic configuration, structural repertoires and corporate expertise and cultures, or parallel work, for example in Pennings and Buitendam (1987), seemingly have no influence on BPR proponents, despite their obvious relevance. Prophetically for BPR, Clark (1987) pointed out that innovation has been largely assumed, with the problems of innovation and relatedly, exnovation, less central to organization studies. Clark and Staunton (1989) list nine limitations of the mainstream innovation literature, each of which applies to the way BPR in its radical manifestations is promoted. Again, the BPR literature proceeds as if long-standing and much debated models of transition in the post-Fordist period (see Amin, 1994), for example the regulation, neo-Schumpeterian and flexible specialization approaches, have not provided a conceptual depth, and empirical findings that render the BPR analysis of the 'crisis' and prescriptions for the 'call to arms' all too shallow. Studies of the complexities of organization and of strategic change (Pettigrew, 1988; Jermier et al., 1994) and their lessons, for example the importance of continuity as a basis for change, the political and cultural difficulties radical reengineering may store up for itself by taking the 'don't automate, obliterate' route, are all too easily lost in the rhetoric of transformation through simplification. But then, simplicity and collective forgetting may be BPR's central appeal (Grint et al., 1995).

This chapter seeks to take the critique further by firstly locating the claims, rhetoric and actual organizational practices labelled BPR within a historical perspective. It finds the claim that BPR represents novel, discontinuous change exaggerated both theoretically, and as embodied in actual BPR organizational practice. We locate the particular appeal of BPR within an 'externalist' as well as an 'internalist' account of its messages; that is, we consider the extent to which the persuasive utility of the account rests not within the 'rational' or 'logical' content of BPR but within the relationship that is established between BPR and its external environment and context. Subsequently, we consider the levels of success achieved and some reasons for why, on our evidence, the record continues to be generally more disappointing than, and at odds with, the rhetoric. We argue throughout that political interpretations can throw considerable light on central concepts in the mainstream BPR literature – on discontinuous change and deracination; on BPR as a form of Utopian thought applied to work organizations; on decision-making and outcomes; and on the espoused central role of IT. We also argue for a theoretical development, pointing out the key weaknesses but also the applicability of Actor-Network theory to the study of IT-enabled re-engineering projects.

RESEARCH BASE

Additionally, recognizing that many of the published discussions and critiques of BPR are all too short on empirical evidence (see for example Burke and Peppard, 1995; Coulson-Thomas, 1994) throughout we draw on a range of case and survey findings, by ourselves and others, concerning BPR practice. We argue that the empirical evidence emerging on BPR practice, and the types of results emerging from what organizations have called BPR, do not prove, but are certainly suggestive at many points of, the political interpretation that we detail in this paper. The studies we refer to throughout cover the 1991–95 period and stem mainly from work by Bartram (1992), Douglas (1993), Hall *et al.* (1993), Harvey (1995), Maglitta (1995), Moad (1994), Willcocks and Currie, (1996), Willcocks and Smith (1995) and Willcocks (1995). Our own work covers six detailed case studies tracked in the 1991–95 period and a survey carried out in the September 1994–January 1995 period reporting on BPR practice in 168 UK-based medium and large organizations. The case research employed participant observation, semi-structured interviews of stakeholders from different levels in the organization, a longitudinal approach and detailed analysis of internal documentation. For the survey, after piloting the questionnaire, a random sample of medium and large organizations was selected from the 20,000 contact database of Business Intelligence, an independent research firm. Respondents occupied senior and upper middle management positions and represented a cross-section of organizational roles. The contact database sufficiently represents the major areas of economic activity in the UK and this was reflected in the sample derived. Full details of the methodologies employed in our studies appear in Willcocks (1995) and Willcocks and Currie (1996).

The case and survey work provide findings on the type and extent of BPR practice, and also the relative successes and failures being experienced. Throughout, this information is used to underpin our arguments. Our own survey was also designed to produce practitioner opinion on the major barriers and critical success factors experienced in BPR programmes, and what, in retrospect, practitioners would have done differently, that is what they have learned from their experiences. In what follows we argue that this latter evidence, together with corroborative evidence from other studies, can be used to support our own political explanations of BPR behaviours and failures, though we also recognize that the survey was not explicitly designed to provide such political explanations, and that the findings are open to other interpretations.

BPR: THE RHETORIC OF DISCONTINUOUS CHANGE

Much of the rationale for BPR was developed initially in a North American context, then generalized across the developed economies. The focus can be summarized as: how did corporate America lose its way in Paradise and how can Paradise be regained? The argument underlying much of the BPR management literature suggests that current failure is a direct result of previous success and a radical break from current managerial practices is required (Hammer and Champy, 1993a; Harrington, 1993; Johansson et al., 1993). The extensive divisions of labour, functional divisions and economies of scale derived from Adam Smith, F.W. Taylor and Henry Ford worked when demand was high, competition low and customers indiscriminate, but now all these have been reversed and complacency has to be removed by shifting the focus from producer to consumer. It is a shift from vertical functions to horizontal processes. Every process redesign should be concerned with the customer rather than the producer, the process rather than the function, and a multitude of disparate activities that must be amalgamated into a hybrid if the redesign is to work. This approach is presented as simultaneously radical, holistic and novel.

So what is it that has to be done? The radical claims, according to Hammer and Champy, are not driven by technical innovations, even though IT provides a critical enabling device and IT-related BPR provides the most significant examples. Rather, they concentrate on 11 inter-related changes (Hammer and Champy, 1993b). We have argued elsewhere that no individual change is novel – each has previously appeared, if in a different guise (Grint, 1994). Other authors also support the case that there is much that is not so new in BPR (Earl and Khan, 1994; Willcocks and Smith, 1995). The more novel element lies in combining the transformation of organizational performance with the more holistic approach to change embodied in BPR, and the significance allotted to technology, not as a determinant of change but as a critical enabler. Two questions follow: first, why is BPR so popular? Second, why do so many of the radical attempts appear to fail?

There can be no doubt about the relatively recent popularity of something called BPR; at the beginning of 1995 we found 59 per cent of organizations planning or undertaking BPR activity. This is in line with the general findings of earlier surveys in the UK and USA suggesting a 55–70 per cent take-up rate for something called business process re-engineering (Moad, 1993; Preece and Edwards, 1993; Price Waterhouse, 1994). Moreover, BPR as a holistic approach to change is a recent phenomenon. The real take-off point would seem to be 1993/94 when 64 per cent of BPR programmes in our sample began. On a reading of the literature, one explanation for BPR's popularity would need to address its seeming newness, together with the promise of transformation embodied in it. We have also argued elsewhere that the contextual resonances embodied in the dominant accounts of BPR provide an explanation for its popularity. Moving through Taylorism and Fordism, human relations and neo-human relations, each finding a resonance with external events, and for each of which an externalist explanation can be given, one can posit the arrival of a fourth wave, the cultures of excellence approach where the limits of modernism and Fordism are perceived as the stimulus of change. Re-engineering, in this perspective, rather than being considered as the most advanced point in the rational progress of management, and rather than appearing to be just one more manifestation of the dialectical play between science and morality as outlined by Barley and Kunda (1993), is merely the latest in a wave of managerial fashions (see Grint, 1994). The point is supported by a number of more recent publications now seeking to go 'beyond' business process re-engineering (for example McHugh et al., 1995; Watson, 1994).

It is not coincidental that the rise of functional accounts of organizations, and subsequently integrated systems approaches to organization, developed at a time of business organizational stasis, or even more appropriately during the long boom from the end of the Second World War to the 1974 oil crisis. But when old stabilities like the East–West conflict crumble in the Berlin Wall collapse; when American, and even Western economic domination withers under pressure from Japan and the Asian Tigers; and when the long boom turns into the long collapse, the conditions for organizational radicalism are set fair.

BPR can be read as portraying an external and internal crisis to which it can provide a manageable response. An important part of its attraction is in the idea of organizational forgetting, of wiping the slate clean, of starting anew. However, part of BPR's persuasive essence also lies in the resonances that it 'reveals' between the old and the new, particularly between American past glories and future conquests. Thus Hammer is concerned to remind potential American customers that the novelty element is actually an historically rooted part of American culture. Success can be achieved not through breaks with tradition but through a radical return to tradition. That the USA's retrospective ideals, manifest in such rhetorical calls as 'back to basics', 'stick to the knitting' and 'protect the core business', appear to have had only limited success can then be read as a result of either not being radical enough, not re-engineering properly (Hammer and Stanton, 1995), or of not returning to the roots of American tradition. Either way, the argument hinges on an interpretation and use of the rhetoric and practice of re-engineering that is fundamentally political. On this account re-engineering is able to provide a new discourse with which contemporary developments can be simultaneously explained and controlled. And, following Foucault, the process of discursive formation necessarily implicates both knowledge and power, theory and practice (Gordon, 1980; Wolin, 1991).

Given this popularity and the projected utility of BPR, why then do so many radical BPR projects seem to disappoint? As previously discussed, one can point to the focus on process that makes re-engineering multidisciplinary and cross-functional and implies difficult cultural change. Also, the focus on transforming performance could lead to radical, and so high risk, approaches to organizational transformation being adopted. Finally the concern for IT-enabled BPR brings in a technology dimension that always adds further risk of failure to any major project (Stringer, 1992; Willcocks and Griffiths, 1994). In what follows we take the analysis further and discuss how politics, together with organizational histories and cultures may well help to explain why most organizations are in fact seeking incremental, less radical approaches in their practices labelled BPR. The predominance of 'rationality' has prevented us from assessing how far the success, failure and more incremental approaches to organizational change can be linked to the significance of management's politics. This raises a related, prime issue: how much the 'back to basics' and 'return to the roots' movements also imply a 'back to politics' movement. As with 'culture' and 'excellence' in the 1980s, BPR rhetoric and practice emerge from our evidence as ways of talking about and conducting political activity by seemingly other, more acceptable means. Let us examine this idea in more detail, before turning to the evidence on actual BPR practice.

BPR AS DERACINATION

In this section we use the idea of deracination to consider BPR. Like so many forms of organizational change, BPR is essentially premised on deracination in its assumption that uprooting organizational norms and traditions is necessary for radical increases in productivity. This uprooting not only relates to the organizational form – whether flattened hierarchies or teams – but also to the displacement of 'normal' organizational practices. In effect, the very act of deracination is designed to cut off the oxygen of conventional Machiavellian (selfish or war-like) activities and to facilitate an entirely novel form of management practice under the alien (peaceful) conditions that result from re-engineering. Thus BPR is adopted and deployed as if office politics either do not, should not or will not exist in the re-engineered corporation. The irrationality of the past is cut away by the BPR plough to encourage a conflict-free zone where rationality rules. 'Re-engineering can lead you to a promised land of its own' is the comment Hammer and Stanton (1995) make when comparing the BPR journey to that described in Exodus. But what does this 'promised land' look like? One version is described by Johansson *et al.*, (1993):

> {Managers} should measure everything they can. . . . Once managers know what changes have to take place . . . they will start to influence the behaviour of staff, focus on results, and release their creative talent. They also start changing their roles, becoming less concerned with control and instruction, and more concerned with challenge and discussion. . . . With this change of management style, organizational politics can be cast aside (p. 202).

This statement is fairly typical of the unitary perspective on the organization that dominates so much writing on business process re-engineering, including that of Hammer and Champy. The problem here lies in the truncated theorization of the nature of power and politics inherent in much of what passes for thinking about, and providing the rationale for, BPR practices. From the beginnings of industrial capitalism in the late 18th century in Britain, management tasks and causal explanations have been locked into models of rational behaviour ultimately embedded in the operations of the market: managers do what they do because the imperatives of the market require that it be done.

At the same time, from Dalton's classic *Men Who Manage* and Jay's *Management and Machiavelli*, where political goals were deemed to be critical, to Child's notion of organizations being run by a 'dominant coalition' of senior executives, to Lee and Lawrence's concerns for the power of social networks, and into Hannaway's more recent account of the duality of management – where working for the company and for oneself are the twin aims (and they need not coincide), there have been arguments that management is as much a political process as a rational one (Dalton, 1959; Child, 1972; Lee and Lawrence, 1985; Hannaway, 1989); from a critical perspective, of course, management as a political activity – in the sense of being exploitative – has a history almost as long. From Marx to Braverman and the Labour Process approaches, and from Bendix to Baldamus, management's action has been configured or rationalized as action in the interests of capitalists or managers but not of all (Marx, 1954; Bendix, 1956; Baldamus, 1961; Gowler and Legge, 1983). In effect, management is a political activity either as the politics of competing groups or the politics of personal ascendancy through the corporate ladder (see Stewart, 1993, for a useful review).

If organizational life is as political as some of the literature suggests, then attempting to inhibit it is clearly a difficult task. Moreover, not only might this Machiavellianism undermine attempts to generate more homogeneous corporate cultures but it also moves to shift organizations in radically new directions. There is an illustrative parallel here. When F. W. Taylor, through Scientific Management principles, sought to control and isolate the low-level employee he did so not out of ignorance of human social needs but out of practical experience of how skilled work-groups could operate against management interests. One can read BPR also as an essentially political intervention – normative, metaphorical, and practical – into work organizations. In what follows we suggest three ways that BPR can be understood as a political process.

RE-ENGINEERING UTOPIA

Re-engineering in its radical version can be located as a particular form of Utopian thought applied to work organizations. It does not attempt to improve the way business currently operates (though some of the re-engineering focus on business processes implies this – see Harvey, 1995), but to rethink the way it operates. More importantly, it asserts that the critical feature of re-engineering is that associated with re-engineering management rather than just production processes (Champy, 1995; Padulo, 1995). It does not seek to improve functions' efficiency but to examine whether functions are the best way to run a business. Moreover, it does this against a background in which the larger danger is not in radical change but in the danger of obsolescence. Re-engineering's innovation, then, may lie in its denial of an incrementalist orthodoxy that has prevailed since the mid-1960s. In essence, the ideas imply that only an attack on all fronts simultaneously in which every possible institution, ritual, practice and norm is subject to critique and reconstruction, is likely to succeed (Hammer and Champy, 1993a; Harvey, 1995). The premise of the radical argument, therefore, is that incrementalism is itself a barrier to change. This does not imply that all attempts to change should be Utopian in their scale and direction but rather that Utopian thought here should be considered rather differently from its traditional role, in More's Utopia and Huxley's Island for example, as fit only for dreamers, fit for 'nowhere' (Grint and Hogan, 1994ab). Instead, Utopia might be conceived as a method of outlining the possible alternatives to the status quo as a proactive stimulus to change – as William Morris intended.

Re-engineering, then, can be located as a Utopian form of thought, necessarily political in its use during interventions so as to galvanize organizational practice. However, there is evidence (see below) that the radical extent of the change required explains both the wide rhetorical (but few practical) successes and the many relative disappointments with re-engineering. On this interpretation, the high degree of uncertainty and risk involved unnerves those attempting to re-engineer so that they seek more conservative and instrumental approaches to change that appear both less risky and more plausible. This, of course, is precisely the argument made in the late 1950s by Lindblom's (1959) account of 'disjointed incrementalism' or 'muddling through', after Simon's 'satisficing' behaviour (Simon, 1947). These incisive critiques of rational decision making imply that decision-makers do not approach organizational problems with a clean sheet of paper and an ideal, but with a pre-folded piece of paper and in the light of existing structures and policies (Jabes, 1982).

Of course, such political and organizational realities have already been recognized in several revisionist alternatives to the utopian version of BPR (Heygate, 1993; Craig and Yetton, 1994; Davenport, 1993). Davenport and Stoddard (1994) point to:

> a revisionist alternative that allows reengineering and quality to exist in tandem, applying the radical approach only where it is absolutely necessary, and being happy with 10 per cent improvements elsewhere.

Our own survey evidence shows a complementary picture. High risk, radical BPR approaches were generally not being taken. One indicant of this was low expenditure, with 43 per cent of medium and large organizations each incurring BPR related expenditures of under £1 million. Many of the processes being re-engineered seemed to be existing ones to which improvements were being sought rather than those identified as a result of a radical rethink of how the organization needed to be reconfigured and managed. Radical BPR is portrayed as achieving sizeable job losses, yet we found that for all completed BPR projects and all types of process, staff redundancies averaged less than 5 per cent of total BPR costs. Generally, whatever the process being re-engineered, organizations did not seem to be aiming high when they looked for improvements from BPR. This is in fact a common finding across much of the reported case and survey work (see Hall *et al.*, 1993; Maglitta, 1995; Moad, 1993). There may well be a cause and effect here, with organizations aiming low and hitting low, because the actual improvements being achieved were also relatively low. The best performance on actual improvements were found to be with core processes, though these were impressive in relatively few cases (see Figure 4.1). Across the eight main improvement areas identified,

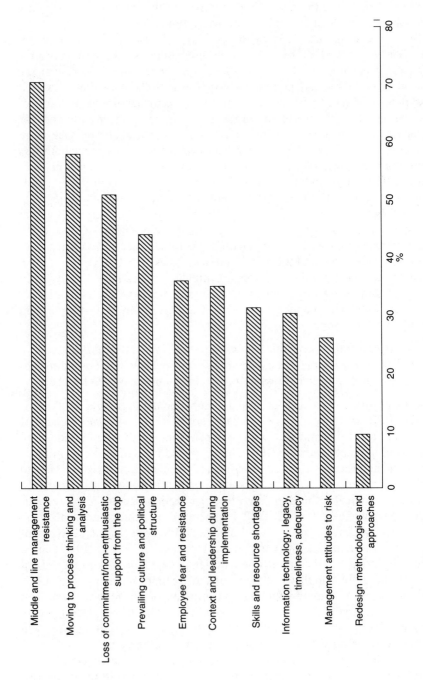

Figure 4.1 Core process improvements

the highest average improvements were in speed cycle times (61 per cent), improved external service (50 per cent), improved internal service (40 per cent) and more flexible response (36 per cent). Support, management and cross-boundary process re-engineering produced consistently lower improvements than these.

Very few organizations are achieving what could be called 'break-through' results. In the literature breakthrough results suggest order of magnitude improvements in process performance, feeding through into significant turnaround in an organization's financial performance. Looking at the organizations that have completed BPR programmes, and using a relatively conservative 'breakthrough' benchmark of 20 per cent profitability gain, 20 per cent revenue gain and 10 per cent decrease in costs of doing business, only 18 per cent of organizations have achieved significant financial benefits from BPR on all three measures. The politics of Utopia – seen at the level of both rhetorical flourish and practical/methodological prescription – are being suborned to achieving tangible improvements rather than radical change. The picture of discontinuous change represented in the BPR literature is not clearly underscored in BPR practice.

Politics intrude in another way. Even if the form and extent of the change is as utopian in its radical result as re-engineering suggests, it is unlikely that the end product will emerge as a depoliticized 'promised land' in a Machiavellian sea but, rather, as an island where managerial life may have changed while remaining essentially political: there are still careers to be carved out, clans to join and gangs to avoid. Indeed, in the revitalized, dynamic and slimmed down re-engineered organization the operations' transparency may mean that political life has to be, if anything, more subtly handled than before, but handled nonetheless. If William Morris's *News From Nowhere*, and the works by More and Huxley were utopian they nevertheless represented visions where political ideas, interests and actions were strongly represented. As evidence from our survey will show (see below), there is nothing inherent in BPR as a process or outcome that depoliticizes organizational life; if anything, politics breed in times of major, IT-enabled change (Pettigrew, 1985; Willcocks *et al.*, 1996). Even more political resonances occur when re-engineering is presented as a permanent revolution. Thus for Hammer and Stanton (1995) the 'promised land' is, in fact, never finally arrived at: 'There are no plateaus anymore, only a mountain with no summit' (p. 318). Not only will change create politics, but depoliticization will be forever destabilized. This repoliticization of Utopia will be familiar. For managers, such Utopias may be the CEO's latest dream that involves all members of staff wearing uniform or watching 'corporate vision' videos. Here Utopia becomes a straitjacket that warrants no deviation, that considers all protest as a sign of indiscipline or conspiracy or worse; it becomes the politicized nightmare rather than the de-politicized dream because it implies that the originator of the dream has a universal wisdom that simply cannot exist. In the business field we can consider a litany of gods that failed, or at least failed to revolutionize our businesses permanently: Taylorism, Fordism, Management by Objectives, Measured Day Work, Payment by Results and Collective Bargaining. We might even note how these gods recur in time when today's executives forget yesterday's Utopias. For example, individual payment systems were an essential principle for F.W. Taylor, but were tried and found wanting in the tendency to decay which appears to undermine all such schemes as individuals and groups protect their political position by 'working the system' to their own advantage. That they are now back in favour is not the issue, but we should not expect them to be any more rational or to last indefinitely any more than last time.

THE POLITICS OF DECISION-MAKING AND ACTION

It has been a convention of Western thought since the Enlightenment that the same rationality that persuaded us to think analytically rather than synthetically also operates to persuade us that rationality, rooted in reasoned individual action and the application of scientific principles, is the means by which individuals are persuaded to execute decisions made by others or to change their opinion, their attitude or their behaviour. And indeed, the dominant line in management texts presents politics as an aberration from a rational norm. However, another strand of management studies presents managers experiencing organizations as Machiavellian Princes running political institutions in pursuit of what appears to many to be their own private interests (Pettigrew, 1985; Pfeffer, 1992). Hence, decisions are effectively executed by (successful) political infighting, by (successful) networking, by making the right friends and the right enemies, by going to the right school and university, by choosing the right parents, gender and ethnicity, and by a whole host of related aspects that have little to do with any form of rationally legitimated criteria for ensuring success.

If this is the case in organizations, if managers operate politically rather than rationally and succeed or fail on political-rational rather than organizational-rational criteria, then we might consider the extent to which change programmes, such as re-engineering, succeed or fail on the same grounds. In effect, explaining the rational implications of continuing the traditional way of doing things and the rational effects of a re-engineered process may be considerably less effective than setting out to achieve the same ends through a political process. In short, this might mean moving from a campaign to persuade people through an appeal to their minds to a campaign to enrol them through an appeal to their hearts.

In the BPR case rhetoric is, of course, an important power resource, as pointed out by Grint (1994) and Jones (1994). Rhetoric is also implicated in power relations to the degree to which it supports the legitimacy of change.

On a broader front legitimacy is tied in with politics as the management of meaning (Willcocks *et al.*, 1996). In the BPR programmes surveyed we constantly found a high degree of difficulty experienced in, firstly, developing shared norms and beliefs among stakeholders; and, secondly, in getting those values to translate into co-operation and commitment over process and IT changes and their operationalization. Thus in our survey, the top problem encountered in the design stage of BPR was gaining 'buy-in' from all stakeholders; during BPR implementation it was resistance to change. Similar results are reported from other studies (Douglas, 1993; Haughton, 1992; Heygate, 1993; Maglitta, 1995).

Despite this, most conventional perspectives on organizational decision making and action are predicated on a very traditional theory of power. These perspectives tend to imply that where organizational power is in the hands of an individual or a small elite, then power emanates from the centre to the periphery with the causal influence similarly centrifugal (Handy, 1985). In short, a leader's power causes others to act. In practice, of course, leaders do not 'do' very much by way of actually performing the acts required to secure change. On the contrary, leaders generally get others to do the performing. Having said this, in our survey, gaining and sustaining top and senior management support was rated consistently as the major single critical success factor in BPR programmes. Clearly other stakeholders expected regular practical assertion of influence by their superiors. It also emerged that this quite frequently did not emerge, with loss of top/senior management support ranked as the third most significant barrier in BPR programmes. Such findings are in fact typical across all the empirical work on BPR that we have analysed.

An interpretation of this confusion over roles relates to reassessing the analytics of power. If subordinates themselves do not act a leader has little power; only as a consequence of subordinate actions can leaders be deemed to have power. One can see from Figure 4.2 the difficulty that a BPR programme can then encounter. If middle and line management resistance is the first most significant barrier, and the prevailing culture and political structure the fourth, then even assuming senior management support for BPR, it inevitably runs into political problems. That such political difficulties emerge is endorsed by a range of other empirical studies (for example Bartram, 1992; Hall *et al.*, 1993; Moad, 1994; Watkins, 1994). Power, in this perspective, therefore, is contingent on producing and reproducing a network of associations that facilitates 'acting at a distance' (Latour, 1993). Thus power is a consequence of action, rather than a cause of action.

This shift from the 'principle' of power to its 'practice', as Latour terms it, or from power as a possession to power as a relationship, as Foucault's writing implies, also suggests that subordinate action occurs only through the subordinate's interpretation of self-advantage: subordinates obey

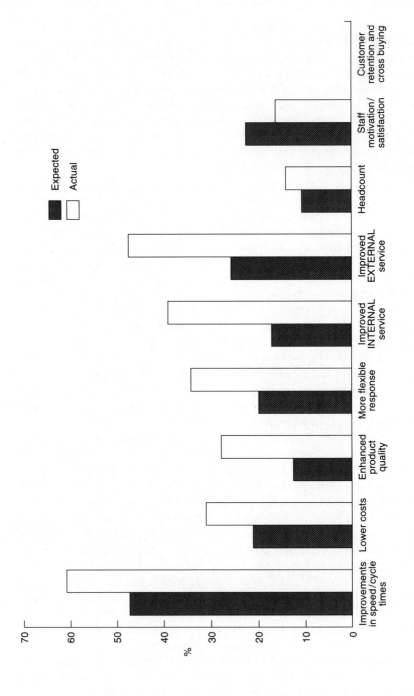

Figure 4.2 The 10 most significant barriers in BPR programmes

because they consider it in their interests to do so (Gordon, 1980; Latour, 1986). In turn, it is likely that the leader's command will become distorted through what Latour calls the 'translation' process: not only do leaders depend on their subordinates but a subordinate's translation of their edicts may well be a distortion of the leader's intention. This implies that rather than power spreading out from the centre to the periphery in a determinate and unmediated fashion it is both highly contingent and the subject of constant interpretation and renegotiation. Such a revision in this context implies that the existence of policies or rules does not ensure such policies or commands are enacted. Moreover, difficulties in BPR initiatives may lie in the misrecognition of power: if subordinates are ultimately in control of their own destinies then whether BPR – or any change programme – fails or succeeds ultimately depends on their being persuaded to act in particular ways. In practice, as Giddens (1984) describes, a dialectic of control operates. It is also useful, following Foucault (1988), to refer to power as a relationship, and therefore to power relations in which resistances are formed at the point where relations of power are exercised. In short, a degree of self-government is not so much an ideal to aim at as a fact of life.

That the conceptualization and analytics of power are important in studying BPR emerges strongly from both our survey and case work, and a range of other studies on BPR. In our own survey four of the top five, and seven of the top ten, most significant barriers to BPR relate to human and political issues, broadly conceived. Furthermore, as far as interest groups are concerned, it is notable that managers rate lower-level employees' fear and resistance as much less significant barriers to BPR than middle and senior management's. This would seem to relate to the comparatively greater power middle, line and senior managers have in the prevailing cultures and political structures in the organizations under review, a finding replicated in other studies (Douglas, 1993; Watkins, 1994; Willcocks and Smith, 1995). The importance of political/human issues in BPR was endorsed when we asked respondents to identify the critical success factors and what they would have done differently in their BPR programmes. Six of the nine top critical success factors relate to human/political issues: top management support, gaining employee 'buy-in', project management, implementation style, communication processes and establishing the need and the levers for change. These themes and type of finding also emerge strongly from the range of extant published empirical work on BPR. As just three examples, survey work in the UK financial services sector found the most common barriers to be lack of top level agreement, commitment, drive and vision, and politics and vested interests, especially at middle management level. Douglas (1993), in US case studies, concluded that: 'the CIOs we spoke with say they have spent a year or two just trying to soften up defences formed by business unit heads and top-level management to the point that they can begin discussing re-engineering'. In researching a

BPR project in the NHS, Willcocks and Currie (1996) report a senior clinician's comments: 'End-games are difficult in the NHS . . . you . . . get political opposition, given the range of professional groups and stake-holders. In information systems there are many interests to look after . . .' Such extant work helps to underline the strongest single finding in our survey when respondents were asked what they had learned from their BPR experience. Their collective response can be summarized as 'pay much earlier and more focused attention to the human and political issues inherent in BPR.'

THE ROLE OF INFORMATION TECHNOLOGIES

In the management literature, most commentators in BPR theory identify IT as a critical enabler of business process re-engineering. But IT also emerges from practice as an important enabler of BPR activity and support for redesigned processes. Thus, in our 1995 survey 58 per cent of respondents rated the IT role in enabling radical process redesign as 'critical', 32 per cent rated it as 'marginal' while 10 per cent said IT had no role to play in their BPR projects. For even more organizations IT played an important role in supporting redesigned processes. 68 per cent of respondents rated IT process support for BPR as 'critical' in their organizations. IT, or rather its management, also figured as one of the top ten critical success factors for BPR programmes, while technical deficiencies together with poor IT management were also rated as seventh out of the ten most significant barriers to BPR. IT represented between 24 and 45 per cent of total spending on each of the BPR programmes we reviewed.

IT was regarded as a critical element in the success of the top 'best performers' that had completed BPR programmes. This group consisted of the 'breakthrough' organizations and the organizations gaining significant profitability, revenue and cost reduction improvements as a result of BPR. In practice over 75 per cent of the top 30 per cent best performers in BPR saw IT as critical in both enabling radical process redesign and supporting redesigned processes. Over half the top best performers were incurring over 40 per cent of their total BPR spend on IT, though for the others IT spend was average or below for the type of process being re-engineered. This finding is based on a small sample, but supports other research findings that there tends to be little or no correlation between size of IT spend and organizational performance (Willcocks, 1994; 1995).

In our reading of the BPR message and the degree of IT utilization, IT has a highly significant role in how BPR is constructed and implemented. In this section we reconsider perspectives on technology in organizational settings, with a view to reconstructing the relationship between technology and politics, and indeed the possibility of technology as politics.

One common perspective on technology can be referred to as essentialist:

some objective view of technical capacity is in principle available and this technical capacity is viewed as inherent to the technology (artefact or system). But what happens if we reconsider technology as no more nor less of a black box than any other element in the BPR equation? This general approach has been referred to as anti-essentialist (see Grint and Woolgar, forthcoming for an extended review of this approach). It encompasses a broad church of perspectives, including 'social shaping' (e.g. MacKenzie, 1990), 'social construction of technology' (e.g. Bijker *et al.*, 1987; Bijker and Law, 1992) and what has been called 'designer technology'. These otherwise different approaches share the view that the nature, form and capacity of a technology is the upshot of various antecedent circumstances involved in its development (mainly taken to include design, manufacture and production). These antecedent circumstances are said to be 'built into' and/or 'embodied in' the final product; the resulting technology is 'congealed social relations'.

One particular approach within the broad anti-essentialist model that provides a further perspective on IT-enabled BPR is Actor-Network theory. Recent developments in Actor-Network theory suggest that the academic and analytic division between the 'human' and 'non-human' is a major stumbling block to comprehension since there are virtually no conditions under which humans exist other than within networks of other humans and non-humans (Callon, 1986; Law, 1991; Latour, 1986, 1988, 1993; Ormrod, 1995; Singleton, 1995). In the words of Latour (1991), 'Technology is society made durable.' These 'hybrids' or 'Monsters' (Law, 1991) run counter to the analytic tradition set up under the procedures and rules of the Enlightenment philosophers (Latour, 1993), and pose formidable problems of analysis since our understanding of the world is premised on divisions between people and things. They are also, of course, problematic because our tradition has been one in which the specific 'effect' of any variable can be readily assessed. Thus, for example, how can we differentiate between the 'effect' of IT in the re-engineering process and the 'effect' of all the other elements? Since BPR is, by its very nature, a holistic hybrid it becomes difficult to evaluate the significance of the discrete elements. As a second point, Actor-Network theory suggests not just that a holistic analysis is necessary but also that we should avoid 'switching registers' (Law, 1991, p. 8) when we move from analysing the human and the non-human. This symmetry of analysis runs not just counter to the entire Enlightenment tradition but has profound implications for understanding the significance of both the human and the non-human. Callon (1986), for example, in his account of certain French scallops, poses it in a counter-intuitive form that talks of the 'interests' of the scallops in aligning themselves to one particular actor-network rather than another. For studying re-engineering, the point here is that since we probably know as much about the real interests of scallops as we do about those of other people perhaps we can learn from Actor-Network approaches both by discarding the different registers that inhibit understanding and by reconsidering our universally all too easy attribution of interests, cause and effect.

A third relevant aspect of Actor-Network theory is the notion of the network's strength being derived from the robustness of the links rather than the 'inherent' strength or power of any discrete element. This idea of technology being 'society made durable' is especially relevant to BPR's radical claim to better performance since it asserts that the holistic union of the social and technical is the key to the approach's strength and influence. But to what extent is the radical garnering of a heterogenous network within BPR premised on taken for granted claims about the capacity and effects of its component parts? Capacities and effects of both human and non-human elements are themselves the result of constructive or constitutive rather than descriptive efforts.

In sum, Actor-Network and other anti-essentialist approaches to technology can offer a more heuristic purchase on the significance of technology and have considerable policy implications for technology design, development and use. These, in turn, may be critical for explaining the success or failure of various BPR initiatives. At the same time it is important to note that these anit-essentialist perspectives bring a number of compromising problems with them. The first is the ambivalence associated with the idea of antecedent circumstances being 'built in', since this seems to imply that a technology is 'neutral' and can be objectively evaluated until such time as the politics or values are built in. Since, to borrow a phrase from Levi-Strauss, technologies always arrive 'cooked' and never 'raw' it is difficult to accept that a non-evaluative account, i.e forgetting the political dimension in the initial analysis of technology, is plausible. Relatedly, with regard to 'antecedent circumstances' one needs to problematize the assumption that 'interests' are transparently available to the analyst and do not require considerable interpretive activity. Unless we can be certain that we can 'read' the interests of various groups into various technologies we might be wary of this. Thirdly, one can question the view that technologies, albeit those at the end of a cycle of embodying antecedent circumstances – the final stabilized technological products – are capable of having effects; that is effects which do not require interpretive action – they speak for themselves (see Grint and Woolgar, forthcoming, for a detailed critique).

However, in our view, Actor-Network theory and other anti-essentialist approaches have much to offer. If the world is composed of 'hybrids', of 'monsters', then the implications are that many conventional approaches to change management – whether they focus wholly on people or on technology – are severely limited in their applicability. An essential aspect of the most radical formulations of Actor-Network theory is the emphasis on the problematic nature of agency. Only in Actor-Network theory do the 'things' appear to have the same status as 'humans' in the development of interests. In radical versions of BPR, as among our survey respondents, there is a stress on redesign through the notion of process. There is also high stress on IT as 'critical enabler'. This type of finding features strongly in a wide range of studies (Bartram, 1992; Douglas, 1993; Maglitta, 1995; Moad, 1994; Price Waterhouse, 1994). Hammer and Stanton (1995), from an essentialist perspective, perhaps state the central role of artefacts the most clearly:

> technology should not be adapted to processes, but processes must be totally configured to exploit the full potential of technology. (p. 172)

But artefacts – in the case of BPR information-based technologies and redesigned processes – can themselves be interpeted as having political properties (Winner, 1985). Clearly as part of the politics of BPR, 'things' as well as people need to change radically, and in doing so the actor network that results can make concrete the repoliticized, re-engineered organization. Actor-Network theory can assist further in the synthetic analysis that is needed here. The importance of such an analysis becomes clear when the symbolic nature of IT within change projects such as BPR is considered. Not only is the technology a visible sign of BPR being implemented, but stakeholders may utilize and interpret IT as a symbol of progress, cultural change, investment and progress (Scarbrough and Corbett, 1992; Willcocks et al., 1996). As such, IT as 'artefact' has considerable political resonances in the context of BPR.

CONCLUSION

Business process re-engineering is revealed as essentially political in its rhetorical and practical manifestations. Its claims for newness are exaggerated, and its application generally less startling in its outcomes than its promotional literature predicts. One defence offered by Hammer and Stanton (1994) is that organizations that do not achieve such results are not doing 'real' re-engineering. There is some evidence from our survey that this is the case, though one would need to ask why this is so. On the other hand the further defence that 'success or failure is determined by a company's understanding of it, the ability to execute it and the executives' commitment to it . . . . those who do it right succeed; those who do not fail' would seem to be largely tautologous.

The paths organizations are tending to take in practice under the BPR labelling, and the barriers being encountered, would indicate reason for greater recognition of, and sensitivity to, human, social and political issues and processes in change than that registered amongst BPR's more ebullient proponents. It is not that such issues are ignored, of course. Indeed, Hammer's most recent book adresses itself almost entirely to the problem of 'resistance to change' (Hammer and Stanton, 1995). Rather the human, social and political issues are viewed from a unitarist, senior management perspective, informed by a mechanistic, largely technicist, almost 17th-century view of how organization's function and can be changed – if the clock is broken, replace it with a new one. This is supported in a review of the 1991–93 BPR literature where Tinaiker *et al.* (1995) found 95.9 per cent of articles concerned with only technical issues. They also found the dominant depiction of BPR as a top-down approach to restructuring organizations to increase efficiency on the basis of technical design criteria highly reminiscent of the principles of Scientific Management. All this flows into how human issues are conceived and problematized and how 'resistance to change' and 'counter-revolutionaries' are to be dealt with. In Hammer and Stanton (1995), for example, there is a violence and self-belief inherent in the approach that could easily become dysfunctional:

> Dramatic improvement has to be paid for in some way, and the coinage is usually denominated in units of suffering. (p. 174) . . . it is necessary to deal with them ('resisters') gently but insistently by pointing out the gaps in their understanding and the errors of their ways. By means of repeated communication and clarification they can be brought onto the straight and narrow . . . . However, those who are deliberately trying to obstruct the reengineering effort . . . need the back of the hand'. (p.183)

In this respect the use of the word 're-engineering' among BPR proponents is not accidental but symptomatic of a world view seeking to treat politics as aberrant and dysfunctional, and providing mechanisms for depoliticizing organizations in the pursuit of the 'promised land' of the re-engineered organization. As such BPR is both radical and political, but also probably builds in a range of difficulties for itself.

References

Amin, A. (ed.) (1994) *Post-Fordism: A Reader*, Blackwell, Oxford.

Baldamus, W. (1961) *Efficiency and Effort*, Tavistock, London.

Barley, S.R. and Kunda, G. (1993) Design and devotion: surges of rational and normative ideologies of control in management discourse, in *Administrative Science Quarterly*, 37, pp. 363–399.

Bartram, P. (1992) *Business Reengineering: The Use of Process Redesign and IT To Transform Corporate Performance*, Business Intelligence, London.

Bendix, R. (1956) *Work and Authority in Industry*, John Wiley, New York.

Bijker, W., Hughes, T. and Pinch, T. (eds) (1987) *The Social Construction Of Technological Systems*, MIT Press, Cambridge, Massachusetts.

Bijker, W. and Law, J. (eds) (1992) *Shaping Technology/Building Society*, MIT Press, Cambridge, Massachusetts.

Briday, R. (1992) Forging a new culture at Capital Holdings' direct response group, in *Insight Quarterly*, 4, pp. 38–49.

Burke, G. and Peppard, J. (eds) (1995) *Examining Business Process Reengineering*, Kogan Page, London.

Cafasso, R. (1993) Re-engineering: just the first step, in *Computer World*, 19 April.

Callon, M. (1986) Some elements of a sociology of translation, in *Power, Action and Belief* (ed. J. Law), RKP, London.

Champy, J. (1995) *Reengineering Management*, Nicholas Brealey, London.

Child, J. (1972) Organizational structure, environment and performance, in *Sociology*, 6, 1, pp. 1–22.

Clark, P. (1987) *Anglo-American Innovation*, de Gruyter, New York.

Clark, P. and Staunton, N. (1989) *Innovation in Technology And Organization*, Routledge, London.

Clark, P. and Starkey, D. (1988) *Organizational Transitions and Innovation Design*, Pinter Publishers, London.

Coulson-Thomas, C. (ed.) (1994) *Business Process Reengineering: Myth And Reality*, Kogan Page, London.

Craig, J. and Yetton, P. (1994) *The dual and strategic role of IT: a critique of business process reengineering*, working paper 94–002 Australian Graduate School of Management, University of New South Wales, Kensington.

Dalton, M. (1959) *Men Who Manage*, McGraw-Hill, New York.

Davenport, H. (1993) *Process Innovation: Reengineering Work Through Information Technology*, Harvard Business Press, Boston.

Davenport, H. (1994) Saving IT's soul: human-centred information management. *Harvard Business Review*, March–April, pp. 119–131.

Davenport, T. and Stoddard, D. (1994) Reengineering: Business Change of Mythic Proportions? in *MIS Quarterly*, 18, 2, pp. 121–127.

Douglas, D. (ed.) (1993) The role of IT in business reengineering, in *I/S Analyzer*, 31, 8, pp. 1–16.

Earl, M. and Khan, B. (1994) How new is business process redesign? in *European Management Journal*, 12, 1, pp. 20–30.

Foucault, M. (1988) The ethic of care for the self as a practice of freedom, in *The Final Foucault*, (eds J. Bernauer and D. Rasmussen), MIT Press, Cambridge, Massachusetts.

Galliers, R. (1994) *Information technology and organisational change: where does BPR fit in?* Paper at information technology and organisational change: the changing role of IT and business conference, Nijenrode University, Breukelen, Netherlands, 28–29 April.

Gordon, C. (ed.) (1980) *Foucault, M. – Power/Knowledge: Selected Interviews and Other Writings 1972–77*, Harvester Press, Brighton.

Gowler, D. and Legge, K. (1983) The meaning of management and the management of meaning, in *Perspectives on Management: A Multidisciplinary Analysis* (ed M. Earl), Oxford University Press.

Giddens, A. (1984) *The Constitution of Society*, Polity Press, Cambridge.

Grint, K. (1994) Reengineering History, in *Organization*, vol. 1, no. 1. pp. 179–202.

Grint, K., Case, P. and Willcocks, L. (1995) *Business process reengineering reappraised: the politics and technology of forgetting*, Proceedings of the IFIP WG 8.2 Conference Information Technology And Changes In Organisational Work, Cambridge University, December 7–9th.

Grint, K. and Hogan, E. (1994a) *Utopian Management*, management research paper, Templeton College, Oxford.

Grint, K. and Woolgar, S. (forthcoming) *The machine at work*, Polity Press, Cambridge.

Hall, G., Rosenthal, J. and Wade, J. (1993) How to make reengineering really work, in *Harvard Business Review*, November–December, pp. 119–131.

Hammer, M. and Champy, J. (1993a) *Reengineering the Corporation: A Manifesto for Business Revolution*, Nicholas Brealey, London.

Hammer, M. and Champy, J. (1993b) Reengineering the corporation, in *Insights Quarterly*, Summer, pp. 3–19.

Hammer, M. and Stanton, S. (1994) No need for excuses, in *Financial Times*, 5, October, p. 20.

Hammer, M. and Stanton, S. (1995) *The Reengineering Revolution*, Harper Collins, New York.

Handy, C. (1985) *Understanding Organizations*, Penguin, London.

Hannaway, J. (1989) *Managers Managing*, Oxford University Press, New York.

Harrington, H. (1993) *Business Process Improvement*, McGraw Hill, London.

Harvey, D. (1995) *Reengineering: The Critical Success Factors*, Business Intelligence, London.

Haughton, E. (1992) Business reengineering: moving the corporate Goalposts, in *Computer Weekly*, 30 July, pp. 20–21.

Heygate, R. (1993) Immoderate redesign, in *The McKinsey Quarterly*, 1, pp. 73–87.

Heygate, R. (1994) Being intelligent about 'intelligent' technology, in *The McKinsey Quarterly*, 4, pp. 137–147.

Jabes, J. (1982) Individual decision making, in *Decision Making: Approaches and Analysis*, (eds A.G. McGrew and M.J. Wilson), Manchester University Press.

Jay, A. (1967) *Management and Machiavelli*, Benton Books, New York.

Jermier, J., Knights, D. and Nord, W. (eds) (1994) *Resistance And Power In Organizations*, Routledge, London.

Johansson, H., McHugh, P., Pendlebury, A.J. and Wheeler, W.A. III (1993) *Business Process Reengineering: Breakpoint Strategies for Market Dominance*, John Wiley, Chichester.

Jones, M. (1994) Don't emancipate, exaggerate: rhetoric, 'reality' and reengineering, in *Transforming Organizations With Information Technology*, (eds R. Baskerville, S. Smithson, O. Ngwenyama and J. DeGross), Elsevier, Amsterdam.

Klein, M. (1994) Reengineering methodologies and tools, in *Information Systems Management*, spring, pp. 31–5.

Latour, B. (1986) The powers of association, in *Power, Action and Belief: A New Sociology of Knowledge*, (ed. J. Law), Routledge Kegan and Paul, London.

Latour, B. (1988) The prince for machines as well as machinations, in *Technology and Social Process*, (ed. B. Elliott), Edinburgh University Press.

Latour, B. (1993) *We Have Never Been Modern*, Harvester Wheatsheaf, Hemel Hempstead.

Law, J. (ed.) (1991) *A Sociology of Monsters*, Routledge, London.

Lee, R. and Lawrence, P. (1985) *Organizational Behaviour: Politics at Work*, Hutchinson, London.

Lindblom, C. (1959) The science of muddling through, in *Public Administration Review*, vol. 19, pp. 79–99.

McHugh, P., Merli, G. and Wheeler, W. (1995) *Beyond Business Process Reengineering: Towards The Holonic Enterprise*, John Wiley, Chester.

McKenzie, D. (1990) *Inventing Accuracy: A Historical Sociology Of Missile Guidance*, MIT Press, Cambridge, Massachusetts.

Maglitta, J. (1995) Reengineering the workplace: weak links, in *Computerworld*, 6, February, pp. 94–97.

Markus, L. and Robey, D. (1995) Business process reengineering and the role of the information systems professional, in *Business Process Change: Reengineering*

Concepts, Methods and Technologies, (eds V. Grover and W. Kettinger), Idea Group Publishing, Harrisburg.

Marx, K. (1954) *Capital*, vol. 1, Lawrence and Wishart, London.

Moad, J. (1993) Does reengineering really work? in *Datamation*, 1 August, pp. 22–28.

Moad, J. (1994) Reengineering: report from the trenches, in *Datamation*, 15 March, pp. 36–40.

O'Hara, M. and Watson, R. (1995) Automation, business process reengineering and client server technology, in *Business Process Change: Reengineering Concepts, Methods and Technologies* (eds V. Grover and W. Kettinger), Idea Group Publishing, Harrisburg.

Ormrod, S. (1995) Feminist sociology and methodology: leaky black boxes in gender/technology relations, in *The Gender-Technology Relation*, (eds K. Grint and R. Gill), Taylor and Francis, London.

Padulo, R. (1995) *Reengineering management learning*, management research paper, Templeton College, Oxford.

Pennings, J. and Buitendam, A. (eds) (1988) *New Technology As Organizational Innovation*, Ballinger, Cambridge.

Pettigrew, A. (1985) *The Awakening Giant: Continuity and Change in ICI*, Blackwell, Oxford.

Pettigrew, A. (ed.) (1988) *The Management Of Strategic Change*, Blackwell, Oxford.

Pfeffer, J. (1992) *Power in And Around Organizations*, Free Press, New York.

Preece, I. and Edwards, C. (1993) *A Survey of BPR Activity in the UK*, working paper, Cranfield University Business School.

Price Waterhouse (1994) *Price Waterhouse Review 1994/5*, Price Waterhouse, London.

Scarbrough, H. and Corbett, J. (1992) *Technology and Organization: Power, Meaning and Design*, Routledge, London.

Simon, H.A. (1947) *Administrative Behaviour*, MacMillan, New York.

Singleton, V. (1995) Networking constructions of gender and constructing gender networks: considering definitions of woman in the British cervical screening programme, in *The Gender-Technology Relation*, (eds K. Grint and R. Gill), Taylor and Francis, London.

Stewart, R. (1993) *Managerial Behaviour*, management research paper MRP94/1, Templeton College, Oxford.

Stringer, J. (1992) Risks in large projects, in *Operational Research Tutorial Papers*, (ed. M. Mortimer), Operational Research Society, London.

Thackray, J. (1993) Fads, fixes and fictions, in *Management Today*, June, p. 41.

Tinaiker, R., Hartman, A. and Nath, R. (1995) Rethinking business process reengineering: a social constructionist perspective, in *Examining Business Reengineering*, (eds G. Burke and J. Peppard), Kogan Page, London.

Walsham, G. (1993) *Interpreting Information Systems in Organisations*, Wiley and sons, Chichester.

Watkins, J. (1994) *Business Process Reengineering in the Financial Services Sector: Survey Report*, Bristol University.

Watson, G. (1994) *Business Systems Engineering*, John Wiley, New York.

Whipp, R. and Clark, P. (1986) *Innovation And The Auto Industry*, Frances Pinter, London.

Willcocks, L. (ed.) (1994) *Information Management: Evaluation of Information Systems Investments*, Chapman & Hall, London.

Willcocks, L. (1995) *False promise or delivering the goods? Recent Findings on*

The Economics and Impact of Business Process Reengineering, Paper on proceedings of the second IT Evaluation Conference, Henley Management College, July 5–6.

Willcocks, L. and Currie, W. (1996) Information technology and business process reengineering: emerging issues in major organizational innovation projects, in *European Organizational and Work Psychologist*.

Willcocks, L., Currie, W. and Mason, D. (1996) *Information Systems At Work: People, Politics and Technology*, McGraw Hill, London.

Willcocks, L. and Griffiths, C. (1994) Predicting the risk of failure in major information technology projects, in *Technological Forecasting and Social Change*, 47, 2, pp. 205–228.

Willcocks, L. and Smith, G. (1995) IT-enabled business process reengineering: organizational and human resource dimensions, in *Journal of Strategic Information Systems*, 4, 3.

Willcocks, L. and Margetts, H. (1994) Risks and information systems: developing the analysis, in *Information Management: Evaluation of Information Systems Investments* (ed. L. Willcocks), Chapman and Hall, London.

Willmott, H. (1995) Will the turkeys vote for christmans? the reengineering of human resources, in *Examining Business Reengineering*, (eds G. Burke and J. Peppard), Kogan Page, London.

Winner, L. (1985) Do artifacts have politics? in *The Social Shaping of Technology*, (eds D. MacKenzie and J. Wajcman), Open University Press, Milton Keynes.

Wolin, S. (1991) On the theory and practice of power, in *After Foucault – Humanistic Knowledge, Postmodern Challenges*, (ed. J. Arac), Rutgers University Press, New Brunswick.

Chapter 5

Advanced technology and the development of new forms of work organization

Patrick Dawson

The system is a combination of technology and people. Neither is the sole provider of the total system, it's the combination of the two. Technology has to be capable of doing what you want it to do. People have to be accepting of the way of working with that technology. It's not until you get the two together with the appropriate balance working in harmony that you get the best out of the system.

(CSIRO Interview, 1995)

INTRODUCTION

The ongoing debate around new-wave manufacturing strategies (Storey, 1994) and technological change at work (McLoughlin and Clark, 1994) centre on a range of issues from Piore and Sabel's (1984) thesis on 'flexible specialization', the question of whether technology is used to 'informate' or 'automate' (Zuboff, 1988), claims of 'Japanization' (Oliver and Wilkinson, 1988) and the so-called emergence of 'lean production' (Womack, *et al.*, 1990). The character of these changes for the future of organizations and the nature of work remains open to competing claims (Dawson and Webb, 1989). Although there is increasing agreement that companies are undergoing significant organizational innovations, whether these 'innovations' represent a radical departure from conventional conceptualizations of organizations (Atkinson and Meager, 1986) or are occurring within existing frameworks (Tuckman, 1994), continues to generate debate across a broad and increasingly fragmented set of literatures (Storey, 1994, pp. 1–15).

The design of new technology and the development of new forms of work organization is an important and generally under-investigated area which may provide useful insight to our current understanding of the process by which these new innovations unfold in practice. While new technologies and techniques may provide enormous potential to transform the world of work, they may also impose a number of intended and unintended rigidities. These restrictions can result from decisions made during the design process in setting what John Bessant terms the 'design space' or options for organizational restructuring around technology (Bessant, 1983, pp. 14–30). As such, design is a critical period in which key decisions may be made based on certain 'common-sense' assumptions about the nature of organizations. Once design is complete and change implemented, the contsraints built into the technology may become manifest. For example, the early work of Boddy and Buchanan indicated how organizational and human dimensions are often ignored by systems designers who work in isolation from the context in which the equipment is to be used (Boddy and Buchanan, 1986, p. 28). As a consequence, the implementation of new technology into the workplace can generate a number of negative reactions and unforeseen outcomes.

One response to companies' failure to reach their full potential from investments in new technology and work arrangements has been the development of collaborative projects through government funding. The Alvey project, with a budget of over £350 million over five years, was one such example (see Bench-Capon, 1991; Dawson, 1994, pp. 143–9); more recent projects include the UK Manufacturing Organisation, People and Systems Programme (MOPS) and the parallel European EUREKA programme entitled Integration Technology and Organisation for Quality Production (INTO) (Gillis, 1994, pp. 3–8). In addition, with a trend towards closer customer-supplier relations in the creation of more co-operative network arrangements, there is also a growing number of non-government funded collaborative initiatives (Limerick and Cunnington, 1993). In this chapter the Australian examples of the Commonwealth Scientific and Industrial Research Organisation (CSIRO) collaborative agreement with General Motors-Holden's Automotive Limited and the Boeing Commercial Airplane Group are used to illustrate the process of industrial collaboration in the development of new production arrangements; they are comparable and pertinent in highlighting key issues surrounding industrial collaboration, design of new technology, and development and implementation of cellular forms of work organization. The relationship between these elements and how the process unfolds over time is detailed in two summary case study analyses. Data are used to illustrate the political nature of collaborative projects and to spotlight the processes involved in transferring research innovation into programmes of organizational change. Before this analysis the chapter first outlines key problems associated with the dominant Lewinian model to understanding change, and advocates an alternative processual framework. This approach is utilized in the empirical section and the chapter concludes with a processual analysis of the case material in order to draw out new insights on the practice of innovative collaboration in the development and implementation of new forms of work organization.

DISCARDING LEWINIAN ORTHODOXY AND ADOPTING A PROCESSUAL APPROACH TO CHANGE

The seminal work of Kurt Lewin has had a significant and long-lasting effect on the way academics have researched and taught topics on change management. The ghost of Lewin in the form of an established orthodoxy has generated considerable resistance to new frameworks for understanding change. This is perhaps ironic, given that Kurt Lewin championed minority claims, questioned conventional assumptions and prejudices and throughout his life remained a strong advocate for democracy at the workplace (Board de, 1978). For those practitioners and academics within the field of management known as Organisational Development (OD), his classic work on intergroup dynamics and planned change has proven to be particularly influential (see Kreitner and Kinicki, 1992, pp. 723–61). Essentially, he argued (1951) that for change to be successfully managed it is necessary to follow three general steps (Robbins, 1991: p. 646) identified by him as unfreezing, changing, and refreezing. Unfreezing is the stage where a need for change is recognised and action is taken to change existing attitudes and behaviour. This preparatory stage is deemed essential to generating employee support and minimizing resistance. According to Lewin's technique of force-field analysis (1947, pp. 5–42) there are two sets of forces in operation within any social system: driving forces that operate for change and restraining forces which attempt to maintain the status quo. The example of drink-driving illustrates this where, although there may be strong driving forces to stop drinking and driving, such as public condemnation, fear of losing driving licence, cost, new laws, publicity campaigns, disapproval of spouse and the concern of harming others, the restraining forces of habit, camaraderie, relief of tension, friends drinking, social pressure and the dislike of coercive methods may act to maintain the status quo. If these two opposing forces are equal in strength, they are in a state of equilibrium. Consequently, to bring about change you either need to increase the strength of the driving forces or decrease the strength of the resisting forces. Furthermore, as these two sets of forces are qualitatively different it is possible to modify elements of both in managing change. In practice, however, the emphasis of OD specialists has been on providing data that would unfreeze the system through reducing the resisting forces rather than increasing the driving forces (Gray and Starke, 1988, pp. 596–629; Weisbord, 1988, p. 94). Once these negative forces have been reduced through disconfirming information, the consultant embarks on moving the organization towards the desired state. This is the second general step of changing or moving an organization, and involves the actual implementation of new systems of operation. Once this is complete, the final stage of refreezing occurs which may involve the positive reinforcement of desired outcomes to promote the internalization of new attitudes and behaviours. An appraisal of the effectiveness of the change programme is the final element used in the last step to ensure that the new way of doing things becomes habitualized.

This three-phase model of change is currently an integral part of the conventional orthodoxy taught in business departments and management schools around the world. While the strength of the model lies in its simple representation (which makes it easy to use and understand), it is also its major weakness as it presents a uni-directional model of change. The linearity which this three-stage model suggests is not supported by the empirical evidence on the introduction of new technologies and management techniques (see Dawson, forthcoming). In addition, this approach adopts a normative framework and assumes that there is one best way to manage change that will increase both organizational effectiveness and employees' well-being.

In managing large-scale change, revision of implementation strategies to overcome or tackle unforeseen contextual difficulties is often needed. Organizational change is a complex and dynamic process which is also influenced by powerful coalitions within organizations and the history and context within which change is taking place. This is illustrated in the empirical sections which follow where the expected outcomes detailed in initial plans are revised and modified as a result of the ongoing interplay between the politics, context and substance of change. These three main groups of determinants form part of a less prescriptive and more analytical processual approach to understanding organizational change which is outlined in the author's (1994) book: *Organizational Change: A Processual Approach*.

Following a processual approach, the context of change is taken to refer to factors within the external environment and those internal to the organization, such as administrative structures, technology, human resources, history and culture and the product or service of an organization. The substance of change refers to the type of change (whether new technology or management technique), scale of change (whether incremental or radical transformation), and defining characteristics of the change initiative (content rather than labels). Finally, the politics of change is used to refer to the process by which certain well-placed individuals, groups or powerful coalitions can influence decision-making and agenda setting at critical junctures during the process of organizational change. By combining these three dimensions (the politics, substance and context of change) it is possible to engage in a processual analysis of the design of technology and its implementation in the development of new forms of work organization. In the sections which follow the technology design and implementation process are examined and new technology and work restructuring are subjected to processual analysis.

PROJECT PROPOSAL IN THE FORMULATION OF AN AGREEMENT WITH GMHAL

In April 1985, the Commonwealth Scientific and Industrial Research Organisation's (CSIRO) Division of Manufacturing Technology (DMT) and General Motors-Holden's (GM-H) Automotive Limited (GMHAL) agreed that DMT would prepare a confidential proposal on the benefits of integrating the manufacturing facilities of GMHAL's Plant 1. The following month three members of DMT spent a week at the plant observing and documenting operations. From their initial analysis they concluded that cellular manufacture should be a central element of a modernization scheme which sought to optimize all aspects of operation, from the supply of raw materials to the delivery of finished goods. The DMT group argued that their preliminary data indicated significant opportunities for major cost reductions. Furthermore, they advocated that a collaborative arrangement with CSIRO would ultimately benefit GMHAL by increasing the profitability of Plant 1. From their perspective, the GMHAL plant would enable the newly formed DMT group to gain valuable experience in applying their research knowledge to a practical 'real-world' problem. According to their project leader, the industrial collaboration would serve as a 'loss-leader' project for DMT in the development of commercial software. For these reasons, CSIRO were willing to do the work at a third of commercial rates (on condition that they held the intellectual property rights), offering a comparatively cheap solution to GMHAL's problem:

> A collaborative arrangement between GM-H and DMT is seen as having considerable benefits for both parties. The combination of expertise and skills should lead to a project team with expert knowledge of both the products and processes of the GM-H plant, and of advanced manufacturing information technology. For GM-H, the development and installation of a flexible manufacturing facility, with substantially increased profitability, is an obvious immediate benefit. The development of a facility tuned to the specfitic needs of GM-H will require more than the application of 'off-the-shelf' technology – a significant research component is involved, which is of benefit to DMT.
>
> (CSIRO, 1986, p. 2)

The DMT proposal advocated industrial collaboration in four phases, with each phase subject to a separate agreement based on the experience gained in preceding phases. The first, three-month, phase centred on analysing current manufacturing operations to identify opportunities for cost reduction and to specify (and possibly establish) a demonstration manufacturing cell as a test bed for further development. Three or more CSIRO employees and two full-time GMHAL staff members would work together on collecting and analysing data and installing the proposed demonstration cell.

In the second phase the lessons learned and the concepts developed over the first few months would be further refined and expanded to formulate a completely revised manufacturing system for Plant 1. Using the same resources over a six-month period, this part of the collaboration was intended to culminate with a report recommending revised plant arrangements, outlining expected implementation costs and projected productivity gains.

The third and fourth phases were to run concurrently over 12 months, with the latter involving the design, relocation, procurement and commissioning of all the required hardware for implementing the new methods of work organization. The implementation process was to be managed by GMHAL with advice and assistance from DMT. At the same time DMT would develop an Integrated Production Management System (IPMS) which would be tailored to the specific cell manufacture needs at Plant 1. As the proposals outlines:

> When installed on the GM-H computer system, the IPMS would give GM-H an in-house capability to analyse all aspects of the operation of the revised manufacturing plant. In particular it would enable the on-going optimization of the plant under conditions of changing costs, throughput demand and part mix, or when new processes and products are to be introduced. The simulation capabilities of the package would also assist in the determination of optimum maintenance schedules.
>
> (CSIRO, 1986, p. 11)

In February 1986 a formal agreement was signed between GMHAL and CSIRO. As it turned out, both the timeframes and the phased approach to industrial collaboration and organizational change were continually redefined through ongoing processes of consultation and negotiation between the two major parties. For example, the actual plant-wide implementation of cellular manufacture occurred between 1989 and the end of 1990 (when the author was engaged in the study). Three years later in June 1992 (in a series of repeat interviews) there were still a number of changes to be completed and it was generally agreed by those interviewed that the plant was operating at around 90 per cent cellular manufacture.

In all the GMHAL cellular manufacturing project spanned ten years, during which the CSIRO's DMT established a collaborative agreement to formulate a technical design for Plant 1 and to develop software for a shopfloor scheduler. In 1995 the plant was operating under cellular arrangements with six manual 'Kanban' systems. They no longer have a formal set of plans, such as was anticipated with the shopfloor scheduler, but rather use a Kanban document where segments can be torn off and used as a traveller document with the production pieces. Hence, they only produce components requested by the Kanban card issued by production control, and by simply walking around a cell you can quickly assess the state of operations by referring to these cards. Moreover, under this visual form of work organization they no longer measure their performance against a set platform but set themselves an improvement target then measure themselves against their achievements.

Another major change from the original proposal centred on the need to produce quantifiable results which the plant manager could used to justify continuing the change programme. As a result a pilot cell was implemented in parallel with the development of cell-build software for full plant layout. Originally DMT had intended to formulate a total design before any shopfloor implementation of this new form of work organization. In short, internal GMHAL politics placed pressure on the plant manager to show real gains for funding purposes, which in turn put pressure on the DMT team to produce workable pieces of the system.

Further constraints on the DMT team included a request that no more than 15 to 18 machines be allocated to any one cell; that there should be no more than 100 and that there should be a maximum of 12 people per cell. These requirements imposed by the local management group led to a series of consultations before the presentation of a first-cut for cellular manufacture. Thus, the cell-build software was not used in isolation from plant concerns to develop a technical solution, but was used to draft a design within pre-defined organizational constraints, which were then forwarded and discussed with plant management, modified, and then forwarded again. While technology did not determine plant design, it did set the parameters for a cellular form of work organization within which local requirements could be accommodated through close and ongoing collaboration.

In building on the knowledge and experience gained from their cellular change project with GMHAL, DMT have further developed their collaborative initiatives with other south Australian manufacturing companies, through membership of a national research project (involving university and company collaboration), and through their involvement in an American change programme. In the section which follows, their relationship with the Boeing Commercial Airplane Group and the development of cellular manufacturing at Boeing's Wichita Division is briefly examined. This programme is comparable to GMHAL, although the size of operations were significantly larger and more complex.

THE BOEING COLLABORATIVE PROJECT

The contract that we had with Boeing was initially a three year contract. The support originally started off in Seattle and so I guess the last 18 months or year was down in Wichita, and that was extended slightly to complete this project, but our contractual agreement has essentially ended. However, we agreed that we would continue to provide remote support on a 'as-needed' basis, which is what I am doing.

(CSIRO interview, 1995)

The DMT made initial contact with Boeing in 1990 following some industry publications and publicity in the area of their cell-build software. This happened within the context of a broader agreement between CSIRO and Boeing who were party to a corporate memorandum of understanding (i.e. an umbrella agreement), under which individual projects were developed. Each of these projects were agreed independently between various groups within CSIRO and Boeing. As a project member recounted:

> It probably took about 12 to 18 months to get a cellular manufacturing project agreed to. Essentially, we worked under the original agreement although it changed in content somewhat from originally anticipated over the three years. And for the Wichita end there was some extension to the original contract tacked on the end. . . . It grew and was modified, and I think that round about the right resource commitment was placed into the project over the time. But it ended up being directed at somewhat different things. We had anticipated originally, that after a trial pilot cell installation in Boeing, we could probably work with Boeing to enhance our technology and make it a more robust useable product, and that would be part of that project. But it wasn't until the end of the project time that we got to the pilot cell stage and there was no intention to go further. Going through that exercise Boeing feel comfortable enough with the software as we've got it and skilled enough to be able to drive it in-house for their own use. So they see no real advantage in developing it into a product. So there was quite a change in the content of the programme.

> (CSIRO interview, 1995)

Initially, DMT attempted to work with the manufacturing research and development group in Seattle to introduce cellular manufacturing into one of their factories. As it turned out, they were unable to get the agreement and support of key personnel at Seattle and as a consequence the project failed. However, at an internal Boeing conference, personnel from Boeing's Wichita Division became interested in DMT's technology and expertise. They had already spent two years investigating the possibility of cellular design using John Deere's group technology software, but had not been successful. A closer relationship developed between Wichita and DMT, and it was decided that a CSIRO team member should be located on site in the US. As a result, in September 1993 a member of the DMT went to the Wichita Division of the Boeing Commercial Airplane Group to work on an existing cellular change project. The possibility of restructuring into cellular form was already on the divisional agenda and considerable time and effort had already been put into improving and maintaining the validity of manufacturing data:

Two years prior to us arriving they had a technical team which was trying to grapple with this manufacturing problem. So I did have an advantage that the data that we had was in reasonable shape.

(CSIRO interview, 1995)

However, the technical problem or reorganizing huge numbers of parts and manufacturing steps into an appropriate form of work organization necessitated a reconceptualization of the notion of cell design:

We started off with the 80,000 parts and 1.6 million manufacturing steps and somehow had to devise a procedure that would take them from status quo – I have a slide, which I can probably give you a copy of, which shows the extent of the spaghetti of the traffic between buildings. Essentially, what we were trying to do is to take their information, which we believe is fairly reasonable, and say for this manufacturing business unit these are self-contained mini-factories. So this raises the notion of a cell to a higher level, to a factory level . . . at GMH and Hardies and Hoovers and so on, we were working at the detailed level. Whereas now you are coming back up almost at an organizational level. This next step is to then take each mini-factory and to break those out into sub-autonomous groups and then if necessary, stage three would be detailed cell design.

(CSIRO interview, 1995)

In other words, given the scale of operations at Boeing, the DMT team had to consider the implications and relationships between cellular forms of work organization at a number of different levels. The area of concern, the Manufacturing Business Unit (MBU) Fabrication comprised a complex of different buildings, including plants, warehouses and an engineering laboratory. Within this multi-building site DMT set about identifying mini-factories which consisted of groups of related cells. They identified four potential mini-factories within the Wichita Division. Conceptually, these mini-factories comprise a number of cells plus appropriate hub(s). A hub is defined as a dedicated cell which can service a number of interlocking work cells. For example, the parts family of clips, angles and other components of the pilot Brakeform Cell followed two distinct flows. The first, which involved blank, brake, and heat treatment accounted for the majority of all parts and the second, which followed the sequence of blank, heat treatment and brake accounted for the remainder. As heat treatment was also a process requirement of other components, it was designed as a dedicated focal cell (a hub) within a group of cells which made up a mini-factory.

During the first phase of their collaboration with Boeing CSIRO assessed their current operating situation and formulated a range of possible routes to change. After three months at the Wichita Division (just before Christmas

1993) the Cell Design Team put forward a four-option proposal comprising full plant design, following a pilot cell route, taking a parallel but staggered approach – as they did with GMHAL (see Dawson, 1994, pp. 111–19) – or to do nothing. After a period of consultation and discussion with senior management the Cell Design Team convinced Boeing of the benefits of a staggered approach involving setting up and running a pilot cell in conjunction with developing a full plant design (DMT's preferred option):

> I believe that by adopting that parallel approach it's given Boeing the opportunity to go through the rather significant learning curve of tackling all of those issues, particularly the multi-skilling and pay issues, which they had not previously perceived as being integral to the change process.

> (CSIRO interview, 1995)

During phase 1 the Cell Design Team also identified some candidates for the pilot cell. Eventually they opted for establishing a Brakeform cell (which manufactures clips, brackets and angles). Phase 2, which began in January 1994, centred on the logical design of a pilot cell (shopfloor people were incorporated into the design team), a full plant design, and training Boeing personnel to take control of the change process.

The pilot cell route to work reorganization

The CSIRO software identified a family of 6,500 part numbers which were similar in their processing requirements. Before the formation of a Rapid Fab Brakeform Cell each component underwent a series of operations involving considerable travel time around the complex. Components would often travel between Plant I and Plant II, as well as being stored and moved significant distances even within the plants. Under the trial cell this family of parts was to be bounded within a self-contained area, drastically reducing transportation costs and distance travelled in shop-to-shop routings. In determining final cell layout the Cell Design Team members formed a small team of process experts who were familiar with each piece of equipment and associated processes to identify and agree on the most appropriate design for the physical layout of the cell. This group also decided on the control responsibilities of each operator and the physical layout of the benches.

In selecting operators for the Brakeform Cell, interested employees had to first submit an application which was assessed by a committee before their acceptance. The chosen employees were then given some pre-cell training before the pilot work cell became fully operational. After only two months of operation the cell demonstrated considerable benefits, for example, the average actual flow (material issue to inspection) was reduced from 17 to 10 days and there were considerable savings in transport costs. Some of the broader change benefits which the cell provided include proving that the process of cell design and implementation can work; educating Boeing personnel about the importance of non-technical factors; and highlighting and addressing business process changes required to support cellular manufacture:

> I think that I've come to appreciate that certainly the technical issues form only a small and often relatively simple portion of the whole exercise. I also think it's fair to say that up until the time that we got involved in Wichita the team there was primarily technically oriented. And so the first day that I arrived there – I obviously gave an overview of some of our capabilities in that area – then very quickly went onto other issues and stressed that our expertise lay in the project management side of things, and that if we were going to succeed that essentially we needed a team which was going to consist of two types of expertise. On the one hand, those that have experience and expertise in the design of cellular manufacturing systems, which was essentially what we were asked to bring to the party over there. And on the other hand, and this was crucial, to have their own people that were extremely knowledgeable about their processes, their products, and their environment. The other thing that I stressed at the opening presentation, was that if we were going to be successful not only did we have to have more or less an holistic approach to this project, but we needed an appropriate team with an appropriate balance of expertise, and that the composition of the team would change overtime. . . . The [pilot cell] is certainly a major success story within Wichita. An excellent sales vehicle for what cellular manufacturing is all about.
>
> (CSIRO interview, 1995)

Although the pilot cell has been a success, as indicated in the opening section, Boeing have not opted to extend their collaborative agreement to examine the possible development of the cell-build technology. Using their own in-house expertise, they are currently driving the CSIRO system and only actively seek DMT support as they need it. From their perspective, the main benefits they have gained though collaborating with the CSIRO are as follows:

- comprehensive, top-down design methodology and tools
- emphasis on cross-functional teaming
- transition from drawing board to the factory floor
- input from outside the company
- project management, to help navigate the process of change

(Fox *et al.*, 1995, p. 6)

DMT's first proposal of a plant design was presented to Boeing in July 1994. Since then, there has been a change in management and the full plant design activities have been shelved, with no indication of its further uptake during 1995, although work continues on the design and implementation of a number of cells.

A PROCESSUAL ANALYSIS OF NEW TECHNOLOGY AND CELLULAR MANUFACTURE

Throughout the life of these two projects there were a number of changes to expected outcomes outlined in the initial proposals. With the processual approach three main groups of determinants, the substance, context and politics of change, can be used to explore the changing nature and character of these collaborations over time. The substance of change is taken to refer to the scale of the proposed change, in this case plant restructuring; the defining characteristics of the change in the development of technology (CSIRO) for the purpose of implementing a cellular form of work organization (GMHAL and Boeing); and the type of change programme, in being an industrial collaboration between two separate organizations.

In these two examples there is a close similarity and overlap in the substance of change proposed at GMHAL and Boeing. Both involved the use of DMT's cell-build software which has been developed to aid the design of a particular form of work organization, namely, cellular manufacture. The technology does not promote a number of alternative forms of work organization, but rather sets out a range of possible options under a cellular design format. As such, it defines the parameters and character of work from which decisions about the physical location of equipment and materials within predefined cells can be made. It is only at this stage that employees may (if supported by management) get involved in intra-cell design issues, such as the individual allocation of a predefined group of tasks. As one interviewee explained:

> We moved from some of the initial investigations to identifying, for example, candidates for pilot cells. We didn't see a need at that stage – in working our way through some of the politics of change projects – to involve people from the shopfloor. But we saw them as being critical partners at a time when we had identified a candidate or number of candidate pilot cells, and then we got them involved in the further detailed design of those cells.
>
> (CSIRO interview, 1995)

In both cases the project involved collaboration between a hardware fabrication facility which had already shown an interest in workcell design and the DMT, although the scale of the project within Boeing was far larger. In many ways Boeing is following a similar route to GMHAL, taking the pilot cell path with the potential of moving towards full-plant design. Currently, they are still at the stage of implementing and evaluating early cell development. From an analysis of the data, Boeing initially viewed the technical issue as the main inhibiting factor or problem to be solved and only later recognized the wider social and organizational implications of trying to manage such a major change. In contrast the hardware plant at GMHAL did go the route of full cellularization. Although the scale of change was a contributing factor (being a self-contained unit in a single location), the process of changing plant conditions and involving employees, unions and their representatives, was instigated before work reorganization into cellular form (see also Dawson, 1994, pp. 104–22). In this way the substance of the projects also interlinked and overlaid aspects associated with the context and politics of change.

In relation to internal context, these included factors such as human resources, administrative structures, existing technology, product and knowledge (in this example the automotive and aircraft components produced and existing software developments and expertise), and the history and culture of GMHAL (Plant 1) and Boeing's Wichita Division (the Fabrication MBU) and the CSIRO (DMT). The history and culture of these particular organizations were important in setting the scene under which decisions were made and shaped, and in influencing group and individual response and reaction to the change projects. DMT's experience with GMHAL led them to recognize the importance of the social aspects of technical change early on during the Boeing collaboration. As a result, they perceived this as a high priority area throughout the life of the Wichita project:

> I saw myself as an adviser to a Boeing team. From day one I was conscious of the fact that if we're going to sell this project to top management it's Boeing people who have to get up and say: 'We the sheet metal folks think within sheet metal we can to this'. I'm happy to sit in the background and pull all the strings and push people in the right direction and make sure that everything's done right.
>
> (CSIRO interview, 1995)

Furthermore, although there were a number of similarities in context – in both being involved in hardware fabrication – the GMHAL plant serviced just over 3,000 individual parts and small assemblies whereas Boeing MBU processed some 80,000. Other differences included the very different external pressures faced by the two facilities: for example, while Wichita was not under commercial threat, the GMHAL plant manager had been instructed to either transform the plant into a viable operating unit or else GMHAL would sub-contract their fabrication needs to other small local manufacturers. The threat of closure did, in this case, create an environment which was not only tolerant of change, but actively supported the initiatives by local management (particularly as it offered the possibility of job security).

Once again, context can be seen to interweave and overlap the substance of change programmes and the politics of work reorganization schemes. A company's history and culture and the nature of the change programme proposed shape decision-making through presenting perceived boundaries for change initiatives. This political element is central to a processual approach for understanding change and refers to both internal organizational politics and external influences and activities. For example, in the first collaborative exercise the comparatively low position of the plant manager in the GMHAL hierarchy influenced the speed and direction of the project and on a number of occasions the hardware fabrication implementation team was constrained by funding decisions made at more senior levels within the organization. In the case of Boeing, the absence of political backing by key personnel in Seattle prevented the uptake and development of the initial collaboration. It was not until contact was made with the Wichita Division (which had already taken steps towards cellular forms of work organization) that the potential for change through collaboration could be further developed. Even within this environment, the problem of restructuring was largely viewed as a technical problem and as a consequence, DMT had to spend considerable time stressing the importance of the social and organizational issues:

> My role was as an ambassador, to make sure that issues such as multi-skilling, even in a large organization such as Boeing in which change – because of union agreements which had been in place for five years, the plethora of job codes they have – you're not going to make changes in these types of area over night. So I saw myself more as an ambassador to make sure that these things were continually on the agenda. The fact that we got involved fairly early on with the unions and had an open, honest dialogue with them about what we were intending to do, certainly made life a lot easier for us.

> (CSIRO interview, 1995)

These three groups of determinants (substance, context and politics of change) have all acted to shape the process and outcomes of the two collaborative projects outlined above. Although the technology employed set the design constraints on options for cellular work arrangements, the setting up and operation of these new forms of work organization was also determined by political agendas and context. In both cases gaining senior management support was a major issue and in the GMHAL case the threat of plant closure and union support facilitated the transition towards full plant cellularization. In the case of Boeing, while technical constraints were foreseen as the major anticipated barrier to change, in practice non-technical aspects became far more critical in determining the process of organizational change. In short, it has been the complex interplay between the substance of the change project (cellular manufacture), contextual conditions and the political dimension of embarking on this type of large-scale change which have shaped the speed, direction and outcomes of change.

CONCLUSION

This chapter has attempted to illustrate some of the key issues in developing and applying computer software in the collaborative design of work into cellular form. The case studies of the relationship between a national research-based organization and two multi-national corporations spotlight the political nature of collaborative projects. In particular, how changing company agendas can redefine the expectations and involvement of the various and changing co-operative parties in these types of developmental initiatives. In both cases data has been used to demonstrate some of the main processes involved in transferring research innovation into programmes of organizational change. The workplace change venture between GMHAL and the Australian CSIRO outlined how organizational requirements can influence design output under industrial collaborations, the potential timescale of these type of projects and how internal politics (in the form of funding negotiations) significantly altered DMT's strategy for managing technology development in the formulation of cellular layout. The collaboration between the DMT and the Wichita Division of the Boeing Commercial Airplane Group usefully demonstrates the dynamic character of industrial collaborations and the limitations of change projects where the prime focus of management rests with technical design.

In highlighting the dynamic nature of change, the empirical data question the validity of conventional change models which are wedded to Lewinian categories of unfreeze, change and refreeze. The notion of a neat linear progression between a number of predefined stages in managed change is problematic in belying the reality of the muddied and processual nature of large-scale organizational change initiatives. Moreover, Lewin's model, in assuming an uncontested and clear view of the desired consequence of change, has a tendency to overlook organizational politics and to solidify (through the concept of refreezing) what is a dynamic and ongoing process. From the author's research into technology, the change process can more aptly be described as an odyssey, which while generally being planned, requires the continual revision of navigational decisions to meet unpredictable and unfolding conditions. In the examples cited in this chapter, the processual analysis of the case material illustrates the dynamic interplay between the politics, context and substance of change as determinants of the character, direction and outcomes of industrial collaborations.

REFERENCES

Atkinson, J. and Meager, N. (1986) *New Forms of Work Organization*, Institute of Manpower Studies report no.121, Sussex University.

Bench-Capon, T.J.M. (ed.) (1991) *Knowledge-Based Systems and Legal Applications*, Harcourt Brace Jovanovich, London.

Bessant, J. (1983) Management and manufacturing innovation: the case of information technology, in *Information Technology in Manufacturing Process: Case Studies in Technological Change*, (ed. G. Winch), Rossendale, London.

Board de, R. (1978) *The Psychoanlysis of Organistions. A Psychoanlytic Approach to Behaviour in Groups and Organisations*, Tavistock, London.

Boddy, D. and Buchanan, D. (1986) *Managing New Technology*, Blackwell, Oxford.

Dawson, P. (forthcoming) *New Technology and Quality Management: Change in the Workplace*, Routledge, London.

Dawson, P. (1994) *Organizational Change: A Processual Approach*, Paul Chapman Publishing, London.

Dawson, P. and Webb, J. (1989) New production arrangements: the totally flexible cage? in *Work, Employment & Society*, 3(2), pp. 221–38.

Fox, J., Edwards, A., Watt, J. and Taylor, B. (1995) *Successful Techniques to Realize the Benefits of Cellular Manufacturing*, Boeing Commercial Airplane Group Wichita Division.

Gillis, J. (1994) Human factors collaborative research within manufacturing, in *Advances in Agile Manufacturing: Integrating Technology, Organization and People*, (eds P. Kidd and W. Karwowski), IOS Press, Amsterdam.

Gray, J.L. and Starke, F.A. (1988) *Organizational Behavior: Concepts and Applications*, Merrill, Columbus, Ohio.

Kreitner, R. and Kinicki, A. (1992) *Organizational Behaviour*, 2nd edn, Irwin, Homewood, Illinois.

Lewin, K. (1947) Frontiers in Group Dynamics, in *Human Relations*, 1, pp. 5–42.

Lewin, K. (1951) *Field Theory in Social Science*, Harper and Row, New York.

Limerick, D. and Cunnington, B. (1993) *Managing the New Organisation: A Blueprint for Networks and Strategic Alliances*, Business and Professional Publishing, Chatswood.

McLoughlin, I. and Clark, J. (1994) *Technological Change at Work*, 2nd edn, Open University Press, Buckingham.

Oliver, N. and Wilkinson, B. (1988) *The Japanization of British Industry*, Blackwell, Oxford.

Piore, M. and Sabel C. (1984) *The Second Industrial Divide. Possibilities for Prosperity*, Basic Books, New York.

Robbins, S.P. (1991) *Organizational Behaviour: Concepts, Controversies, and Applications*, 5th edn, Prentice-Hall, Englewood Cliffs, New Jersey.

Storey, J. (ed.) (1994) *New Wave Manufacturing Strategies: Organizational and Human Resource Management Dimensions*, Paul Chapman Publishing, London.

Tuckman, A. (1994) The yellow brick road: Total Quality Management and the restructuring of organizational culture, in *Organization Studies*, 15(5), pp. 727–51.

Weisbord, M.R. (1988) *Productive Workplaces: Organizing and Managing for Dignity, Meaning and Community*, Jossey-Bass, San Francisco.

Wilson, F. (1994) Introducing new computer-based systems into Zenbank, in *New Technology, Work and Employment*, 9(2), pp. 115–26.

Womack, J.P., Jones, D.T. and Roos, D. (1990) *The Machine that Changed the World*, Rawson Associates, New York.

Zuboff, S. (1988) *In the Age of the Smart Machine*, Heinemann, New York.

Chapter 6

Role-taking and role-switching in organizational change: the four pluralities

David Buchanan and John Storey

INTRODUCTION

What skills are required to introduce effective organizational change? A satisfactory answer requires exploration of a number of related themes. We are concerned here with the demands on those who would present themselves as drivers of change in the organization, in contrast to those who welcome, are neutral towards, or actively resist the initiatives promoted by others. (This simple dichotomy, between change drivers and others, should not disguise the fact that they are two potentially overlapping and shifting populations.) It is necessary to consider critically the term 'change agent', and to examine different conceptions of that position. It is necessary also to consider the sequencing of change processes as factors generating differential demands on organizational actors and to examine how much change drivers are constrained by historical conditioning and current context, or whether equipped with appropriate knowledge and tools they can overcome and exploit historical factors and manipulate contemporary conditions to their advantage.

This chapter develops an approach to understanding organizational change by considering the behavioural repertoire deployed by change agents through the various stages of the change process. It also seeks to offer new insights concerning the plurality of change agents' roles, and how these, through their interaction, shape both the process and its outcomes. The central aim is to elaborate our understanding of the notion of 'agency' in the context of organizational change.

The chapter reviews the literature concerning phase models of change, identifying the broad similarities in the approaches available, and identifying the extensive contributions or inputs that phase models implicitly demand of change agents. The main critique of such models has traditionally been concerned with their attempt to impose an order and a linear sequence to processes that are in reality messy and untidy, and which unfold in an iterative fashion with much backtracking and omission. Here, a second critique of phase models is introduced; this concerns the lack of elaboration of the notion of change agency, through preoccupation with change context, substance and process. One line of argument advanced in the chapter thus concerns the multiple individual interventions in the change process on the one hand, and the organizational and social setting of interacting change agents on the other.

The chapter also draws from the literature concerning role models of change agency. Such models typically seek to establish the differential role sets and behavioural repertoires of change agents. The main critique of such models lies with the oversimplified representation of organizational positions and of how they interact. However, it is argued that individual actors consciously take up and switch roles depending on their perception of needs, personal competences, the positions of other actors, and personal self-interest. The chapter will also consider how this role-adoption and role-switching represents an accomplished and contingent selection of behaviours designed to achieve particular aims in an evolving and uncertain context.

Commentators who advocate a pluralist perspective on organizational change typically point to the plurality of actors engaged in the process. This useful, but oversimplified, notion is extended in this chapter to a consideration of 'four pluralities'. Pluralist accounts of change, it is argued, must consider first, the plurality of organizational actors; second the plurality of change drivers; third, the plurality of change phases; and fourth, the plurality of roles that change drivers are required to perform. These themes form the four main sections of this chapter.

What does a pluralist perspective on organizational change entail ? In the opening bars of Edward Elgar's first symphony, first performed in 1908, the melody, scored *andante, nobilmente e semplice*, is carried by the flute, clarinet, bassoon and viola following two long pianissimo rolls from the timpani (see, for example, Mundy, 1980, p. 75). During these opening bars, the rest of the woodwind and the brass are silent, while the cello and bass sustain a slow march tempo with pizzicato crotchets. This is a conveniently simple illustration of the way in which orchestral composers manipulate texture, mood and tone through different combinations of instruments, scored to play in different modes. The opening of the second movement of this symphony, for example, relies extensively on the violins, brass and timpani in an exciting *allegro molto* scherzo.

The orchestral symphonic score serves as a somewhat crude metaphor for the view of change shaped by a plurality of organizational actors. This is simply a point of departure, an artifice for illustrating the theoretical stance that we wish to develop. As with all such metaphorical and illustrative devices, it collapses when pushed too far. No special claims are made for this device other than for its use-value in helping us to improve our understanding of change processes in organizations. While the pluralist perspective on organizational change finds widespread support, it has been relatively underdeveloped particularly with reference to the practical implications for the change management process.

Just as some (particularly contemporary) orchestral music may seem chaotic or disorganized until one understands the composer's purpose in scoring it in that manner, so organizational change processes may appear as untidy cocktails (Pettigrew, 1985) of confused and irrational behaviour until one understands the players and how they have chosen to act. And here is the first crucial point at which the metaphor crumbles. The B flat clarinet player in the third bar of Elgar's first symphony plays just what Elgar wrote for him or her to play at that point, *nobilmente* and *piano dolce*. The composers of symphonies do not allow for the intentionality of the musicians. Actors in an organizational setting have considerably more latitude in choice of objectives and roles and how they will play those roles. The constraints on that latitude arise from the wider context and history of the organization (including certain key figures and personalities), and not from the pen of a master composer or with a conductor's baton. The orchestral metaphor is thus in danger, if taken too seriously, of obscuring the constructivist paradigm which underpins our main argument.

We wish, then, to use this metaphor simply to highlight particular aspects of the perspective developed here, and to point to specific departures from current thinking and theorizing in the change management field. Is it possible to identify and label the players in the organizational change process? Can we characterize the different modes in which they play their parts? Can we advance our understanding of change by examining the inter-relationships between the actions of the players? The key issues to which we wish to draw attention thus include the following:

- Any portrayal of the 'change agent' as a singular role is flawed.
- Adequate explanations of organizational change processes should recognize a plurality of players, of multiple agents of change.
- Furthermore, the multiple agents of change choose and switch roles in an intentional and creative manner in the progression of change.
- The detailed story of how those roles are activated in the organizational change process, to secure personal and group advantage, and in the formation of alliances and loyalties, has not been effectively analysed.
- The research focus should thus lie with developing our understanding of the orchestration or interplay between the different actors – drivers and others – in organizational change.

The nature and texture and pace and climate of change can be seen to depend on the ways in which the actors choose to engage in and disengage from the process in different ways, in different roles, in different modes, and at different times. As the performance of the symphony, with its harmony and discord, with slow and rapid passages, with shifts in mood between (for example) excitement and tranquillity, relies on the shifting engagement and combinations of the orchestral players, so too does the performance of organizational change. We hereby have access to a view of organizational change as a creatively orchestrated performance, rather than a carefully planned and managed process. Our understanding of change, and of that performance, will thus be advanced by our understanding of how the various players attempt intentionally to score or to construct their interlocking contributions.

The processual approach to change gives organizational actors supporting parts, moving them onto the front stage occasionally in special roles. The unit of analysis for Pettigrew (1985; 1987) is 'the process of change in context'. Context is regarded as a critical variable with explanatory power, not merely the playing field on which the actors manoeuvre. Our intention is to explore the implications of a shift in attention within the processual perspective, concentrating on change agency, on the players in the game. One distinct advantage of this should be to allow the practical managerial implications to be identified in a way not so far achieved (see the critiques of the work of Pettigrew and colleagues by Argyris, 1988, and Buchanan, 1994). The current interest in and emphasis on processes of strategic change has diverted attention away from the issue of change agency, the roles involved, and the expertise required.

THE VARIED AND ESCALATING DEMANDS OF CHANGE

The demands placed on drivers of organizational change are likely to be shaped by the nature of the change itself. These demands appear to be escalating, as appropriate and rapid internal change is increasingly linked with market success and competitive advantage. A number of commentators have sought to differentiate between types of change. Pettigrew (1985; 1987) focuses attention on 'strategic' change. The term, 'strategic' in this context is 'descriptive of magnitude' (Pettigrew, 1987, p. 668). This implies an analytical focus on large-scale or radical or fundamental organizational changes, and perhaps also carries the prescriptive implication that organizations should now be more concerned with changes at this level than with minor or operational alterations to structures and procedures. Pettigrew et al. (1992) distinguish strategic change from 'more operational matters', implying that the former concerns major structural alterations.

There are other commentators who offer more specific approaches to the characterization of strategic change. Boddy and Buchanan (1992) argue that organizational change can be classified on two dimensions, concerning degree of centrality or peripherality to the primary task of the organization, and the extent to which the change is perceived as radical or incremental. Changes peripheral to the primary task of the organization, and that are introduced incrementally, are likely to cause agents of change few technical or organizational problems, and the penalty for error is consequently low.

Radical changes that are central to the primary task of the organization are likely to be significantly more problematic, and the penalties for mistakes consequently higher. The nature of the change in its organizational setting thus conditions the change agents' experience of tranquillity or harassment. Boddy and Buchanan (1992) fail to distinguish the differential contributions of change drivers and address their remarks to 'the change agent' who will experience 'high hassle and high vulnerability' with strategic changes.

Dunphy and Stace (1990; 1993) define 'scale of change' with a four-level typology. Fine tuning is characterized by the refinement of policies, methods and procedures. Incremental adjustment is characterized by modifications to strategies, structures and processes in response to a changing environment. Modular transformation involves the major re-alignment of one or more departments or divisions in the organization. Finally, corporate transformation concerns radical shifts in strategy and revolutionary changes throughout the whole organization. These researchers advocate a contingency approach which argues that a dictatorial or coercive style of change leadership is appropriate for managing corporate transformation, whereas a collaborative, consultative style of change leadership (typically advocated by OD practitioners) is more effective for implementing minor adjustments. Dunphy and Stace do not pursue the issue of expertise beyond the advocacy of management styles. However, the expertise required to implement 'participative evolution' may be quite different from the methods and behaviours required to bring about 'dictatorial transformation'.

Davenport (1993, p. 171) argues that five main factors condition the experience and management of change. These concern the scale of the change, level of uncertainty about the outcomes, breadth of changes across the organization, the depth of 'penetration' of attitudes and behaviour, and the time scale of the implementation. The demands on drivers when change is narrowly focused, predictable, superficial and brief could thus be expected to be quite different from the demands created by change which is broadly conceived, unpredictable in many dimensions, protracted in its implementation, and requires significant changes in thinking and behaviour.

Storey (1992) adopts a four-cell model to classify types of managed change in his analysis of organizational transformations. This relies on two key dimensions. One concerns the extent to which change is unilaterally devised by management, or brought about by joint agreement (the organizations studied all being unionized). The second dimension concerns the extent to which change is introduced as a complete package of interlocking measures, or as a series of discrete initiatives. From these two dimensions, a four-fold typology of change is revealed.

Top-down systemic change involves major restructuring which is far reaching in both breadth and depth of change in the organization. Such change is planned and follows close guidelines. The vision is drawn up. The gap between 'then' and 'now' is identified. Department and personal action plans are constructed. Timetables are established. Progress is measured against milestones. There is, however, a lack of participation, and lower level managers and other participants in the organization may feel little sense of ownership of or involvement in the change process.

Piecemeal initiatives may be devised by a variety of mangers from different functions and levels. Storey (1992, pp. 130–1) notes how in one organization a whole series of initiatives had been launched, many of them of a disparate nature, with emphasis shifting between employee involvement, flexibility, payments system redesign, quality programmes, and so on. There was no attempt in that example to bring these initiatives together in any coherent manner.

Bargaining for change echoes traditional productivity bargaining. Here a series of target issues are identified and tackled in a piecemeal way, but with the objective of winning acceptance of change from trade union representatives. This pattern has been relatively common in Britain.

Systemic jointism refers to those situations in which a total package is negotiated. In Britain, this is undoubtedly the rarest type of change because union-management relations are mainly confined to a circumscribed arena of pay and conditions. But in America, Kochan et al. (1986, p. 175) report some significant corporate transformations where union leaders have been involved in strategic issues. A similar pattern emerges in Walton (1987).

Storey (1992) also identified a fifth type of change, falling between the two dimensions mentioned earlier. This is not a 'pure' type, but it is worth noting that a characteristic form is where the broad features of the desired change are set out at corporate level, but local business units are charged with developing detailed plans and proposals to fit their particular circumstances. Each type of change, in this model, can be seen to require its distinctive areas of expertise. Top-down systemic change may rely on autocratic project management skills. Piecemeal initiatives require the ability to identify and articulate the 'issues of the moment', to position these in the management agenda, and to sustain commitment. Bargaining for change clearly requires negotiation skills of a high order. Systemic jointism also requires negotiation skills, combined with strength of vision, long-range planning, and the maintenance of strong relationships with trade union organizations. Composite change patterns demand a combination of skills in motivating local and independent managers while co-ordinating activity across different business units.

It is thus reasonable to conclude that change drivers may be required to develop a broader and more sophisticated behavioural repertoire, if and as the demands they are likely to face both escalate and differentiate in the face of current trends and pressures. Our understanding of organizational change agency thus has both practical and theoretical significance.

THE FIRST PLURALITY: MULTIPLE ACTORS

Most commentators now accept a pluralist notion of organizational change agency, rather than a focus on a single change agent. This departs from notions of a singular, multi-talented individual with a set of near-universal competences. Ohmae's (1992) influential work on 'the mind of the strategist' falls into that category, however, as do Tichy and Devanna (1986) when describing 'the transformational leader'. Boddy and Buchanan (1992), while seeking to establish a broad repertoire of change expertise, conflate the terms project manager and change agent into a singular role. Similarly, Bott and Hill (1994) identify ten personal qualities required for effective organizational change under the headings 'setting an engaging direction', 'fostering independent relationships', 'providing systematic support' and 'stabilising beliefs'.

The label 'change agent' in the American literature is typically synonymous with the term 'OD practitioner'. Hunsaker and Cook (1986, p. 669) define the term change agent as 'the generic title for a person who seeks to initiate and manage a planned change process, usually employing OD techniques'. Gray and Starke (1984, p. 586) equate the title of change agent with an internal or external consultant – also described as a 'behavioural scientist consultant' (p. 587) – responsible for an OD programme, pointing out that this role can vary from an active decision-making one to passive counselling. Gibson et al. (1982, pp. 541–3) similarly distinguish the roles of internal and external change agents with respect to OD interventions, identifying also different models of the relationship between agent and organization based on different degrees of collaboration.

More recently, Cummings and Worley (1993, p. 30) elaborate the 'core and advanced skills for the future OD practitioner'. Their list of skills includes intrapersonal, interpersonal and general consultation skills, and knowledge of organizational development theory. This list covers the basic capabilities which Cummings and Worley regard as central to OD effectiveness. The additional areas identified include knowledge of research design and evaluation techniques, data collection and analysis methods, presentation skills, line management experience, knowledge of generic management functions, and collateral knowledge areas (such as social psychology, policy analysis, and systems engineering). The full list includes over 80 separate headings, of which 34 are 'starred' as 'advanced skills' (such as transorganization theory, unobtrusive measurement, telephone intervention skills, and psychopathology and therapy). This can be viewed, therefore, as a comprehensive agenda for an on-and-off-the-job training course for the aspiring multi-talented OD practitioner. These citations merely represent a literature which, while perhaps recognizing a pluralist stance, in the abstract often treats the change agent as a singular, identifiable, and highly influential individual.

The processual perspective on organizational change presents a more complex and diffuse view of change agency. For example, at some points in his analysis, Pettigrew (1985) appears to marginalize the role of agents of change, subordinating such positions' significance to wider organizational and environmental factors. He claims that it is necessary

> to conceptualize the major transformations of the firm in terms of linkages between the content of change and its context and process and to regard leadership behaviour as a central ingredient but only one of the ingredients in a complex analytical, political, and cultural process of challenging and changing the core beliefs, structure, and strategy of the firm.
>
> (Pettigrew, 1987, p. 650)

However, he also emphasizes that, from his study of change in ICI, 'all these cases indicate the importance in managerial terms of strong, persistent, and continuing leadership to create strategic change' (1985, p. 454). The leadership role is here concerned with articulating the issues that need to be tackled, with defining the problems to be considered important, with 'problem finding', and with 'visionary presentation' of plans and ideas often in imprecise ways. Pettigrew does not, therefore, deny the significance of the change agent's role, but is concerned to locate that position firmly in the wider organizational and environmental context which both constrain and facilitate the change agent's actions. The moving and shaking role of 'exceptional people' has to be balanced with an understanding of the 'extraordinary circumstances' in which they find themselves acting.

Pettigrew *et al.* (1992, p. 27) point to 'the often competing versions of reality seen by actors in change processes'. Dawson (1994, p. 4), also working within a processual perspective indicates how, 'the co-existence of a number of competing histories of change can significantly shape the process and outcomes of ongoing change programmes'. This perspective, generates opaque answers to questions like, 'who are the change agents?' and 'what do they do?'.

Pettigrew is understandably critical of the OD approach for its lack of attention to process and context factors (internal and external, current and past). The OD focus is with the players, not the field. Skill requirements can be identified independently of the organizational context. Pettigrew's focus in contrast is with process in context, which influences the how and why of change, and the tradition, culture, structure, business sector and socio-economic environment of the organization, which can also constrain and facilitate change processes. Pettigrew further claims that the real problem of strategic change is anchoring new concepts of reality, new issues for attention, new ideas for debate and resolution, and mobilising concern, energy and enthusiasm often in an additive and evolutionary fashion to ensure these early illegitimate thoughts gain powerful support and eventually result in contextually appropriate action.

(Pettigrew, 1985, p. 438)

In defining 'the real problem of change' in this way, Pettigrew clearly places quite a different set of items on the change agent's agenda from those typically found, say, in Cummings and Worley (1993). The latter include a short section on the topic of 'developing political support', dealing with three themes: assessing the power of the change agent, identifying key stakeholders, and influencing stakeholders. One can infer from Pettigrew's analysis that effective intervention in the organization's political system involves more sophistication, and further techniques, than Cummings and Worley have to offer.

The traditional change implementation concerns with involvement and ownership acquire different connotations in attempts to stimulate debate and to mobilize concern. The emphasis on goals, responsibilities, deadlines, controls and sympathetic involvement are here replaced with a concern for legitimacy. From this perspective, the management of change becomes the management of meaning. As Pettigrew thus argues:

A central concept linking political and cultural analyses particularly germane to the understanding of change and continuity and change is legitimacy. The management of meaning refers to a process of symbol construction and value use designed to create legitimacy for one's ideas, actions, and demands, and to delegitimize the demands of one's opponents. Key concepts for analysing these processes of legitimization and delegitimization are symbolism, language, ideology and myth.

(Pettigrew, 1985, p. 442)

Change agency in this perspective is partly reactive, responding to environmental or contextual threats and opportunities, and partly proactive in exploiting contextual factors to promote and support change proposals. The change agent's skills from this perspective thus concern the ability to intervene in the organization's political and cultural systems and simultaneously to manage the content, context and process of change. However, from a practical managerial point of view, it is not clear what is meant by such intervention. The value of the processual perspective to the practising change agent is not entirely clear; analytical strength thus reflects a prescriptive weakness (Boddy and Buchanan, 1992).

It may be useful at this point to distinguish clearly between two facets of a pluralist perspective. First, it is clear that the nature and pace of change can be influenced by a plurality of organizational actors. Egan (1994) offers rather humorous guidance to the change agent on a stakeholder analysis which in his view should consider partners, allies, fellow travellers, fence-sitters, loose cannon, opponents, adversaries, bedfellows and the voiceless. Second, it also seems clear that those who seek to promote organizational initiatives adopt a plurality of change roles. The remarks of, for example, Cummings and Worley, Dawson, and Bott and Hill, seem to be directed towards 'change drivers' rather than to recipients, spectators, victims, or other contributors.

THE SECOND PLURALITY: MULTIPLE DRIVERS

Not all the actors concerned with organizational change are proactive: some are spectators or passengers. Several commentators have sought to identify the differential roles of change drivers. It is clear from these analyses that change is typically driven by the interlocking (but not neces-sarily consistent and mutually supportive) activities of several actors in the organization. Williams *et al.* (1993, p. 112) in their text on managing organizational culture change identify the 'three roles which change agents play' as initiator, co-ordinator and facilitator. The initiator is the charis-matic and visionary leader, who could be the founder or the new chief executive. The role is, 'primarily one of giving direction, inspiration and support' (p. 115), and the main input is likely to come at the beginning of the change process. The co-ordinator is concerned with successful imple-mentation and this role can be carried out either by an individual or a team. The main input from this role comes, they argue, at the end of the primary decision-making cycle. The facilitator is involved throughout the change process in helping others to change and to learn. This is the role also of the trainer, the instructor, the OD manager. Goals here are achieved through direct action with others, and this person could be an outside consultant or a line manager.

In their work on business process re-engineering, Hammer and Champy (1993) answer their question, 'who will re-engineer?' by identifying five different driving roles: leader, process owner, re-engineering team, steering committee and re-engineering czar. The leader is a senior executive who authorizes and motivates the overall re-engineering effort. The process owner is the manager with responsibility for a specific process and the re-engineering effort focused on it. The re-engineering team is a group of individuals dedicated to the re-engineering of a particular process, who diagnose the existing process and oversee its redesign and implementation. The steering committee is a policy-making body of senior managers who develop the organization's overall re-engineering strategy and monitor its progress. Finally, the re-engineering tsar is an individual responsible for developing re-engineering techniques and tools within the company and for achieving synergy across the company's separate re-engineering projects. Hammer and Champy (1993) open this account of 'the toilers in the vineyard of re-engineering' (p. 116) by summarizing their interrelationships in the following terms: 'The *leader* appoints the *process owner*, who convenes a *re-engineering team* to re-engineer the process, with the assistance from the *tsar* and under the auspices of the *steering committee*' (p. 103).

Also writing about the toilers in the vineyards of re-engineering, Davenport (1993) identifies five major change drivers: the advocate who proposes change, the sponsor who legitimizes it, the targets who undergo it, the agents who implement it, and the process owner – typically the most senior target. Davenport emphasizes the role of the visionary leader as the initiator, creator and primary proponent of the vision. This individual requires four qualities, according to Davenport, including commitment and the ability to inspire, conceptual skills, impatience for results, and an ability to handle the 'soft' behavioural aspect of change. He also points to uncertainty as a generator of anxiety and resistance, and to the role of pain and hope as motivators and catalysts. Along with many other commentators in this field, Davenport (1993, p. 173) thus emphasizes the significance of the 'bold outline of a compelling future state' provided by the change leadership.

THE THIRD PLURALITY: MULTIPLE PHASES

The emphasis of much of the (European) literature on organizational change during the 1980s was with the process of strategic change. That emphasis was encouraged by dissatisfaction with (American) OD models, and by a preoccupation with strategy formulation at the expense of strategy implementation. Pettigrew (1985), echoing Bennis (1969) describes the OD approach as the 'truth, trust, love and collaboration model' of organizational change, arguing instead for change strategies that are sensitive to the context, the history and the process of change.

Pettigrew's work has conditioned both thinking and the research agenda with respect to organizational change through the 1980s and into the 1990s (Wilson, 1992). However, this research tradition has consistently avoided prescription, in the interests of 'empirical integrity' (Pettigrew and Whipp, 1991). The analytically complex, multi-variate, multi-dimensional, multi-level, longitudinal model which Pettigrew advocates from the theoretical high ground disables attempts to distil guidance of value to those at the coal face. The manager seeking advice from this genre will find only broad and generalized statements . The researcher exploring the nature of the management process will similarly find only vague (and sometimes apparently contradictory) indications and little specific practical illustration. 'No checklists', the Tom Peters acolyte would complain.

The position advanced here seeks to build on the work of Quinn (1980), Kanter (1983), Pettigrew (1985; 1987; 1988), and Pfeffer (1992), among others, in considering both the rational-analytic aspects of change agency as well as what Quinn called the 'power-behavioural' components of that role, and what Tom Burns (1961) called the 'micro-politics' of change. Boddy and Buchanan (1992) review some of the literature relating in particular to the power, political and symbolic dimensions of the role of the change agent, and the intent here is to extend that work.

Attempts to describe and explain processes of change in organizations are typically based on phase models seeking to identify the stages through which changes unfold through time. Greiner (1967), for example, identifies six phases of successful change implementation, each involving a stimulus to, and reaction from, the power structure of the organization. These phases proceed through pressure on top management, intervention at the top, problem diagnosis, invention of new solutions, experimentation, and then reinforcement. Greiner's thesis is that successful change depends on an effective sharing or redistribution of power, through a developmental process reflected in this patterned sequence. Kanter (1983) describes the process of change more parsimoniously as three 'waves of action' which respectively concern problem definition, mobilizing a supportive coalition, and completion. Pettigrew (1985) uses a four-phase model of the change process (drawing on Beckhard and Harris, 1977). These phases are:

- the development of concern about the status quo
- acknowledging and understanding the problem
- planning and acting
- stabilizing the change process.

Burnes (1992) offers a more elaborate 'nine-element' approach to strategic change implementation. This involves creating a vision, developing strategies, creating readiness for change, creating the culture for change, assessing the type of change needed, planning and implementing the change, managing involvement and communications, sustaining the momentum, and organizing for continuous improvement. Dawson's (1994, p. 3) processual framework, echoing Kanter, admits to three 'general timeframes' in change implementation, concerning:

- *conception* of a need for change
- process of organizational *transition*
- *operation* of new work practices and procedures.

There are in the literature many such phase models of change, some fine-grained and others broad-brushed depending on the authors' purpose. The phase delineation does not imply discrete steps. On the contrary, however specified, it is clear that these phases overlap, and that the process is often an iterative one with much backtracking (for example, as senior management attention is diverted, as diagnoses are revised, as mistakes are recognized, as experimentation throws up new solutions). One may therefore assume that these models are post-hoc rationalizations, tidied-up versions of a much messier reality, and that they may thus be of more value in structuring accounts of change after they have happened than in planning the implementation process in advance. Such 'hindsight' accounts can, of course, still inform practice.

The metaphor of the orchestral score encourages a focus on both the organizational roles being assumed in the performance, and the manner or style in which those roles are performed. As with the manager who turns the disciplinary meeting into a counselling session on uncovering domestic problems affecting work performance, we may expect individual agents of change to switch roles and styles, from planning, to experimenting, to lobbying for support, and so on. The choice and flexibility implied by the ability to switch styles gives the agent of change potentially more freedom than the simple notion of role, bounded as that concept typically is by individual preference and by the expectations of fellow actors in the organization.

THE FOURTH PLURALITY: MULTIPLE ROLES

Is it possible to infer the various organizational roles of change drivers from models of the change process? Can we identify the components of what Kanter (1983) calls 'change architect skills' across the overlapping 'waves of action'? As the implementation process unfolds, different types of engagement with the change process will presumably be required. The skills of fostering concern are different from the skills of planning, which are different from the skills involved in completing and stabilizing. It also seems reasonable to suggest that a close viewing would reveal a range of actors moving into the performance. Different individuals may be expected to play different roles, contributing to the process in discrete, overlapping, identifiable and potentially conflicting ways. However, particular individuals, by virtue of their position in the organization, their relationship to the changes in hand, and the nature of their potential contribution, may be expected to assume multiple roles through time. We should also expect to see the players shifting the behavioural mode of their activity with the action, perhaps playing their part *andante tranquillo* at one stage, shifting (for sake of illustration) to *presto con malizia* (quickly and with malice, as the second movement of William Walton's first symphony is scored) at another.

Suppose we assume that all the demands on change drivers – that is, the requisite variety of roles – can be identified from phase models of change. We may thus be in a position to identify the expertise required in each phase. If this assumption holds, we can presumably construct the jigsaw of skills, knowledge, attributes and behaviours possessed by agents of change in an organization and fundamental to effective change implementation. Precedents for this enterprise include Belbin's (1981) characterization of team members' roles, and managers' and leaders' roles by Quinn and colleagues (1990).

This approach has a precedent in the literature of team building and, as will shortly be considered, in the change management literature also. Here we engage in 'listology' – the art of devising managerial checklists with spurious face validity and dubious practical value. The point is not, however, to present and defend a particular formulation, list or set of labels, but to establish the argument for a further facet of a pluralist account of change – that change drivers contribute in many ways to organizational initiatives. The other three facets of this account concern the multiplicity of actors, of change drivers, and of phases through which change typically progresses. Listology is popular because it is relatively straightforward and because the results have an ostensibly direct appeal and instant applicability.

Examining the phase models summarized here reveals that drivers of change could be expected to function in several overlapping roles such as:

- visionary, catalyst, 'mover and shaker'
- analyst, compelling case-builder, risk assessor
- team-builder, coalition-former, ally seeker
- implementation planner, action driver, deliverer
- fixer-facilitator, wheeler-dealer, power broker
- reviewer, critic, progress-chaser, auditor.

These roles and their underlying competences cover the three general timeframes identified by Dawson (1994), the nine implementation stages identified by Burnes (1993), the four phases identified by Pettigrew (1985), the three waves of action identified by Kanter (1983), and the six phases identified by Greiner (1967). As with the conclusions from the OD perspective, the combined task appears to require a superior multi-talented individual – or as the processual perspective invites us to consider, to focus instead on the interlocking contributions of a multiplicity of drivers.

One conclusion that can be drawn from these accounts is that the expertise required by agents of change depends on role. The expertise required, for example, for effective advocacy or change initiation may be different from that required for effective implementation. Conventional change implementation skills, on the other hand, may not wholly overlap with the expertise of the power broker and wheeler-dealer – who may be uncomfortable in the roles of either facilitator or tsar. From a processual perspective, this conclusion appears premature. Drivers of change in complex organizations are unlikely to slot into predefined roles. One would expect rather to see individuals adopting different roles, and playing those roles differently through time, according to the pressures and demands of events as well as on personal preference and expertise. The manner in which organizational events then unfold may be explained in part by role taking and switching, and on the differential levels of competence with which interlocking agents conduct themselves when engaging in the organizational change performance.

THE CREATIVELY ORCHESTRATED PERFORMANCE: FINAL SCORE

We opened this discussion by considering the skills required by the change agent, and how contemporary trends place a premium in many organizations on appropriate and rapid change. We considered the mutiplicity of organizational actors and also the number of different drivers potentially involved in change. We noted how the activities, or roles of the change driver, can be expected to vary across different phases of implementation. There is, therefore, a need to situate the concept of change agency firmly in the organizational context. That is precisely what the processual perspective offers, but the architects of this stance have been preoccupied with process and content and have not, as yet, brought agents of change, and the practical managerial implications of a pluralist perspective, clearly into focus.

This discussion suggests that a pluralist account of change should take into account four facets or dimensions of plurality. The first concerns the plurality of organizational actors involved in change, the second the plurality of change drivers, the third that of phases of organizational change, each generating different conditions and making separate demands, and the fourth the multiple and shifting roles that change drivers may be called upon to play throughout the implementation process. The following list seeks crudely to summarize these 'four pluralities'.

- organizational actors
  recipients, spectators, victims, opponents, subversives, enemies, fence-sitters, loose cannon, allies, the voiceless
- change drivers
  initiator, co-ordinator, project manager, facilitator, advocate, sponsor,

(re-engineering) tsar, process owner, deliverer-implementer, steering group members, task force participants
- change phases
waves of action concerning: conception, developing concern, planning and acting, transition, operating, stabilizing
- change-driving roles
visionary, catalyst, analyst, influencer, coalition builder, lobbyist, planner, reviewer, wheeler-dealer, political fixer, resistance-blocker

As we shift the focus from the organizational level of analysis to that of the individual, a number of implications follow. First, we see different individuals playing different roles as the change process unfolds through time, selecting and switching roles depending on their understanding of organizational circumstances. This may involve more or less successful attempts by change drivers to adopt, capture and establish particular roles in the pursuit of personal gain or organizational advantage. We are confronted, therefore, with a 'shifting pluralism'. The composition of the population of organizational actors is not constant with respect to those who are change drivers and those who are not, with respect to the roles of the change drivers, or with how those drivers choose – creatively and in the spirit of experiment – to act out their various roles.

Restating our central question, is it helpful to characterize the roles of change drivers? We can presumably expect individual actors to adopt, capture, define and shift roles through time as their understanding and definition of the situation changes. The flexibility and creativity implied in this perspective gives the agent of change more freedom than either 'singular' concepts of role, or the processual perspective allow. To constrain that flexibility within a list of roles would be counterproductive, and contrary to the thrust of the argument which concerns the need to adapt change-driving behaviour in a creative manner to the circumstances.

The analysis thus results in the following propositions:

- an adequate explanation of organizational change must be alert to the multiplicity of players involved in the process
- the multiple players adopt, define, capture and switch roles in the change process
- role taking and switching and defining and capturing depend in part on the type of change, on the timing of the process, and on individual perceptions of what constitutes effective intervention in the pursuit of individual and corporate goals and projects
- the multiple players adopt and change behavioural styles in acting out different roles – there is no fixed prescription, for example, for the 'effective sponsor'
- role taking and switching also depend on the type and timing of change

and on perceptions of what will work; this presupposes a creative-experimental stance on the part of change drivers

- role taking and switching are conscious and creative acts which rely on the players' resources of position, competence, and power (e.g., Pfeffer, 1992)
- adequate understanding of change processes lies in the interplay of multiple agents of change in the organization and their shifting interactions
- that interplay is not always harmonious and effective, and an adequate perspective must allow for and explain discord, conflict and error
- organizational change processes do not move smoothly and predictably from phase to phase but are characterized instead by alterations in pace and by back-tracking.

The systems theory concept of 'equifinality' implies that there may be multiple routes to the same end point. If the process of change management is a creative performance, then different styles of performance may ultimately have the same or similar organizational implications. The players in this performance are not diligently following a predetermined score; the metaphor collapses at this point. They are instead constructing their own lines of action through time, in concert – but not necessarily always in harmony – with the other players in the organization around them. This is not, therefore, a contingency perspective on change agency in the sense of finding 'optimal fit'. It is from this new point of departure, we conclude, that the next research challenge arises, and from where practical guidance may be derived to greater effect than the processual perspective has been able to offer.

References

Argyris, C. (1988) Review essay: first- and second-order errors in managing strategic change: the role of organizational defensive routines, in *The Management of Strategic Change*, (ed. A.M. Pettigrew), Blackwell, Oxford, pp. 342–51.

Beckhard, R. and Harris, R. (1977) *Organizational Transitions: Managing Complex Change*, Addison Wesley, Reading, Massachusetts.

Belbin, R.M. (1981) *Management Teams: Why They Succeed or Fail*, Heinemann, London.

Bennis, W. (1969) *Organization Development: Its Nature, Origins and Prospects*, Addison-Wesley, Reading, Massachusetts.

Boddy, D. and Buchanan, D. (1992) *The Expertise of the Change Agent: Public Performance and Backstage Activity*, Prentice Hall International (UK), Hemel Hempstead.

Bott, K. and Hill, J. (1994) Change agents lead the way, in *People Management*, August, pp. 24–7.

Buchanan, D.A. (1994) *Theories of change*, Loughborough University Business School research series, paper 5, March.

Burnes, B. (1992) *Managing Change: A Strategic Approach to Organizational Development and Renewal*, Pitman, London.

Burns, T. (1961) Micropolitics: mechanisms of institutional change, in *Administrative Science Quarterly*, vol. 5, pp. 257–81.

Cummings, T.G. and Worley, C.G. (1993) *Organizational Development and Change*, (5th edn), West Publishing, Minneapolis/St Paul, Minnesota.

Davenport, T.H. (1993) *Process Innovation: Re-engineering Work Through IT*, Harvard Business School Press, Boston, Massachusetts.

Dawson, P. (1994) *Organizational Change: A Processual Approach*, Paul Chapman, London.

Dunphy, D. and Stace, D. (1990) *Under New Management: Australian Organizations in Transition*, McGraw-Hill, Sydney.

Dunphy, D. and Stace, D. (1993) The strategic management of corporate change, in *Human Relations*, vol. 46, no 8, pp. 905–20.

Egan, G. (1994) *Working the Shadow Side: A Guide to Positive Behind-The-Scenes Management*, Jossey Bass Publishers, San Francisco, California.

Gibson, J.L., Ivancevich, J.M. and Donnelly, J.H. (1982) *Organizations: Behaviour, Structure, Processes*, Business Publications, Plano, Texas.

Gray, J.L. and Starke, F.A. (1984) *Organizational Behaviour: Concepts and Applications*, Charles E. Merrill, Columbus, Ohio.

Greiner, L. (1967) Patterns of organizational change, in *Harvard Business Review*, vol. 45, no. 3, pp. 119–30.

Hammer, M. and Champy, J. (1993) *Re-engineering the Corporation: A Manifesto for Business Revolution*, Nicholas Brealey, London.

Hunsaker, P.L. and Cook, C.W. (1986) *Managing Organizational Behaviour*, Addison-Wesley, Reading, Massachusetts.

Kanter, R.M. (1983) *The Change Masters: Corporate Entrepreneurs at Work*, George Allen & Unwin, London.

Kanter, R.M. (1989) *When Giants Learn to Dance: Mastering the Challenge of Strategy, Management and Careers in the 1990s*, Simon & Schuster, London.

Kochan, T.A., Katz, H. and McKersie, R.B. (1986) *The Transformation of American Industrial Relations*, Basic Books, New York.

Mundy, S. (1980) *Elgar*, Omnibus Press, London.

Ohmae, K. (1992) *The Mind of the Strategist*, McGraw Hill, New York.

Pettigrew, A.M. (1985) *The Awakening Giant: Continuity and Change in ICI*, Blackwell, Oxford.

Pettigrew, A.M. (1987) Context and action in the transformation of the firm, in *Journal of Management Studies*, vol. 24, no. 6, pp. 649–70.

Pettigrew, A.M. (ed.) (1988), *The Management of Strategic Change*, Blackwell, Oxford.

Pettigrew, A.M. and Whipp, R. (1991) *Managing Change for Competitive Success*, Blackwell, Oxford.

Pettigrew, A.M., Ferlie, E. and McKee, L. (1992) *Shaping Strategic Change: Making Change in Large Organizations – The Case of the National Health Service*, Sage, London.

Pfeffer, J. (1992) *Managing with Power: Politics and Influence in Organization*, Harvard Business School Press, Boston, Massachusetts.

Quinn, J.B. (1980) *Strategies for Change: Logical Incrementalism*, Richard D. Irwin, Homewood, Illinois.

Quinn, R.E., Faerman, S.R., Thompson, M.P. and McGrath, M.R. (1990) *Becoming a Master Manager: A Competency Framework*, John Wiley, New York.

Storey, J. (1992) *Developments in the Management of Human Resources*, Blackwell, Oxford.

Tichy, N.M. and Devanna, M.A. (1986) *The Transformational Leader*, John Wiley, New York.

Walton, R.E. (1987) *Innovating to Compete: Lessons for Diffusing and Managing Change in the Workplace*, Jossey Bass, San Francisco.

Williams, A., Dobson, P. and Walters, M. (1993) *Changing Culture: New Organizational Approaches*, 2nd edn, Institute of Personnel Management, London.

Wilson, D.C. (1992) *A Strategy of Change: Concepts and Controversies in the Management of Change*, Routledge, London.

Chapter 7

Implementing vulnerable socio-technical change projects

Richard Badham, Paul Couchman and Ian McLoughlin

INTRODUCTION

There is now a growing enthusiasm for self-managing, self-directed or empowered work teams (Wellins *et al.*, 1991; Osburn, *et al.*, 1991). While such ideas are not new and have enjoyed considerable currency in the past, it is now conventional wisdom that modern production conditions – driven in particular by changes in product markets, technology and work-related legislation-favour autonomous team-based working far more than ever before. As a result, management is said to attach strategic rather than operational importance to team-based forms of work. For some this is a key difference between team-based working initiatives of the 1980s and 90s and their predecessors of the 1960s and 70s (Buchanan, 1994).

Team-based cellular manufacturing (TBCM) is one such initiative which has attracted considerable interest in Europe, North America and the Asia-Pacific region. TBCM involves grouping machines (lathes, drills, presses etc.) into groups or cells according to the particular processes and their sequence which are required to produce parts or families of parts. The *technical* redesign of production in this way creates the potential for the *social* redesign of work so that workers operating as a semi-autonomous team can perform the tasks in the cells. For this to happen cell members need to become multi-skilled – able to operate different machines and carry out maintenance tasks for example – and empowered to take day-to-day operating decisions in the planning, execution and monitoring of cell operations. In place of the traditional first-line supervisor, teams have 'leaders', who may be elected by other team members rather than appointed by management. In addition, teams may be able to stop production as and when they see necessary to discuss work-related problems and so on. In their most advanced form, team-based cells might have considerable responsibility for interacting with their environment to the extent that they have direct contact with 'customers' both inside and outside the organization. Ultimately they might operate, in effect, as mini-business units themselves. The upshot is a radically different approach to designing the technical and social aspects of production from the traditional layout of machines according to function and the organization and control of work according to the 'Taylorist' principles of a detailed division of labour and hierarchical supervision. The various levels of team-based working said to be enabled by cellular manufacturing techniques are summarized in Figure 7.1.

It is these characteristics and possibilities that have made TBCM and similar initiatives attractive to those who are interested in promoting more human-centred, humanized or socio-technical approaches to work redesign. However, in practice, the potential for using cellular manufacturing as a vehicle for persuading management to pay more attention to the social aspects of production system design has, to date, been restricted. First, despite the claimed greater commitment of senior management to team-based working, it has not necessarily resulted in the unambiguous transfer of substantial autonomy to work teams in the vast majority of cases of TBCM implementation (Jurgens *et al.*, 1993) – a finding echoed in reviews of the effects of other new production and organizational techniques (see Beer *et al.*, 1990; Schaffer and Thomson, 1992; Hill *et al.*, this volume; Willcocks and Grint, this volume). Second, as with most work humanisa-tion and 'socio-technical' work redesign projects of the 1960s and 70s, contemporary initiatives have encountered severe implementation pro-blems and often failed to progress beyond isolated pilot schemes (Kelly, 1982; Badham and Naschold, 1994).

It is the argument of this chapter that the change-management process is crucial to successful implementation of human-centred/socio-technical work redesign projects such as TBCM. Advocates of human-centred work redesign of this type need a better understanding of the process of change within organizations and how it can be managed, in particular its micro-political dimensions and characteristics. This is especially so given the inherent 'vulnerability' of complex and novel projects which seek to accomplish both technical and social change of this type. We begin our discussion, therefore, by considering the peculiar 'vulnerability' of socio-technical projects. What follows draws heavily on the experience of a socio-technical change project conducted in Australia in the early 1990s – the 'SMART project'. As we will see, this involved collaboration between social scientific and engineering researchers with three manufac-turing companies to introduce TBCM. These efforts met with varying degrees of success and the experiences in the three companies serve to illustrate both the vulnerability of this kind of change project and the importance of change management to their success. Finally we outline and explore what we term a configurational-process model of change. This is intended as a framework for understanding and explaining events in the case studies and as a potential guide to more informed intervention by action researchers in promoting socio-technical ideas in similar projects in the future.

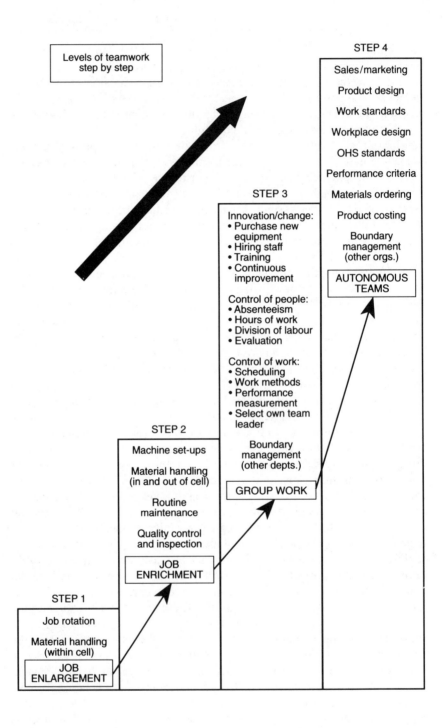

Figure 7.1 Levels of teamwork in team-based manufacture

VULNERABLE CHANGE PROJECTS AND THE POLITICS OF SOCIO-TECHNICAL CHANGE

There is now a growing literature on new project management (Frame, 1994) and the role of the 'change agent' in dealing with the 'people' issues in running organizational change projects. For some this involves supplementing a 'harder' technically-oriented approach to the management of complex projects with a 'softer' people-centred approach using established organizational development methods (McCalman and Paton, 1992). For others, it means going beyond traditional technical project management and organizational development methods, and developing the political 'backstage' skills and techniques of the change agent (Boddy and Buchanan, 1992). A common theme in all such accounts, is the difficulty of dealing with the 'people' issues and controversial politics that surround more 'complex', 'uncertain', 'softer' or 'vulnerable' projects.

In using the term 'vulnerable' projects here, we are pointing to two sets of conditions that make projects more subject to organizational disruption and, consequently failure: their degree of complexity and how radical they are, two key features, we would suggest, of contemporary work humanization or socio-technical change programmes.

With complex projects, in contrast to more routine mechanistic types of change, there is a large degree of uncertainty about what is to be done and how to do it. Objectives are less clear, resource requirements not so well known, activities more often redirected, and schedules reorganized. As McCalman and Paton (1992) observe, in such conditions it is more difficult to achieve the shared perception of the project's goals and keep the necessary commitment to provide a solution. More time and effort has to be spent ensuring effective communication, addressing people's perceptions, encouraging flexibility, and generating and re-generating involvement in the face of new problems, setbacks and opportunities.

With radical change, problems arise from the degree to which organizational actors, culture and structure have to be transformed for the project to succeed. The radical nature of such projects is derived from two elements: the degree to which the change is central to the organization's strategy and survival and involves modifications throughout the organization (breadth) and the degree to which these modifications are a radical departure from existing ways of doing things (depth). The more major the project in these two senses, the more politically controversial it is likely to be since the activities and interests of a wide range of different groups may be fundamentally threatened. Clearly, such projects will take on many of the characteristics of complex projects listed above. What is added here is the likelihood of political disruption and opposition – a further factor increasing the project's vulnerability.

This feature is emphasized by Boddy and Buchanan (1992), who stress the increasing hassle and 'personal vulnerability' facing change agents implementing large-scale projects that are seen as complex and affecting the organization's 'core task'. The combination of these two dimensions – degree of complexity and radical nature – is summarized in Figure 7.2.

The radical nature of socio-technical projects derives from their attempt to transform both vertical and horizontal structures in the organization. In the case of TBCM, for instance, the creation of self-managing cell teams involves cutting across traditional semi-skilled work boundaries and 'direct' semi-skilled and 'indirect' skilled demarcations. The complementary design of interdependent technical (cells) and organizational (teams) structures imposes greater demands for co-operation between industrial engineers and human resource personnel, ergonomists or human factors engineers and system designers, and design engineering and manufacturing engineering. The self-managing nature of cell teams involves not only transforming line management, as supervisors become 'coaches' to self-supervising teams, but also reverses the traditional relationship between direct production and indirect support departments. As engineering, accounting and personnel functions are devolved to the teams, indirect departments move into a more 'supportive' relationship.

The introduction of such projects therefore requires clear links with corporate strategy as senior management's commitment is crucial in overcoming opposition and securing the levels of investment required. It also involves considerable changes in the skills, attitudes and activities of personnel at all levels. Direct labourers become responsible for far broader aspects of their work, line managers become more concerned with system development and strategic issues, and traditional specialists (e.g. industrial engineers, human resource specialists, accountants) are required to work more in interdisciplinary and interdepartmental teams, often in greater contact with direct production operations. Indeed, for Brandon (1993), it is this necessity for 'interdisciplinary collaboration' that makes such strategic changes inherently vulnerable to the withdrawal of much needed support by different functional groups.

The complexity of such projects also increases their vulnerability. There are a considerable number of unknowns involved in their introduction. To take one example, the redesign of technical systems imposes new demands on information systems – similarity of parts, feasibility of alternatives, layout analyses, performance data on lead times – and needs the combined knowledge of both technical and production staff. The amount of work required to achieve this is typically uncertain at the start of a project. To take another example, in creating new forms of teamwork, both management and the workforce have to overcome traditional distrusts in order to offer rewards, on the one hand, and both effort and commitment on the other. Yet there are inevitable uncertainties about how the other side will

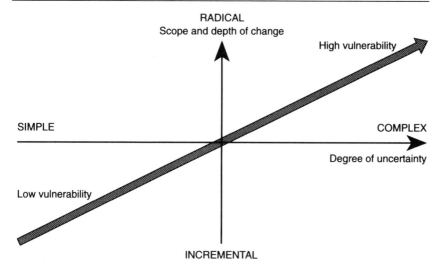

RADICAL
Scope and depth of change

High vulnerability

SIMPLE

COMPLEX

Degree of uncertainty

Low vulnerability

INCREMENTAL

Figure 7.2 Degrees of vulnerability in change projects

behave and how far the final result will be either productive for the firm or rewarding for employees.

In sum, by their nature, socio-technical projects tend to cut across horizontal and vertical boundaries within organizations and impinge on the interests of a broad range of 'stakeholders' who may perceive a variety of 'threats' and 'opportunities'. More than projects which focus mainly on the technical dimensions of change, socio-technical projects may be characterized by political negotiations, alliances and compromises. As such, they are particularly vulnerable to organizational disturbances and micropolitical disruptions. In such circumstances the final nature of implemented change and its impact on productivity, working conditions and so on will be crucially influenced by how conflicts and compromises are managed and resolved during the change process.

This draws attention to the high level of what we term local 'configurational' activity required to adapt general models of 'cellular manufacturing' and 'teamwork' to the particular production and organizational environment of a specific enterprise. Moreover, this activity can impose severe strains on project teams as apparently clear general directives become bogged down in a myriad of details and compromises. In the technical area, for example, the design of product-based cells creating 'whole' products or part families, is always faced by compromises as equipment has to be shared, the scope of production that can be said to be responsible for a 'whole' product has to be decided etc. Crucial socio-technical decisions have to be made in addressing all such questions. In the organizational sphere teams are expected to take on more responsibility and be trained to do so – yet how much responsibility, the speed of introduction, the time and facilities available for training, the educational and cultural content of the training etc. are all far less clear. Decisions in all these areas require considerable investigation, thought and effort to ensure that generic socio-technical ideas are effectively adapted to the specific demands of the organization. As we will see, the uncertainty, frustration and potential for sabotage involved in the lengthy processes of resolving such issues is a further factor which considerably increases such projects' vulnerability.

THE SMART PROJECT: THREE CASES OF 'VULNERABLE SOCIO-TECHNICAL CHANGE'

The Smart Manufacturing Techniques: Team-Based Cellular Manufacturing (SMART) project focused on the practical integration of technical and organizational aspects in the design and implementation of new production systems. The project was called SMART to contrast it with the more conventional view of 'intelligent' manufacturing systems. According to this latter view, 'intelligent' manufacturing is identified with machines incorporating artificial intelligence which are capable of coping with complex and changing conditions, and hence refers to high levels of automation and the automatic control of production operations. By contrast our approach, inspired by a European tradition of skill-based automation, seeks to effectively integrate human and technological components in creating adaptable and flexible systems that support rather than undermine the responsibility and creativity of skilled operators (see for example, Brodner, 1989). Through this approach we argue that the twin goals of increased international competitiveness and more humane work can be addressed.

The project was carried out over two years, from 1993 to 1995, with partners from research (four institutions) and industry (three sub-project firms). The research partners, working in universities and Australian federal and state government research organizations, brought to the project skills and knowledge in the areas of manufacturing systems design and organizational analysis. The overall project was funded by the companies and the Australian Department of Industry, Technology and Commerce.

The three company sub-projects provided some interesting contrasts.

• Koala Irrigation manufactured plastic irrigation systems, and before joining the project had received an Australian federal government 'best practice' grant. The company had previous experience with cellular manufacturing and had developed its own version of semi-autonomous work groups.
• Wombat Plastics (a division of an international motor company in Australia which supplies plastics components for local car assembly) had a

long history of experimenting with work teams, initially in the mid–1980s under its employee involvement programme. Under its innovative plant manager considerable progress had been made in achieving team-led quality and productivity improvements.

- Kangaroo Whitegoods (a division of an international domestic appliance company), manufactured whitegoods and floorcare products. In the late–1980s it had begun to experiment with 'just-in-time' manufacturing methods and with value added manufacturing (VAM) groups, a form of quality circle.

In each of the sub-projects the SMART project researchers defined their role as the introduction and promotion of skill-based or human-centred design principles. This was attempted in different ways in each of the three firms. In Kangaroo Whitegoods for example, the principles were incorporated in job redesign models which spelt out the various options concerning how teams in the firm's press shop might be organized. At the lowest level this would involve no more than some enlargement of team members' jobs. At the highest levels the teams would be fully autonomous and effectively a 'business within a business'. In Wombat Plastics a set of evaluation critera were developed, including some human-centred principles, which were then used to assess alternative production system designs. In Koala Irrigation, socio-technical design principles were already very much part of the company's approach and the task here was to add an already well developed philosophy on the development of team-based working.

The three sub-projects sought to put these proposed design principles into operation in different ways. In Wombat Plastics the aim was to take the opportunity offered by the introduction of a new car model to redesign the way in which instrument panels ('dashboards') were assembled. This would involve replacing a single machine-paced production line (this was 'tightly coupled' through a just-in-time scheduling system to a downstream main assembly line), with team-based assembly cells whose operation would be 'de-coupled' from the main assembly line by 'buffer stocks' of finished instrument panels. In Kangaroo Whitegoods, team-based cells were to be introduced into a press shop which was traditionally organized as a process-based jobbing shop where equipment was laid out according to function and operators' jobs were restricted to a narrow range of tasks. In Koala Irrigation, an existing cellular manufacturing set-up, based on the assembly of irrigation systems components, was to be further extended and developed with particular emphasis on measuring performance in team-based production systems.

Despite the clear formulation of design principles, the definition of sub-project goals, and the specification of detailed plans and timetables for implementation, the ultimate fate of each project varied considerably from what was intended. Progress in each case was by no means linear or straightforward, and some goals were not achieved. In the case of Wombat Plastics, for instance, a cross-functional design team was set up which was meant to be the core of a participatory design process in which shop floor representatives were fully incorporated. The team, facilitated by SMART project representatives, met over four months and explored various ways in which the instrument panel assembly process could be redesigned. However, the whole process was brought to a premature conclusion by the plant engineering manager, who suddenly imposed his own solution to the design problem. Shortly thereafter this solution was aborted. There were various reasons for this second cancellation: first, the company failed to alter a neighbouring line, which meant that floorspace reserved for the cell was no longer available; second, the promise to create a rapid solution to meet the tight deadline for the assembly of the new vehicle created a resistance to radical redesign efforts; and third, the engineering manager and new plant manager generally opposed the project. Thereafter the influence of human-centred principles was restricted to successful contributions to two small and highly marginal projects where the concern was to improve the productivity of specific operations within a conventional approach to production system design.

At Kangaroo Whitegoods, the sub-project began with the establishment of a cross-functional project implementation team and a senior management guidance team. In the project proposal, the sub-project plan was to proceed through five sequential phases: preliminary analysis, definition of the cells, pilot cell design, cell implementation and documentation of case studies. Four issue groups were set up by the implementation team to focus on specific areas within the overall plan. These were to examine: job design, performance measures, production control and scheduling, and layout and simulation. The project did ultimately succeed in creating a pilot cell. This was staffed by a small team which was given an introductory training course on team-based cellular manufacturing and which began to take the first steps towards self-management. However, the project did not follow the sequential plan, the process of cell development and implementation involved considerable political activity within the firm, and not all the project's aspects achieved their planned objectives (e.g. at the end of the project, the job design and reclassification of cell team members had not been finalized, only a rudimentary performance measurement system was in place for the pilot cell team, and key issues relating to production planning and scheduling in the cellularized press shop were not resolved).

In the case of Koala Irrigation, the SMART project built on the success of an earlier project funded under the Australian federal government's best practice demonstration programme, under which the plant had successfully introduced team-based cells. The aim of the SMART Project, in what was seen at the outset to be the easiest of the three cases, was to extend this experience and further develop the cells. Of all three sub-projects, the objectives in the company were the most vague, so the project scope was broad. The sub-project began with the formation of a new cell (manufacturing small plastic irrigation 'drippers') and concluded by facilitating the formation of a management team whose role was to support the shopfloor cell teams. The sub-project initially had a technical focus, applying computer-based layout and process analysis methods to a production problem, but this was later replaced with a largely organizational focus to consider how best to manage and run established cells and organize the plant management team as a support group. However, much of this activity happened against a shifting backcloth of changing company personnel and ultimately the constraint of a parent company which found it increasingly difficult to understand and support the new approach to manufacturing.

In sum, in each company the notion of human-centred design principles being applied to production system and work redesign ultimately proved radical enough to expose conflicts of interest across a variety of horizontal and vertical demarcations within each enterprise. The proposed changes, although their underlying principles, design objectives and implementation plans were relatively clearly specified, proved neither straightforward nor unproblematic. In particular, organizational politics became a key factor in shaping both process and outcomes as the projects developed. For the SMART project team, the task of managing these politics emerged as just as important as defining human-centred principles, specifying objectives and detailing timetabled plans. Ultimately, the degree of success of the three projects seemed to rest on the capacity to understand and manage change projects which, in their varying ways expressed degrees of 'vulnerability' and therefore susceptibility to political resistance and disruption. What is needed, this suggests, is a more detailed understanding of the change process itself when vulnerable socio-technical projects are undertaken.

BEYOND CONVENTIONAL SOCIO-TECHNICAL MODELS: THE CONFIGURATIONAL PROCESS MODEL

The socio-technical approach to work design has long emphasized the central importance of focusing on both technology and organization at the same time in creating new techno-organizational systems. However, traditional socio-technical theory (van Einjatten, 1993; Badham and Naschhold, 1994) has tended to focus on organization rather than technology, has had little to say about the detailed shaping of technological change and has tended to underestimate the political dimensions of the design and implementation of socio-technical systems (Perrow, 1983). For socio-technical systems theory, the problem of implementing new systems is largely one of 'jointly optimizing' 'given' 'technical' and 'social' sub-systems. There is little systemic concern to investigate the role of local and internal political processes which serve to configure the implementation and final outcomes of change. This has tended to support 'generic' views of both 'technology' and the social organization of work. Moreover, while in the past socio-technical systems theorists have quite correctly identified the problems of boundary management as central, they have not turned this into a systematic identification of the full political, organizational and technical role of the people responsible for the range of actions needed to design, implement, run, defend and develop new socio-technical configurations. At worst this supports an elitist perception of change agent activities, as the province of internal and external 'experts' engaged to initiate change in a conservative and essentially passive system. In consequence, the importance of political processes involved in negotiating the technical and organizational outcomes of socio-technical change projects is underplayed. A more direct focus on such issues, we would argue, requires reconsideration of both the way in which socio-technical theory defines the 'system' to be changed and the nature and dynamics of the change process and the role played by socio-technical practitioners when intervening in change themselves. To accomplish this we require some new conceptual tools.

What we have in mind here is an alternative framework that builds on processual models of technical and organizational change developed by organizational/industrial sociologists (see Introducton, this volume). This approach views the organizational outcomes of technological change as bound by both internal and external context but at the same time uniquely shaped by local social choice and political negotiation within adopting organizations (see for example Wilkinson, 1983; Buchanan and Boddy, 1983; Clark et al., 1988, Dawson, 1994 and this volume). This inherently social and political activity has a crucial influence on 'outcome variables' such as productivity and the quality of working life. The suggestion we would make is that not only are the organizational or social outcomes of change subject to such influences but that the technological basis of such change is also one that is shaped by choice and negotiation within adopting organizations. Thus the crucial features of both the social and technical outcomes of change are the result of incremental local/internal customization and adaptation of generic systems and models – albeit shaped and constrained by broader conditions and influences.

We would describe these activities of local incremental customization as configurational processes carried out in the context of existing configurations of technological, organizational and human resources bounded by broader internal and external environmental contexts (Badham, 1995). Configurational processes transform the manner in which material resources are converted into outputs and in so doing the nature of existing social and technical configurations of technological, organizational and human resources.

This model is represented in Figure 7.3. Its key elements can be summarized as follows:

- Technological configurations are the specific constellation of knowledge, equipment and procedures that make up the structured, material, technical, non-human elements of a production system. In contrast to more traditional views of technology as having generic, fixed characteristics, capabilities and requirements to make it work, the concept of technological configuration points to the loosely systemic, complex and locally-constituted character of working technological systems (Badham, 1993). Specific generic technological elements are, within this view, merely a resource that can only become a working technology when they are appropriately configured within a production context. Here the process of technological configuration (or reconfiguration) may involve, for example, (a) putting into place the rules and procedures necessary to operate the technology in the local environment, (b) customizing the technology to fit into an organization's larger technological system and so perform the operations required of it in a specific production context, and (c) learning about, exploiting and developing the capabilities of the system, either by utilizing the technology as given or by adding extra elements to it. A technological configuration will also include the set of meanings or interpretations of the characteristics, capabilities and requirements of a technology that, to a degree at least, can be seen as socially constructed rather than as entirely technologically determined.
- Operator configurations are the local set of operation and control personnel and their skills, attitudes, interests and roles. The relevant personnel, at the point of production, would include operators, some indirect labour (e.g. setters, maintenance), and some lower level supervisory personnel. Despite some drawbacks in the use of the term 'operator', it is used here to focus attention on the clear relations of mutual definition, enablement and constraint existing between the technological and operator configurations. Thus, operators can be understood as shaping or engaging in the process of technological configuration (or reconfiguration), while the nature of the technological configuration will both enable and constrain their capacity to do so. This may occur in the process of the design, selection, implementation and running of the technology, in the training, selection, and routine operating actions of system operators, and in the implementation of new forms of work organization.
- Configurational 'intrapreneurs' are a crucial feature of the configurational process model in the production and maintenance of new configurations or reconfigurations. Configurational intrapreneurs play

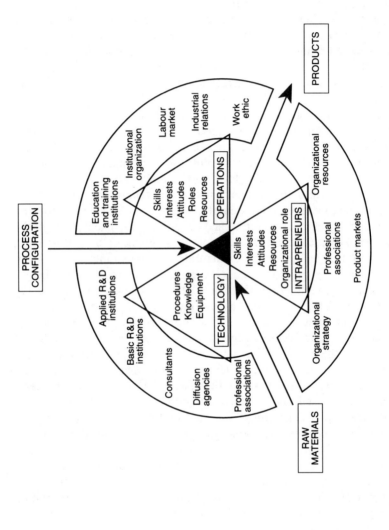

Figure 7.3 Configurational process model

the key role of organizational 'champions', establishing and operating new configurations, managing their boundaries, as well as ensuring their survival and guiding their development. Organizational actors playing this role might include, among others, relevant line managers, manufacturing engineers, human resource managers, and senior executives. The term 'intrapreneur' is used here to emphasize the internal organizational role played by such actors. However, their scope should not necessarily be reduced solely to such an internal role as it may involve crucial interventions in inter-organizational relations and in the activities of other organizations. The term also directs attention onto the active, uncertain and risky process of ensuring that production processes run smoothly, continue to receive support, and are allocated the resources necessary for their further development. Such actors manipulate both technical and social elements, and overcome obstacles in both areas in order to design and implement working technical systems. They include both the workplace 'drivers' and higher level 'initiators' and 'sponsors' of change (see Badham and Buchanan, 1995; Buchanan and Storey, this volume).

- Internal and external environmental contexts influence, and are influenced by, the paths taken by configurational processes. These contexts comprise broader organizational, institutional and cultural environments and events at the corporate, sectoral, national and even trans-national level. In the case of the technological configuration, for example, this is primarily through the interaction with external sources of knowledge, equipment and procedures supplied by, for example, research institutions, professional agencies, consultants, and technology diffusion agencies. These influences will, in turn, reflect factors such as the national R&D system, government technology strategy, international technology linkages (e.g. from parent firm in one country to its subsidiary in another) and so on. For the operator configuration, this occurs through the medium of such things as the industrial relations system, vocational education and training provision, and the history and sub-cultures of occupational groups and the communities from which occupational members are draw. All this will influence the skills, attitudes, interests and roles of 'operators'. Configurational intrapreneurs also have skills, attitudes, personal career interests and roles, and these will reflect such factors as their location within the organizational hierarchy, the organization's objectives, structure and resources, and the influence of external professional cultures.

The interaction between configurational processes and their internal and external environmental contexts is not to be understood in any simple unilinear or deterministic framework. Nor is there any simple demarcation between the configuration and its environment. For the configurational process to survive and develop, decisions have to be made to adapt to or transform the environment. As Aicholzer's (1991) study of systemic rationalization through information technology and organizational change in Austrian firms found, an analysis of the activities at all these levels is essential in understanding local changes. While the impression this gives is one of great complexity, it is just this type of complexity that the effective configurational intrapreneur operates with (often at the level of 'gut feel' or 'instinct') in the creation and perpetuation of a configurational process.

The configurational process model in practice

The configurational process model can now be applied to assist in understanding the problems, issues and context of change in the three sub-project firms. First, we outline the technological, operator and intrapreneur configurations in the three companies and their influence on the sub-project process and outcomes in each case. Second, some issues from the sub-projects which illustrate the configurational process in action are outlined, and in particular the strategic importance of 'local configurational' activity in the context of broader environmental factors such as resource constraints and industrial relations factors.

In Wombat Plastics, the technological configuration in the plant was dominated by industrial engineering and Taylorist/Fordist approaches to the organization of production. This was reflected, as we observed, in the operators' jobs, which involved machine-paced line assembly, tight coupling and short task cycles. The features of such a configuration constituted a major constraint on the development of meaningful team work (e.g. it was impossible for operators to stop work to hold a team meeting without halting downstream operations) and the ability to explore alternative production systems (e.g. most of the company representatives on the design team found it very difficult to accept that a non-linear and integrated assembly process was practical). Secondly, the operator configuration was characterized by low-skilled work performed by mainly male workers of diverse ethnic backgrounds who were generally seen to be the 'hardest cases' in the plant. Attitudes towards managers were mainly negative, and there was little trust between operators and management. Discipline on the line was seen to be a problem, the solution to which was control through ever-present supervision and machine pacing. This managerial reaction to the trust and discipline problem mitigated against the introduction of what was perceived to be a system with inadequate production control (as one engineer put it: 'I doubt whether they would voluntarily meet their production quotas and maintain product quality'.) Finally, the role of configurational intrapreneurs was central to the development of the project. Initially, we had a plant manager who very enthusiastically supported the project and its aims. He retired and was replaced by a manager who was not convinced of the project's benefits. Further, during the project key engineering personnel remained committed to the traditional Taylorist/Fordist configuration, and therefore many of them obstructed change. The retirement of the original enthusiastic plant manager and the failure to enrol the support of the plant's engineering manager contributed to the marginalization of the project and its eventual demise (despite an earlier belief among the members of the SMART project team that the sub-project would be a relatively easy one).

Within Kangaroo White Goods, the technological configuration was of a traditional process-based jobbing shop producing batches of components for downstream assembly lines. The machines were mainly operated manually, with a limited amount of automation. The machines and tools were fairly old, which placed considerable demands on maintenance and toolroom staff to keep the technology operational. The management of this system was dominated by the requirements of ensuring materials flows in and out of the shop and of allocating resources. The production system required a constant process of juggling (carried out exclusively by the supervisory staff), of people, machines, tools and materials to meet the demands of the assembly lines. The fragility of this batch production system (with machine set-up times in the region of 30–45 minutes and many parts progressing through a series of separate press operations) often led to tensions with the supervisors of downstream operations (single-item flow lines with virtually zero set-up times) and the production manager when stock-outs looked inevitable or even became so. The possibility that cellular manufacturing might help to resolve these problems, for example through process simplification and greater control at the shopfloor level, therefore looked good at the outset. However, most press machines were old fashioned manual machines requiring constant operation, severely constrainting the degree of possible redesign of operators' jobs. Problems of noise, temperature and cleanliness in the shop (when compared to assembly work in the plant) also created obstacles to improvements in working conditions.

Operator configurations were characterized by low skilled and low autonomy jobs, requiring hands but not brains. The operators were mainly male long-term employees from diverse ethnic backgrounds. The operators had never received any training other than basic on-the-job 'show and tell' sessions, they had very little experience of team work and there was no active human resource development policy for shopfloor employees. Press shop operators were commonly perceived to be performing among the least desirable jobs in the plant, and various groups had a low opinion of the capabilities of the operators (some tool room tradesmen even referring to them as 'monkeys'). Given these factors, SMART project team members needed initially to do a great deal to create suitable conditions for change within the company.

The project was established and a sustainable momentum built up in the early days through the informal political activities of a key group of organizational intrapreneurs, which included the VAM group co-ordinator, the press shop supervisor and a product engineer with broad new project responsibilities. These activities later came to be supported by the manufacturing director. These intrapreneurs had to work against the antipathy of some other managers in the factory, a lack of active support from top management, and a firm which was organized along traditional hierarchical and bureaucratic lines (factors which contributed to making the project a vulnerable one). These obstacles were overcome over time, and the project achieved, indeed in some cases exceeded, many of its initial objectives. Furthermore, while the impetus for the project, and the source of all initiatives, was initially provided by the SMART project team members, over time this role was taken over by key intrapreneurs (notably the press shop supervisor) within the firm.

Within Koala Irrigation, the technological configuration centred on the manufacture and assembly of mainly plastics products. The technology consisted of automated injection moulding machines which supplied manual assembly processes consisting of a simple and easily configurable set of benches, chairs etc. This was a batch processing environment, producing an extremely wide range of products to meet a wildly-fluctuating (but seasonal) demand. The 'technical' issues of plant layout and process flows had largely been resolved before the SMART project began; this aspect of the configuration was therefore temporarily 'frozen'.

The operators were mainly female casual workers in an area where there were few alternative employment opportunities. Before the cellularization process began, there was considerable distrust towards management – a situation that was exacerbated by a wave of redundancies shortly after the first cells were created. The establishment of largely self-managing cell teams, involving the active support of a plant consultative committee, helped to mitigate this distrust. The assembly work remained repetitive and relatively low-skilled, but increased team autonomy required a degree of horizontal job enlargement as the teams took on more indirect functions. Relationships between the operators in the cell teams and the skilled die-setters (who were allocated to, but did not see themselves as part of, the cell teams) continued to be on the whole problematic. With increasing pressure on the plant to improve performance and cut the costs of production to become more competitive, the most important issues to emerge during the project were organizational ones. These mainly stemmed from the operator configuration.

The project was initiated and supported by an enthusiastic group manufacturing manager and a plant manager. The manufacturing manager ensured that the plant was given enough space within the organization to proceed with radical change, and the plant manager was a major source of stimulus, delegating and inspiring wherever he thought was necessary. Both these key intrapreneurs left during the project, but their intrapreneurial roles were carried on by the special projects co-ordinator and the engineering manager, supported by the national personnel manager. All these intrapreneurs were dynamic drivers of change, and subsequently the projects co-ordinator and the engineering manager were instrumental in bringing the organizational issues at the plant to the fore.

Internal and external environmental context

As we have already noted, the configurational process model draws our attention to how local activities within an adopting organization shape – or configure – the final form or outcomes of both the technical and social dimensions of change. This activity is essential to adapt generic models of technical concepts such as 'cellular manufacturing' and social concepts such as 'teamworking' to the specific production and organizational context of a particular enterprise. The manner in which this happens is also more or less strongly influenced by both internal and external environmental factors. We can illustrate this by looking in more detail at one of our sub-projects – Kangaroo White Goods – where the introduction of TBCM was significantly influenced by internal contextual factors such as existing production conditions and culture, and external environmental factors such as then current changes in the Australian system of industrial relations and national competency standards.

A major issue when introducing cellular manufacturing is how far it is deemed feasible in practice to equip cells with the technical resources necessary for all the operations required to produce 'whole' products or part families. For example, in practice decisions frequently have to be made about which and how particular pieces of equipment are to be shared by cells. This emerged as an issue at Kangaroo White Goods when production engineers decided that the cells would have to share a post-production de-greasing machine. This meant component products would have to queue for the machine before being passed onto assembly, which imposed a technical constraint on the autonomous operation of the cells since each would have to plan its production in relation to other cells' output to avoid bottlenecks at the de-greasing machine. This clearly violated the project implementation team's socio-technical design criteria which aimed to maximize team autonomy. In the face of this criticism production engineers at first argued that technical and financial constraints meant 'there was no option'. They then investigated the possibility of alternative de-greasing technology which would enable this task to be done independently by each cell, to conclude a month later that it was 'technically' not possible.

This, and a whole series of other relatively minor detailed technical considerations, had substantial implications for the final socio-technical design of the cells. This meant that their final form departed considerably from generic models of TBCM. Interestingly, a major difficulty here for the SMART researchers was being able to either fully address or question the judgements of internal production engineers whose expertise combined both engineering knowledge and detailed local in-house experience and understanding of production conditions and techniques. Moreover, this presented the researchers with a dilemma since, while they doubted that 'technical constraints' were as immutable as sometimes presented, to challenge such judgements too far would threaten to undermine the support of the production engineers. Indeed, in retrospect, the SMART researchers felt that the desire to be sceptical about 'technical constraints' had undermined some engineers' commitment to the project and taken up valuable time and effort that might have been more effectively directed towards organizational questions such as job design, job classifications and training.

Similar difficulties emerged about the precise form of team working to be adopted, in particular in relation to detailed questions of job design and training. Concerning the former, the project implementation team, facilitated by the SMART researchers, reached agreement on a range of options for work redesign. These ranged from an 'as is' choice through 'minor change' to 'major change' choices. The last would involve a major reconfiguration of production organization and was seen as a desirable long-term objective. In the short term the minor change option, mainly involving redesign through broadening and enriching of individual members' jobs, was deemed the most practicable. However, this formal agreement was immediately undermined by the press shop supervisor who – despite being a member of the project implementation team – adopted a particularly conservative stance towards the delegation of supervisory functions to work teams. Subsequently he made decisions 'on the run', which clearly went against the agreed job design scenario (although ironically he ultimately became the key champion of the project in the press shop). For example, 'technical reasons' were again evoked to justify a decision to retain specialist workers to transport materials and products into and out of the cells, whereas the agreed work redesign plan clearly saw these activities as becoming the responsibility of the cell itself.

In the case of training, a new course was devised by the project team, training provision organized and senior management approval obtained. However, the arrival of a new manufacturing manager introduced a further set of dynamics into the change process. This resulted in a more cautious and less co-operative approach on the part of the company. One consequence after the machinery had been moved into its new cell configurations was that the training programme was delayed for several months. Ultimately, this delay was a major limiting factor in the extent to which team-based working could be established before the sub-project concluded.

While internal contextual constraints proved significant, the project's progress was also significantly influenced by major events and developments in the external environment. Not least of these was the reform of the hitherto highly centralized Australian national system of industrial relations. This had been set in train by the labour government in the late 1980s (see Hancock and Rawson, 1993).[1] The changes to the Federal Metal Industry Award during this period set one of the key framework conditions for the implementation of TBCM at the company. The two most significant changes were a reduction in job classifications from around 350 to just 14 (agreed in 1991) and the establishment of national statutory definition of competency standards in the industry to match the new job classifications (agreed in 1995). At the same time the decentralization of the national system meant pay was increasingly linked to productivity-enhancing enterprise-level agreements to be reached by local management and unions.

At the outset the project to introduce TBCM was delayed by the efforts of local management and the seven unions present at the site to reach their first enterprise agreement. This delay had the important consequence of allowing a senior production engineer championing the project to influence the content of the agreement to support team-based work organization. This served two purposes. First, it facilitated the work redesign proposals which emerged from the project since there was a pre-existing joint commitment to eradicate functional boundaries, broaden operator task range to include responsibility for quality and so on. Second, this intervention ensured that industrial relations issues were given early consideration by the project implementation team and that both union and human resource department involvement in and support for the project was secured. Significantly, a previous attempt to introduce cellular manufacturing in the press shop had been aborted because of the failure to adequately address such issues, in particular enrolling the support of the human resources function. Indeed, a major concern of the human resources manager at the outset was that the existing regulatory arrangements would be disturbed – as he warned at the time: 'you can do anything you like, so long as you don't change wages and job classifications'. In similar vein, press shop management were sceptical about the likely success of the project because the laudable objective of improving operators' jobs would 'not be allowed' by what was termed the 'anti-personnel' department!

The importance of the human resource function and trade union support was underlined by the issues of new competency standards and job classifications. This was given an additional twist since the company was chosen as a trial site for testing the new standards before national ratification. A vexed question that emerged in considering team-based jobs in the cells was the classification of the team-leader and other cell members, among whom the issue of pay increases to reflect new responsibilities and skills was a major concern. In the event, the scope for interpretation provided by the new competency standards suggested new classifications to be given to cell operators which would result in an improved pay grade. The position of the team leader was more difficult since an initial interpretation of the standards suggested the same classification and therefore pay grading as other cell members. The uncertainties created by this situation threatened to disrupt the project when the individual selected to be team leader for the first cell resigned from the programme for a period. However, this potentially damaging incident – the team leader was a key figure in diffusing and defending the team-based way of working on the shop floor – was eventually resolved after strong representations from the press shop supervisor to the human resources department. The company then agreed a provisional upgrading of cell members and the team leader, contingent on the ratification of the new national standards. This would eventually give the team leader a higher classification and thereby pay grade.

CONCLUSION

The experiences of the SMART project reveal a reality of socio-technical change that is messy and political. It also stresses the need for those interested in intervention to promote socio-technical and human-centred ideas to gain a fuller understanding of this process and their role within it on the part of those intervening in organizations to promote socio-technical and human-centred ideas. Traditionally socio-technical theory has, as have most conventional theories of change management, downplayed the significance of the politics of change and the need for it to be managed in the promotion of human-centred principles and concepts. It has also tended towards unilinear sequential models of change, a focus on individual change agents and a concern to evaluate the success or failure of tools to assist in system redesign. The SMART case studies show how an adequate approach to production system redesign needs to address the local and contingent character of the configurational process, the complexity of the techno-organizational environmental context, and the politics of the change process and its management. In practical terms this has led the SMART team to emphasize, among other things, the importance of stakeholder analysis at the outset of socio-technical projects of this type as one strategy to counter their inherent vulnerability (see SMART, 1995).

At a conceptual level, if we turn to organizational studies and industrial sociology to find guidance in this area, the results are disappointing. While placing an emphasis on politics, power and process the resulting complexity of the models derived tend to stress either the resulting impossibility of intervention in change management (Buchanan, 1994) or its dependence on radical societal level changes in political economy (Braverman, 1974). The history and sociology of technology is more helpful on these issues, in particular in relation to questions of agency in initiating and sustaining changes in technical and social systems (see, for example, Law, 1987; Bijke, 1995). Although often abstract and devoid of any systematic attempt to apply them to contemporary issues of technical change in work organizations, the concepts and models deployed in approaches such as 'actor network theory' are potentially relevant and merit further exploration and development for use in understanding changes in production systems.

The configurational process approach presented in this paper has been influenced by both process models of change from organizational sociology and some of the work emanating from the sociology of technology. In particular, the concept of configurational intrapreneurs is equivalent, with important qualifications[2], to other terms utilized in actor network theory such as 'system builders', 'heterogeneous engineers', 'engineer sociologists' and 'Sartrean engineers' (see, for example, Law, 1987). We should stress, however, that our approach has been presented only as a possible model, not as a comprehensive conceptual framework. We are aware, for example, that the concept of configuration and configurational processes require further exploration and substantiation. As it is, the model goes some way in helping us to understand the varied, complex, shifting and political character of the socio-technical change process, at least as we have experienced it. It also encourages a focus on improving understanding of ours, and we would hope others', involvement and effectiveness in local configurational processes.

Notes

[1] The Australian system of industrial relations has developed around a highly centralized system of pay determination and dispute resolution based on federal and state tribunals. These tribunals make sector-specific 'awards' on the basis of representations made by employers' bodies and trade unions. These awards define such things as job classifications and pay rates for the industry which are then applied locally by individual firms. Since the late 1980s, as the Australian economy has been de-regulated and opened up to foreign competition, efforts have been made to link the pay and conditions outcomes of the award-making process to specific productivity enhancing improvements at workplace level. The latest developments have involved enterprise level bargaining and flexibility agreements as part of a trend towards decentralizing the pay determination.

[2] For example, the 'heroic' configurational intrapreneur is not the only source of dynamism and change, nor of the planned development of the system. Depending on the nature of the configurational process, the technology or the operators may be more or less active and influential in determining the course of change and development. The more democratic the system, for example, the more the operators will take on the function of configurational intrapreneurs.

References

Aicholzer, G. (1991) On systematic rationalization in Austria, in *AI and Society*, 5 (4), pp. 110–113.

Badham, R. (1993) Systems, networks and configurations: inside the implementation process, in *International Journal of Human Factors in Manufacturing*, special edition (guest editor R. Badham), 3 (1), pp. 3– 4.

Badham, R. (1995) Managing socio-technical change: a configuration approach to technology implementation, in *Managing Technological Innovation*, (eds J. Benders, J. de Haan, D. Bennett, *et al.*), Avebury Press, Aldershot.

Badham, R. and Naschold, F. (1994) New technology policy concepts, in *Technology Policy: Towards an Integration of Social and Ecological Concerns*, (eds G. Aich-Holzer and G. Schienstock), De Gruyter, Berlin, pp. 125–160.

Badham, R. and Buchanan, D. (1995) *Power assisted steering: the new princes of socio-technical change*, occasional paper, Leicester Business School.

Braverman, H. (1974) *Labor and Monopoly Capital*, Monthly Review Press, New York.

Beer, M., Eisenstat, R. and Spector, B. (1990) Why change programs don't produce change, in *Harvard Business Review*, November–December, pp. 158–166.

Bijker, W. (1995) Sociohistorical technology studies, in *Handbook of Science and Technology Studies*, (eds S. Jasanoff, G.E. Markle, J.C. Peterson, T.J. Pinch), Sage, New York, pp. 229–56.

Boddy, D. and Buchanan, D. (1983) *Organizations in the Computer Age*, Gower, Aldershot.

Boddy, D. and Buchanan, D. (1992) *The Expertise of the Change Agent: Public Performance and Back Stage Activity*, Prentice-Hall, Hemel Hempstead.

Brandon, J. (1993) On the vulnerability of interdisciplinary programmes of strategic change to functional interests: a case study, in *Journal of Strategic Choice*, 2 (1), pp. 151–6.

Brodner, P. (1989) *The Shape of Future Technology*, Springer-Verlag, London.

Buchanan, D. (1994) *Theories of Change*, Business School research series paper, Loughborough University.

Clark, J., McLoughlin, I., Rose, H. and King, R. (1988) *The Process of Technological Change: New Technology and Social Choice in the Workplace*, Cambridge University Press.

Dawson, P. (1994) *Organizational Change: A Processual Approach*, Paul Chapman, London.

van Einjatten, F. (1993) *The Paradigm that Changed the Workplace*, Arbetslivcentrum, Stockholm.

Frame, J. (1994) *The New Project Management: Tools for an Age of Rapid Change, Corporate Reengineering, and Other Business Realities*, Jossey-Bass, San Francisco, California.

Hancock, K. and Rawson, D. (1993) The metamorphosis of Australian industrial relations, in *British Journal of Industrial Relations*, 31 (4), 489–511.

Jurgens, U., Malsch, T. and Dohse, K. (1993) *Breaking from Taylorism: Changing Forms of Work in the Automobile Industry*, Cambridge University Press.

Kelly, J. (1982) *Scientific Management and the Labour Process*, Macmillan, London.

Law, J. (1987) Technology and heterogeneous engineering, in *The Social Construction of Technological Systems*, (eds W. Bijker, T.P. Hughes and T.J. Pinch), MIT Press, Cambridge, Massachusetts, pp. 111–34.

McCalman, J. and Paton, R. (1992) *Change Management: A Guide to Effective Implementation*, Paul Chapman, London.

McLoughlin, I. and Clark, J. (1994) *Technological Change at Work*, Open University Press, Milton Keynes.

Osburn, J., Moran, L., Musselwhite, E., Zenger, J. with Perrin, C. (1990) *Self-Directed Work Teams: The New American Challenge*, Business One Irwin, Homewood, Illinois.

Perrow, C. (1983) The organizational context of human factors engineering, in *Administrative Science Quarterly*, 28, pp. 521–41.

Schaffer, R. and Thomson, H. (1992) Successful change programs begin with results, in *Harvard Business Review*, January–February, pp. 80–9.

Smart Manufacturing Techniques Project Team (1995) *Managing TBCM projects*, Team-based cellular manufacturing booklet series booklet no. 2, Wollongong University.

Wellins, R., Byham, W. and Wilson, J. (1991) *Empowered Teams: Creating Self-Directed Work Groups that Improve Quality, Productivity, and Participation*, Jossey Bass, San Francisco, California.

Wilkinson, B. (1983) *The Shop Floor Politics of New Technology*, Heinemann, London.

Chapter 8

Universal solutions or local contingencies? Tensions and contradictions in the mutual shaping of technology and work organization

Robin Williams

INTRODUCTION

This chapter explores the implications of the 'social shaping of technology' perspective for the analysis of the relationship between technology and work organization. In contrast to prevalent instrumental views, which see technology as being readily adapted to organizational goals, this analysis brings to light the tensions and contradictions in the mutual shaping of technology and work organization. In particular, the paper explores the relationship between 'the local' and 'the global', critically examining the widespread presumption that technology, by offering universal solutions for organizational improvement, would be a powerful force shaping and harmonizing working life.

'Technology' is of special interest precisely because it has come to be seen as separate from 'society'; because of its apparent hardness in contrast to the presumed fluidity of day-to-day social interaction; and because of its potential generalizability. Its usefulness derives from the fact that it can be divorced from particular settings and applied more widely – moved from one context to another, where, subject to certain limits, it can be expected to perform reliably. This underpins endeavours at the heart of the 'techno-logical project' – for example, the search for economies of scale and the cumulative development of technological knowledge. Furthermore, tech-nological development has been seen as a patterning force in society, following particular trajectories that reflect dominant techno-economic paradigms (Dosi 1982). In the recent past, attention has been focused on information technology (IT) which offered tools for rationalization and automation of work activities, based on 'universal' mathematical princi-ples, that were expected to have widespread applicability across the widest array of firms and occupations. In contrast to such expectations, recent empirical research points to the continued importance of contingent and local factors, arising for example from specific features of the organiza-tional setting, which impede the search for universal solutions. This paper explores these issues in the development and implementation of three types of industrial application of IT: computer-controlled machine tools, integrated company-wide computer systems and 'inter-organizational networks'. Finally the paper uses this dilemma between the global and the local to throw light upon the relationship between technology supply and implementation and discusses how these may be changing in the face of recent developments in IT.

THE SOCIAL SHAPING OF TECHNOLOGY

In contrast to traditional approaches, which only addressed the outcomes or 'impacts' of technological change, a growing body of socio-economic research has come to examine also the content of technology and the particular processes involved in innovation. The social shaping of technology (SST) perspective highlights a range of factors – organizational, political, economic and cultural – which pattern the design and implementation of technology, as well as its social impacts (see MacKenzie and Wajcman, 1985).

SST emerged from a confluence of various different analytical themes, for example, technology policy studies, sociology of scientific knowledge, labour process theory and industrial sociology and evolutionary economics. It involved a common concern that the form of technologies (including the detailed content of technological artefacts) were amenable to and indeed required socio-economic analysis and explanation (Williams and Edge, 1992).

This approach emerged in reaction to the models of technology within the mainstream, post-enlightenment tradition which, within the rubric of progress, had largely taken technology and its socio-economic implications for granted. These presumed that technology would emerge to satisfy social need and envisaged a steady, smooth and homogeneous development. Against this, a critique was articulated of the 'technological determinism' inherent in widely prevalent views of technology as an external factor 'causing' organizational and social change, with its presumption that the path of technological innovation was socially neutral, or subject to an independent technical rationality (Williams and Edge, 1992).

Two somewhat distinct bodies of scholarly endeavour have been applied to these questions: one concerned with the promotion of technology, and the other with its social assessment and control. The former sought to analyse why technologies had often failed altogether, or had failed to deliver the promised organizational improvements. Exploration of these questions led to a view of technological innovation as an uncertain process, full of setbacks. The latter was primarily concerned with the social and political implications of technology and the sets of choices inherent in the development and application of technology. This included many writers from a background in 'labour process' theory. Early writings (see for example Zimbalist 1979) shared with conventional technocratic and managerial approaches a rather 'determinist' view of technologies as a reliable vehicle for particular values or rationalities (e.g. the 'deskilling' objective that Braverman [1974] suggested was a feature of capitalist economies). The social shaping perspective drew on both these bodies of work – in a way which re-united their hitherto separate concerns with the promotion and control of technologies.

Automatic control of machine tools

Perhaps the classic case study of the social shaping of technology is Noble's (1979) study of the development of automatically-controlled machine tools in post-Second World War USA. Two options existed: 'record playback', whereby the machine merely replicated the manual operations of a skilled machinist, and 'numerical control' (NC) in which tool movements were controlled by a mathematical programme, produced by a technician. Noble showed how the machine tool suppliers and managers in the aerospace companies suppressed record playback in favour of NC as part of a deliberate strategy to reduce their reliance on (often unionized) craft workers. However, achieving these goals proved difficult – the attempt to obviate manual skills encountered practical problems and was contested by machinists. Noble (among others) highlighted conflicts around the introduction of NC between technicians and craft workers as the latter sought to retain their centrality to, and control over, the production process. Noble noted how the subsequent development of computer numerical control (CNC) in some ways subverted the original intentions of the developers of NC by allowing programmes to be edited and then written at the machine. Subsequently machines were developed – notably in Japan and Germany – for programming on the shop floor, allowing greater productive flexibility and a lower division of labour. Machine tool manufacturers wanted products that could be sold to the potentially much larger market of small and medium sized firms which tended to have a lower division of labour and skill than the early NC users (Wilkinson, 1983; Fleck *et al.*, 1990).

This case highlights several features that became central to the 'social shaping of technology' perspective:

- that a range of choices existed at every stage in the development and implementation of technologies
- which of these was chosen could not simply be reduced to 'technical' factors, but was influenced by a range of groups and the broader socio-economic setting
- it is therefore unhelpful to talk of the 'impacts' of technology, as if technology was an extraneous factor 'causing' social change. Instead

technology is a deeply social product, and the outcomes of technological change are importantly negotiated and socially mediated.

The case points to the mutual shaping between 'technology' and 'society'. However, this is by no means a straightforward and harmonious process, but is contradictory and fragmented in time and space.

Another theme in the emerging social shaping perspective was a critique of conventional linear models of innovation. These see innovation as restricted to Research and Development, and presume one-way flow of ideas and artefacts from R&D to production, diffusion and use/consumption (Fleck, 1991). This was criticized for ignoring processes of feedback from 'later' to 'earlier' stages in the innovation process and the important innovative effort as technologies are implemented. To draw attention to the latter, Fleck (1991, 1993) advanced the concept of *innofusion*, rather than seeing innovation and diffusion as separate stages. These findings contributed towards the emergence of 'interactive' models of innovation. Whereas linear models tend to privilege technological supply – and the capacity of universal technological knowledges to provide solutions for business, Fleck's innofusion model sees implementation as an industrial laboratory, where suppliers and users jointly learn about the utility of technological products and about user requirements (Fleck, 1993).

Innofusion is of particular importance in the complex 'organizational technologies' that are being developed and applied today – for example 'integrated' corporate IT systems that support a wide array of complex activities. Such applications have been sought by many manufacturing and service organizations since mid-1995, as potentially contributing to strategic goals. Better integration of different areas of the business, and, in particular, increased responsiveness to market, was sought by more effective use of internal information that was hitherto distributed between different parts of the organization. However, marked difficulties have been experienced since the mid-1980s in the development and implementation of such systems. Such integrated applications have to be closely matched to the structure, traditions and working methods of the user organization. Lack of fit may result in unwanted organizational adaptation or even the wholesale failure of the system. Alternatively, the struggle to apply and use technologies may also throw up potentially valuable innovations, which can be fed back into future technological supply (Fleck, 1988; Fleck *et al.*, 1990; Webster and Williams, 1993; Fincham *et al.*, 1995). In this way, elements of local work organization can become sedimented within IT applications – crystallized, and thus potentially applied more widely, in the form of technological artefacts.

This analysis highlights two key points in relation to knowledge and knowledge flow. First is the importance of local expertise and experience –

including knowledge of the user organization, its methods and business context, and knowledge of the implementation process – which must be combined with more generic forms of knowledge (of computing techniques and artefacts) to create functioning information systems. While the latter scientific and technological knowledges tend to be formalized, and concentrated in expert groups, the former includes knowledge which is substantially informal, tacit and experience-based, and widely dispersed among various expert, managerial and other groups within the user organization.

The second point, following on from this, concerns the linkages between supplier and user through which this knowledge and experience can be transmitted. Implementation of new systems is often necessarily a joint process – involving supplier and user in collaborative development and application of technologies to the specific user requirements. The need for such joint development is often not anticipated; as a result the learning process in getting systems to work has often been poorly organized and has not been not properly exploited and the implementation experience – and innovations developed within it – has remained localized. The importance of supplier user links are now becoming more widely recognized (not least because suppliers see opportunities for adding value by providing implementation services as well as artefacts).

Social shaping research thus immediately draws our attention to contingencies and the uniqueness of the user organization. Some writers have come to see the process of technological change, and its outcomes, as almost entirely locally constructed, negotiable and contingent. Indeed the very flexibility in use at the heart of information technology would seem to support such a view. However, this only tells us part of the story. It is important to go beyond snapshot studies of the adoption of technologies to analyse the dynamics of technology development and implementation in its broader social and historical context. In particular if we want to understand the complex relationship between technology and work organization we must consider how technologies may emerge in particular firms and contexts and then become more widely diffused and further adapted to other organizational settings: to look at the biography of technologies as they develop over time – as indicated in Figure 8.1.

For example this indicates how local innovations may become globalized. As already noted, new techniques, developed to meet the needs of particular user organizations, may become incorporated into supplier offerings and may in turn be adopted as components of future technological systems. Indeed such innovations may become widely available – in software packages or even hardware – as cheap standardized commodities. Ultimately they may form part of the basic infrastructure of corporate information systems – for example accounting and payroll systems – where

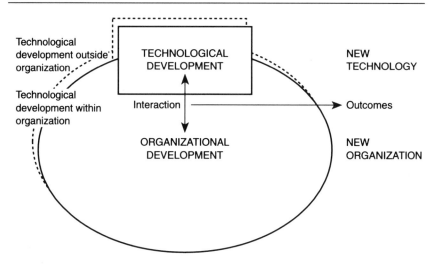

Figure 8.1 Schematic model of the development of technology and organization

a few industry standard packages are used by large numbers of firms (Ward, 1987).

As IT applications become more elaborate they embody ever more knowledge and presumptions about organizational practices, particularly with the shift to 'integrated' applications that support an increasing range of organizational activities. This comprehensiveness increases their utility and value to the user organization. However, as an application becomes more complex it tends to become more specific to a particular organizational user, and its particular range and permutation of activities, which may limit its applicability in other organizational settings – and thus the scope for selling on the application elsewhere. The most complex integrated applications might have a market of one, that is be custom-built to organizational requirements but at great cost, as development costs could not be shared between multiple purchasers. There is a tension, surrounding both supplier and purchaser strategies, between the advantages of increasing an application's scope and specificity (its greater utility and fit to the user organization) and the cost advantages of increasing its market size. 'Discrete applications' relating to finite sets of closely related tasks can readily be supplied as packaged solutions, offering particular economic advantages where they relate to activities that are conducted in broadly and similar ways across a wide range of organizations and can be made available as standardized commodities – such as word-processing packages (Brady *et al.*, 1992). Figure 8.2 summarizes some different strategies that seek to reconcile these conflicting demands, through selling on custom solutions to similar firms, as 'niche-specific' solutions, to the supply of

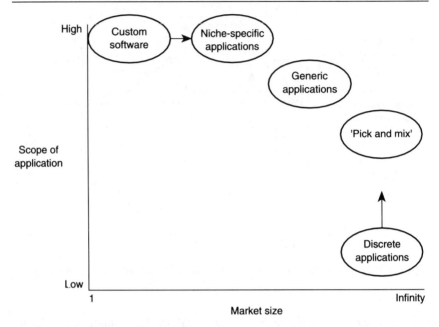

Figure 8.2 Volume/variety characteristics of software supply strategies
Source: Brady *et al.*, 1992.

generic offering – for example applications designed to be readily customized. Of increasing significance is the 'pick and mix' strategy whereby the user organization combines various standard components (hardware and packaged software functions) with unique elements (e.g. customized software) in a configuration that meets its specific requirements. Today, in practice, few applications are developed entirely in-house but are increasingly developed as configurations of this sort (Brady *et al.*, 1992; Fleck, 1993), a point we return to in the concluding section.

We find a complex dynamic in the development of industrial technologies – with novel applications tending to become standardized and sedimented as routine over time (Ward 1987). On the other hand, such mature technologies may become destabilized, may evolve and become differentiated in the face of changing technological opportunities and concepts of business practice (Brady *et al.*, 1992) – as we see below in the re-innovation of computer-aided production management (CAPM) technologies from systems concerned with stock control to becoming aids in production planning – towards goals of just-in-time production.

This is why we can no longer see workplace technologies as an external force, transforming work. Instead, technology and work organization develop in tandem (Webster, 1993). Pre-existing models of work organization, with visions of how these might be transformed, become embedded in information and communications technology (ICT) applications (Fleck *et al.*, 1989). Implementation problems for packaged solutions thus often reflect lack of fit between the social relations in the firms in which a system was initially developed, which become embedded in the software, and the actual circumstances of the user. We can illustrate this in the case of CAPM (Clark and Newell, 1993).

Integrated applications: the case of Computer-Aided Production Management (CAPM)

Ideas about how integrated technologies will proceed have been closely paralleled by concepts of industrial organization (Clark and Staunton, 1989; Webster and Williams, 1993). For example, the goal of computer-integrated manufacturing (CIM), in which the diverse kinds of information involved are to be centralized on an integrated database, finds its organizational correlate in notions of the flexible firm, which has close linkages between its sales, marketing, design and production functions, as well as with its suppliers and customers (Fleck, 1988). Technologies such as CAPM were projected as a stepping-stone towards this vision of CIM. Further, the promotion of these technologies since the mid-1980s has coincided with a growing emphasis on the success of organizational practices of Japanese firms – 'just-in-time' (JIT), 'total quality control', and the like. These concepts of good industrial practice influenced the development of CIM technologies: software systems like CAPM came to incorporate built-in JIT modules and other elements which reflect this new hegemony of industrial concepts (Webster and Williams, 1993).

Though integrated technologies are promoted alongside a vision of the transformation of organizations, in practice it is the former which are more immediately changed. CAPM systems derived from production planning and control systems developed in and for large corporations producing complex assemblages (e.g. vehicle or aerospace manufacturers). The, mainly US, firms involved tended to have well-developed information systems with formalized management decision criteria – reflecting the tradition of management science in these sectors. Attempts to transfer these systems as packaged solutions elsewhere, and in particular to smaller and medium-sized firms in Britain, have met very uneven success – with perhaps as many as half of implementations being abandoned or failing to meet the initial expectations. In reality, in Britain at least, industrial organizations are characterized by highly idiosyncratic production monitoring and decision-making practices, often haphazard data collection techniques, and a frequent absence of expertise or resources to implement coherent, all-embracing information systems (Webster and Williams, 1993). There was a marked lack of fit between the information requirements and practices embedded in the standard software packages that were initially offered by suppliers and the diverse actual circumstances of the firms to which these packages were sold. Users who had bought an apparent 'technical fix' to their business problems found themselves embroiled in a largely unplanned collaborative development process that was often protracted and painful. In this process there was selective implementation of parts of the suites of CAPM software that could be got to work (while other elements were abandoned), combined with customization and general reconfiguration of these supplier offerings to suit particular local circumstances.

The case of CAPM provides an interesting illustration of the forces that tended to align views about the key business problems and technological and other methods by which they should be addressed. In particular it shows how certain technologies and business recipes gain currency – and behind this, the way that particular firms or national economies become widely perceived as exemplars. For example in the late 1980s there was a swarming of supplier offerings in the area of CAPM (accentuated by government initiatives in the area such as the Department of Trade and Industry ACME Initiative of the Application of Computers to Manufacturing and Engineering). Also in relation to CAPM the influence of certain suppliers and consultancies becomes clear. For example we can find IBM as a major player in the promotion of CAPM and its predecessors over a number of years - and across different countries (Clark and Newell, 1993; Clausen and Williams, forthcoming).

Inter-Organizational Network Systems (IONS) and Electronic Data Interchange (EDI)

The example of inter-organizational IT networks and systems, such as Electronic Data Interchange, raises similar themes about the close but contradictory interaction between technology and organization. We will explore two aspects – the uneven development and implementation of EDI technology, and the organizational outcomes of EDI – which both raise questions about the relationship between the 'technical' and the 'social', and about the fit or lack of fit between visions of technology and its outcomes.

EDI relates to the exchange of structured data between the computer systems of different organizations to allow automatic processing of commercial communications – for example orders and invoices (Emmelhainz, 1993). Electronic commerce, through EDI, emerged first among large firms, or groups of similar firms trading intensively, in sectors such as retailing, banking, and automotives. Here the economic incentive to adopt EDI systems was high – in particular where there is a high volume of transactions, and where the costs of standardization required for EDI are not a major obstacle (e.g. in banking where transactions were already highly standardized or in retailing, where a small number of large firms shared similar interests and were, for example, already collaborating in bar-coding, and which, as dominant purchasers, were able to impose standards on their suppliers) (Kubicek and Seeger, 1992; Spinardi *et al.*, 1996). However, in the mid-1980s the trend is towards multi-player systems – as networks spread out from dominant hubs or as new industrial groups emerge to exploit expected 'network externalities' from larger scale EDI systems (Suomi, 1991) in which the benefit for each player increases with every new entrant. As the number of players trading electronically increases, the possible economic benefits increase arithmetically. There is at the same time an increase in the costs of data harmonization (for example in handling a variety of incompatible, proprietary message types or in agreeing data exchange standards). These costs would grow exponentially if these negotiations were handled through bilateral discussions between players. This provides a powerful incentive on organizations to co-operate in developing open EDI standards. Such data harmonization is broadly of two sorts: the agreement of protocols for communication of data between different computer systems, and the agreement about the meaning of the data to be exchanged. The latter includes definitions about the structure and significance of particular messages and the development of product identifiers and addresses.

Fears that incompatible local or proprietary exchange standards would constitute a barrier to trade have led governments to support the development of open standards. In particular the European Commission supported the global EDIFACT process for EDI message development within the United Nations – as a symbol and means of barrier-free trading in Europe. There has been considerable success in developing global or near global standards for the exchange of data between machines (computers, telecoms systems etc.). Moreover, barriers arising from incompatibility between data exchange protocols turn out not to be a key problem insofar as software suppliers can provide packaged solutions to translate between the limited number of industry and open standards of different computers and of the various telecommunication carriers. The key problems encountered have been with the harmonization of the data which is to be exchanged between organizations (e.g. attempts to develop EDI message standards). For example, progress by EDIFACT Message Development Groups has been slow and unwieldy, and has yielded such generic standards that trading communities must then develop their own subsets to trade effectively. These problems arise because what is being standardized is bound up with business and trading practices which differ between countries, sectors, regions and individual firms; it is extremely difficult to accommodate the requirements of many diverse users, who may have different stakes and interests (Kubicek and Seeger, 1992; Graham *et al.*, 1995).

Instead of the harmonious development of global electronic trading communities that had been projected by policy-makers and technologists we can foresee a patchwork of diverse local markets, with their particular flavour. The network externalities that surround EDI are likely to see an increase in the number and size of electronic trading communities, and the cost of maintaining multiple local data exchange formats will mandate in favour of some standardization between them (or at least gateways to facilitate exchanges between electronic trading communities). Some pressures will favour increasingly close links and incremental standardization between these communities. However, there are counter trends which are likely to resist such standardization and promote further differentiation of systems. Take for example the use of EDI to increase the scope of information exchanges between firms beyond routine trading transactions such as orders and invoices to include the exchange of technical and product design data. Simply developing a neutral data format for exchanging data (e.g. engineering drawings) is not sufficient to enable joint design because the data embodies certain working practices and a culture of shared understandings which enable the data to be interpreted. As these cultures and practices differ to a greater or lesser degree from company to company, implementing this data exchange required harmonization of these working practices, and considerable expense in changing internal computer systems (Spinardi et al., 1996).

EDI has been projected as having potentially revolutionary 'impacts' on organizations – not only by improving organizational efficiency, but also by more radical restructuring of practices within and between organizations – for example by dispensing with some of the array of trading transactions including order acknowledgment, delivery schedules, invoices (Spinardi et al., 1996). However, in practice, the direct impacts of using EDI on organization structures and employment in the short and medium term seem to be small, except in organizations processing very high volumes of transactions – and even there the effects appear to be localized (Dankbar, 1991; COST 320, 1992). These considerations suggest the need for caution in assessing the claims of business process re-engineering (BPR) proponents that the strategic application IONS can achieve radical restructuring of organizations (Hammer, 1990). Proponents of BPR cite instances where such radical restructuring has been achieved (Morton, 1990), but examination of these cases reveals that this took the form of incremental programmes of technological and organizational innovation. Only in retrospect could these changes be presented as the result of a programmatic strategy. These points apply with particular force to the most radical forms of change proposed (Business Network Redesign and Business Scope Redesign [Short and Venkatnaram, 1992]) where the process of restructuring takes place across a series of electronically-linked organizations in a supply chain. The uncertainties inherent in managing such a complex transition will present a powerful barrier to such developments in most instances (Spinardi et al., 1996).

THE IMPLICATIONS OF THE SOCIAL SHAPING OF TECHNOLOGY (SST) PERSPECTIVE

This brief examination of research into the social shaping of selected industrial technologies has thrown light on the close interaction between technology and organization seen as a complex mutual shaping process operating at a number of levels (within and beyond individual workplaces) and over time. The implication is not that technologies are plastic and readily available to be shaped to local social requirements. In fact SST research highlights the potential contradictions and disjunctures, for example between suppliers' offerings and users' circumstances. It forces us to be more reflective about certain concepts. For example, although the rhetoric of the user and user requirements is now prevalent in technology policy circles and in the mouths of suppliers, SST studies have highlighted the difficulties in articulating and meeting user requirements.

We cannot take user requirements for granted but must examine how they are constructed at the interface between current practices and systems and expectations about what kinds of technological change may be realizable. In this sense, suppliers and promoters can be seen to articulate the possibility of new user requirements and new solutions and this is, in some ways, to construct users and their requirements. Innovation always involves a leap in the dark – the projection of new needs and new solutions. Developers must inevitably deploy such rhetorics to win resources for their favoured projects. SST highlights the problems that may arise where the rhetoric become too divorced from emerging realities. These are problems that have recurred in different forms since the introduction in the mid 1950s of the commercial application of computer technologies. On the one hand we see the repeated failure of IT applications to live up to the expectations projected for them – a problem which on examination seems to have the same underlying cause: suppliers' promises of a technological fix, and users' willingness to 'buy-in' to these dreams (Fleck *et al.*, 1990). However, this is not a uniform problem. The question is under what circumstances the gearing between expectation and achievement (or for that matter between supplier offering and user requirements) may become particularly and unduly wide. To take the latter, for example; under what circumstances may markets fail to provide appropriate solutions? The CAPM case highlighted the problems that may arise where key promoters become too closely associated with particular approaches (assisted in this case by governmental science and technology policy-bodies), resulting in an overly-programmatic response, and a swarming of supplier offerings around particular approaches (Clausen and Williams, forthcoming). As a result of the latter, IT supply was initially not structured around particular user categories. Suppliers had poor links with current and potential CAPM users; they had little understanding of CAPM implementation and of the actual circumstances of users – for example the diversity of firms and the uniqueness and complexity of their production management problems. In this context, they overestimated the capacity of their own products and underestimated the difficulties of applying them. This also reflects something of the situation of many of the firms buying CAPM packages who often lacked technical expertise in computing and production management techniques needed to evaluate particular supplier offerings and who as small and only occasional players in the IT market lacked market power. Very different experiences can be noted, for example, in the IT acquisitions by large financial service organizations such as banks, who had considerable purchasing power and internal expertise and were able to impose much more favourable conditions and exert greater control over IT suppliers (Fincham *et al.*, 1995).

Similar reservations about other programmatic approaches to the technological and organizational change may be appropriate – notably the concept of BPR, which seems to have rapidly acquired the status of a universal ideology of change management. SST research raises questions about the scope for the kind of top-down, planned strategic change in technology and organization envisaged by BPR (see also the article by Grint and Willcocks, in this volume). In some ways, BPR can be seen to represent a revival of earlier approaches from management science and from IT – a technocratic model that cuts across many of the lessons that have emerged from other approaches which emphasize participative management and treat workforce knowledge as a resource rather than an obstacle.

However, the implication is not one of constant scepticism about the claims of IT. Indeed, the current situation is marked by the increasing pace of uptake of a plethora of increasingly powerful IT offerings. Many of these emerging offerings share certain key features – they are not offered as integral and finished solutions but are often designed to be configurable to various different applications (for example in the way spreadsheets are not specific to particular kinds of organizational use) and/or are designed as component technologies which can be put together and work with other components. (A key requisite here is the development of industry or public interoperability standards to allow different components to work together.) This enables them to be supplied as cheap-mass produced components which can more readily be combined by user organizations into specific configurations and customized to meet to their particular needs. These developments in the era of distributed computing have begun to transform the relationship between systems design and implementation (and between designers and users) – in which some elements of technological design and supply have been further divorced from particular user contexts; while other parts of the design and implementation process (configuration, customization) have moved closer to the user organization and the 'end-user' of particular systems. Some of these applications begin to resemble media insofar as they are communication technologies which can support a potentially enormous range of organizational activities. Their consequent ease of incorporation within existing organizational practices has made possible rapid uptake of such technologies. Over the last decades the main examples have been the fax and the mobile phone. Today expectations are growing around the use of the internet and its enhancement, through the development of broadband networks linking computers, to include video-conferencing and other applications as part of an imputed multimedia revolution.

This is not to suggest that the relationship between technology and organization has suddenly become unproblematic; in many ways this relationship is becoming more intimate while in others it becomes more distant. However, the relationship between global and local has been transformed. Today we can all customize our computer interface to suit our personal preferences. Today we all use (or are familiar with the look and feel of) MicroSoft Windows.

Note

[1] This paper draws on the research programme into the social shaping of technology at Edinburgh University, and in particular a study of 'Organisational Shaping of Integrated Automation' under the ESRC Programme of Information and Communication Technologies (WA 35 25 0006) and an ESRC RGB study of 'Electronic Trading: Patterns in the development and use of Electronic Data Interchange (EDI)' (R000 23 3010). My co-workers were Ian Graham and James Fleck, Department of Business Studies and Dr Graham Spinardi, Research Centre for Social Sciences and Dr Juliet Webster, RCSS, now at East London University.

References

Brady, T., Tierney, M. and Williams, R. (1992) The commodification of industry applications software, in *Industrial and Corporate Change*, vol. 1, no. 3, pp. 489–514.

Braverman, H. (1974) *Labor and Monopoly Capital: the degradation of work in the twentieth century*, Monthly Review Press, London & New York.

Clark P. and Staunton, N. (1989) *Innovation in Technology and Organization*, Routledge, London/NY.

Clark, P. and Newell, S. (1993) Societal embedding of production and inventory control systems: American and Japanese influences on adaptive implementation in Britain, in *International Journal of Human Factors in Manufacturing*, vol. 3, no. 1, pp. 69–81.

Clausen, C. and Williams, R. (eds) (forthcoming) *The Social Shaping of Computer-Aided Production Management/Computer-Integrated Manufacturing*, Proceedings of COST A4 Workshop, Gallileje, Denmark, May 1995.

COST 320 (1992) *The Impact of EDI in Transport*, Commission of the European

Communities/COST, Transport Research, final report September 1992, CEC/ COST, Brussels.

Dankbar, B. (1991) *Werken in Netwerken*, Limburg University, Maastricht.

Dosi, G. (1982) Technological paradigms and technological trajectories, in *Research Policy*, vol. 11, pp. 147–62.

Emmelhainz, M. (1993) *EDI: A Total Management Guide*, Van Nostrand Reinhold, New York.

Fincham, R., Fleck, J., Procter, R., Scarbrough, H., Tierney, M. and Williams, R. (1995) *Expertise and Innovation*, Clarendon/Oxford University Press.

Fleck J. (1988) Innofusion or diffusation?: the nature of technological development in robotics, *Edinburgh PICT Working Paper*, no. 4, Edinburgh PICT Centre/ RCSS, Edinburgh University.

Fleck, J., Webster, J. and Williams, R. (1990) Dynamics of information technology implementation: a reassessment of paradigms and trajectories of development, in *Futures*, vol. 22, pp. 618–40.

Fleck, J. (1991) Information-integration and industry, *PICT Policy Research Paper*, no. 16, Economic and Social Research Council, Oxford.

Fleck, J. (1993) Configurations: crystallizing contingency. *International Jornal of Human Factors in Manufacturing*, vol. 3, no 1, pp. 15–36.

Hammer, M. (1990) Reengineering work: don't automate, obliterate, in *Harvard Business Review*, July–August 1990, vol. 90, pp. 104–12.

Kubicek, H. and Seeger, P. (1992) The negotiation of data standards: a comparative analysis of EAN- and EFTPOS systems, in *New Technology at the Outset: Social Forces in the Shaping of Technological Innovations*, (eds M. Dierkes and U. Hoffmann), Campus/Westview, Frankfurt/New York, pp. 351–74.

MacKenzie, D. and Wajcman, J. (1985) *The Social Shaping of Technology*, Open University Press, Milton Keynes/Philadelphia.

Morton, M.S. (ed.) (1990) *The Corporation of the 1990s*, Oxford University Press.

Noble, David (1979) Social choice in machine design: the case of automatically controlled machine tools, in *Case Studies on the Labour Process* (ed. A. Zimbalist), Monthly Review Press, New York, pp. 18–50.

Short, J. and Venkatnaram, N. (1992) Beyond business process redesign: redefining Baxter's business network, in *Sloan Management Review*, fall 1992, vol. 34, no. 1, pp. 7–21.

Spinardi, G., Graham, I. and Williams, R. (1996) EDI and business network redesign: why the two don't go together, in *New Technology, Work and Employment*, vol. 11, no. 1, pp. 16–27.

Suomi, R. (1991) Alliance or alone: how to build interorganisational information systems, in *Technology Analysis and Strategic Management*, vol. 3, no. 3, pp. 211–32.

Ward, J. (1987) Integrating information systems into business strategies, in *Long Range Planning*, vol. 20, pp. 19–29.

Webster, J. (1993) Chicken or egg? The interaction between manufacturing technology and paradigms of work organization, in *International Journal of Human factors in Manufacturing*, vol. 3, no. 1, 53–68.

Webster J. and Williams, R. (1993) Mismatch and tensions: standard packages and non-standard users, in *Social Dimensions of Systems Engineering: People, Processes, Policies and Software Development*, (ed. P. Quintas), Ellis Horwood, Hemel Hempstead, pp. 179–96.

Wilkinson, B. (1983) *The Shop Floor Politics of New Technology*, Heinemann, London.

Williams, R. and Edge, D. (1992) The social shaping of technology: research concepts and findings in Great Britain, in *New technology at the outset : social forces in the shaping of technological innovations*, (eds M. Dierkes and U. Hoffmann), Campus/ Westview, Frankfurt/New York, pp. 31–61.

Zimbalist, A. (ed.) (1979) *Case Studies on the Labor Process*, Monthly Review Press, New York.

Chapter 9

Information systems as metaphor: the three Rs of representation

Paul Jackson

INTRODUCTION

Throughout the 1970s and 80s it was claimed that modern societies were entering a new social era. With the growth in non-fabricative jobs and services, and the diffusion of information technology (IT), a series of neologisms were coined to capture the shape of this new world: for instance, 'post-industrial society' (Touraine, 1971; Bell, 1973), the 'information economy' (Porat, 1977), the 'computer age' (Dertouzos and Moses, 1979), the 'third wave' (Toffler, 1981) and the 'information society' (Lyon, 1988). While the frameworks which underpin these ideas may lack cognateness, few dissent from the central tenet that a crucial role is played by IT-related innovation.

Notions such as the 'digital economy' (Tapscott, 1995) and 'information age' (for example, Gates, 1995; Birchall and Lyons, 1995) frequently abound, increasingly fanned by the winds of political debate and policy statements. For instance, the European Union's 'Information Society Action Plan' asserts that:

> The Information Society is on its way. A 'digital revolution' is triggering structural changes comparable to last century's industrial revolution with the corresponding high economic stakes. The process cannot be stopped and will lead eventually to a knowledge-based economy.
>
> (Commission of the European Communities, 1994)

In such accounts of the new epoch then, radical changes are envisaged for the way work and service interactions are carried out. But digital and technological developments do more than simply provide new media through which to conduct business transactions; rather, imagery is presented which has consequences for the very way we think about work and organizations. Today, terms such as 'cyber-businesses' (Barnatt, 1995), the 'virtual organisation' (Grenier and Metes, 1995; Birchall and Lyons, 1995), 'virtual corporations' (Davidow and Malone, 1992) and the 'internet-worked business' (Tapscott, 1995) are not only talked about unblushingly, but provide crucial conceptual searchlights for people straining to see the contours of the so-called 'information age'.

The role of new technology in reshaping our perceptions of the world – and, indeed, of ourselves – is nothing new. As Turkle (1987) shows with the rise of the computer, certain technologies have proved extremely evocative objects, providing the catalyst for thinking about social change. Similarly, developments in IT and Virtual Reality (VR) technologies (see Benedickt, 1991) have highlighted possibilities for radical work-related innovation. In the current wave of organizational neologisms, particular attention is focused on the 'informationization' and 'digitalization' of work tasks, and the role of IT in providing for dispersed interaction. Not only have ideas such as the 'superhighway' heightened speculation along these lines, but in so doing, they have brought with them new conceptions of organizational time and space. The picture that emerges is of a world in which information can instantaneously cascade across the planet, and a global economy where the barriers of geography come crashing down around us.

In addressing these issues, this chapter concentrates on what it claims is a key metaphor now underpinning the way we think about modern organizations and work processes: the information system. We will see below why much of the current emphasis on IT-related innovation implies a wider rethink on organizational processes in these terms. For the moment, we need to examine the rise of IT and some of the early discussions of our IT futures.

INFORMATION TECHNOLOGY FUTURES

The term IT was invoked to describe the fusion of computing technologies with the technologies of telecommunications. Developments in this field have been critically dependent on wider improvements to communications infrastructures. By the 1970s, for instance, the development of digital networks provided greater access to information, when terminals were connected to central databases and better support facilities were available within organizations. By the late 1970s local area networks (LANs) and wide area networks (WANs) were established, facilitating distributed data processing and document production. The 1980s saw the arrival of personal computers (PCs) and microcomputers, which could be linked into computer networks. Two further developments in recent years also proved critical to IT usage. The first, the digitalizing of information (including text, voice and image), provided further impetus for the convergence of computing and telecommunications technologies, with the second, the development of integrated service digital networks (ISDN), extending opportunities for such technologies to be linked across space (Gunton, 1990).

The basis for a fundamental transformation in organizational structures is seen to lie in the logical extension of these developments. The convergence of various communications technologies, the formation of a global hardware platform and the increased compatibility of operating systems, suggests that the ability to 'connect' with people and systems not just within but between organizations, makes for a rather different (post)industrial landscape than the one we have known thus far (see Barnatt, 1995; Tapscott, 1995).

For many, its greater ability to handle information makes IT qualitatively different from conventional technology (for instance, Boddy and Buchanan, 1983). Indeed, these authors identify four specific capacities: storage, by converting numerical and textual data into binary form (digitalizing); capture, actively (by automatic sensing) or passively (via human entry); manipulation, for example, calculation and analysis of information; and finally, distribution, by transmitting and displaying information across space (pp. 10–11). This final characteristic soon led to suggestions that workers may be able to operate at a distance from their employing organization – the main thrust of thinking behind teleworking (for example, Huws et al., 1990). More recently, such discussions have led to a more radical rethink, highlighting the possibilities of 'virtualizing' entire organizations (for instance, Davidow and Malone, 1992; Grenier and Metes, 1995).

According to Zuboff (1988), IT has one fundamental function which differentiates it from all previous technology: while it can be used to 'automate' – that is, displace workers and their embodied skills – it can also be used to 'informate'. This term refers to the way IT can be employed to convert material practices into information which can then be recorded and displayed on video screens or computer print-outs. In other words, operating with IT makes certain aspects of the world visible by textualizing them in the form of symbols. As such, tasks can be mediated via information systems rather than by direct physical engagement. Interacting via digitalized and electronic representations not only has important epistemological implications, though (see Heim, 1993); crucial organizational consequences may also follow, particularly where power relations are concerned (for example, see Cooper, 1992). Where work interactions and transactions are mediated through 'cyberspace' – the realm where data is stored, displayed and transmitted – a closer and more critical look at IT and representation therefore becomes vital.

The treatment of IT in the literature has of course varied depending on the scope of the issues under consideration. In discussions of post-Fordism and flexible-specialization, for example (see Hill et al., this volume), IT is often construed as a 'control' innovation, used to break the link extant in assembly-line working between automation and scale. In these cases, attention is focused on such matters as reprogrammable machine tools and flexible production methods (for instance, Piore and Sabel, 1984; Kaplinsky, 1984; Coombs and Jones, 1989; Aglietta, 1979; Harvey,

1989; Phillimore, 1989). Within the broader contours of the debate, IT-mediated working has been contextualized in more general changes to economic and social forms, as found in accounts of the 'service economy' (Gershuny and Miles, 1983) and 'information society' (Lyon, 1988). One early and frequently cited work was Porat's *The Information Economy* (1977), which examined the growth in white-collar working. Porat's particular concern here was the expanding number of information workers, defined as those 'primarily engaged in the manipulation of symbols'.

Approaches to the information economy, such as Porat's, use as their bench-mark a landscape of fabricative activities, involving the manipulation and transformation of material artefacts. Similar contrasts are also redolent where changes to office work are discussed. Here, the move to IT-mediated working reflects optimism inherent in the early 'post-industrial' literature (for example, Bell, 1973), as is evident in such notions as the 'office of the future' and 'paperless office' (Forester, 1989). This is taken further by Giuliano (1991), who develops the idea of the 'information age office'. Such workplaces, we are told, 'preserve the values of the pre-industrial office' – people-centred and skilled – and contrast with life in the industrial office, which Giuliano views as machine-centred, fragmented and standardized. The break with the industrial office is implicit in many scenarios of future office work. Peltu's (1980) contention, for example, that information can be seen as the raw material of office work, also invokes the counterpoint of a world of manufacturing, but does so still within a paradigm resonating with mechanistic analogies.

Accounts of the work-related changes so described make sense only if we accept the premises on which they are built. These concern the role played by IT and information in work processes, and the ontological assumptions about the constitution of organizations. As we will see, trying to sustain the parallel between, on the one hand, the manipulation of raw materials, and, on the other, the manipulation of symbols, can dangerously down-play the socially constructed nature of organizational reality.

As Dunlop and Kling (1991) point out, much 'information age' prophesizing also brings with it a utopian vision of flexible, efficient and co-operative working. Such discourse tends to glamorize offices, implicitly portraying them as 'professional' workplaces, where all employees are 'knowledge workers' (Kling and Iacono, 1989). But as Gunton (1983) and Panko (1984) have shown, modern offices are extremely diverse. As such, many future work scenarios may be premised on a false homogeneity of information work (Prava, 1983). Unfortunately, this complexity is flattened in much of the discourse on IT-related innovation, especially where it concerns virtual corporations and hi-tech teleworking. Nonetheless, such speculation has had a crucial role in shaping expectations of, and anxieties over, the future.

Much of the early images of the information age therefore build up the role of IT in allowing for a reconfiguration of working practices, thanks largely to the representational facilities of IT in allowing for the electronic processing and manipulation of data. The more recent 'wave' of information age prophesying plays on two further issues: the role of IT as a 'space-transcending' technology, and the reworking of the way organizations are constituted in time and space. As with the more narrow changes hypothesized within offices, these ideas also make assumptions about the nature of 'organization' and the role information plays within it. It is to these issues that we now turn.

IT INNOVATION AND THE INFORMATION SYSTEM METAPHOR

It has been suggested above that much of the imagery and speculation from post-industrial writings has found a home in new work concepts such as 'teleworking' and the 'virtual corporation'. An important issue here concerns the way certain facets of information-based organizations dominate new work scenarios. Of particular importance is the centrality of IT-mediated information capture, manipulation, storage and communication. While focusing analysis on IT and information is hardly original, in the context of the 'space-transcending' view of IT, a new twist is given to speculation on organizational forms. As a consequence, talk of 'information age' offices has even been displaced by predictions of the very demise of the central workplace. Huws *et al.* (1990), for instance, talk of the 'elusive office', with Birchall and Lyons (1995) talking of the 'virtual office'. The key metaphor which captures the underlying model of organization here is the 'information system'; as Morgan puts it

> . . . it is possible to see organisations becoming synonymous with their information systems, since microprocessing facilities create the possibility of organising without having an organisation in physical terms . . . Many organisations of the future may have no fixed location, with members interacting through personal computers and audio-visual devices to create a network of exchange and interrelated activity . . ..
>
> (1986, p. 84)

These sentiments, combined with information age imagery, and heightened by such popular notions as the 'information superhighway', infuse much of the more contemporary discussion on organization and work innovation. Certainly, the organization as an information system underpins much speculation on 'telework':

> The office – the site where information is generated, processed and exchanged – has ceased to have any fixed geographical boundaries. It exists only as a network – the 'elusive office' has arrived.
>
> (Huws *et al.*, 1990, p. 220)

Of course, this provides only one lens through which to interpret organizations. Nonetheless, the view it presents – and the new spatial possibilities envisaged of IT – provides a powerful means of conceptualizing innovative opportunities. To balance such ideas, we must remember that organizations are much more complex places than may be implied here. Even virtual organizations and hi-tech teleworkers do not simply vanish into some abstract world of 'organizational cyberspace'; and in wider terms, nor does the so-called 'information economy' suddenly collapse onto the head of a pin. All this makes an examination of temporality and spatiality in organizational constitution vital to understanding the limitations of the information system metaphor. This is all the more important given that the developments mooted tend to illuminate important, and often overlooked, features of conventional 'concentrated' forms, such as the part played by spatial enclosure in surveillance and control (see Foucault, 1979).

It will be argued below that there are three cornerstones to the rise of the 'information system' as the leitmotif of modern organizations. The first is the perceived role of IT in spatial organizational change. Much of this is highly deterministic – not to mention politically naïve – and tends to concentrate on a narrow representation of IT as a 'space-transcending' technology, a matter especially true in early discussions of teleworking (for example, Toffler, 1981). Second is the importance attached to the growth of information work, particularly that mediated by IT. Such developments reflect the trend towards interacting with electronic 'symbols' (or IT-mediated representations) which stand in place of real world contacts and face-to-face encounters (for instance, Zuboff, 1988; Cooper, 1992). As we will see shortly, the epistemological issues raised by 'virtual' forms of engagement provide a particularly profound line of analysis here (see Heim, 1993; Barnatt, 1995). The third cornerstone to the information system metaphor are the assumptions made about time and space in the new work concepts, especially the way they are represented so as to legitimize new (usually 'virtual') models of organization. It is at this juncture that we often see the simultaneous 'de-politicization' of organizational space (and thus the down-playing of the relationship between power and space in organizations), only for the importance of space to be reasserted in global (political) terms, as the arena in which nations meet in head-on (economic) combat. But let us start by examining the way IT has been approached.

REPRESENTATIONS OF IT

One key feature of IT-facilitated teleworking and virtual organization is the concentration on IT in overcoming geographical barriers (for example, Huws et al., 1990; Birchall and Lyons, 1995). Such a perspective is often riven by determinism, presuming a single logical path along which the technology will unfold. But as work carried out by the author in the UK banking sector has shown (Jackson, 1994), while spatial changes to working forms may be deemed organizationally and technically feasible, IT applications which re-affirm the central workplace may still be the preferred innovation option. For instance, although it may well be possible to introduce innovations in telephone banking using home-based teleworkers, the cost and security implications make the option a non-starter. To deal with such empirical retorts, we need to develop a robust understanding of the relation between IT and changes in organizational structures and working practices. To do this, we will examine the contribution of constructivism.

Constructivist theories of technology have their roots in the sociology of scientific knowledge (see, for instance, Latour and Woolgar, 1979; Latour, 1987; Woolgar, 1988). Social studies of science have sought to illustrate that scientific knowledge does not have an epistemologically unique status – that claims as to the 'truth' of scientific findings are played out in the social world, not the natural world, and are therefore socially constructed (see Pinch and Bijker, 1987, p. 19). As such, both scientists and technologists are regarded as constructing their respective bodies of knowledge and techniques, thus making technological artefacts open to sociological analysis with respect to their designs and technical 'content'.

According to Woolgar and Grint, the constructivist approach is best understood by construing technologies as texts that are embedded in and constituted by their interpretive contexts (Woolgar 1991; Grint and Woolgar, 1992; Grint and Woolgar, forthcoming). What the capacities of a technology are, how it should be applied, and what consequences it will have, thus depend on a specific reading of the technology. Interpretive and rhetorical structures are not therefore seen as objective reflections of a given technology, but as the very medium which serves to constitute it.

In addressing the process through which IT is developed and implemented, constructivism leads us to examine the persuasiveness of claims made about it. In doing so, we are urged to reject the idea that humans can acquire knowledge from an artefact in an unmediated way, but instead, following Foucault (1980; 1982), examine the relationship between power and knowledge when constructing and negotiating over representations of technology. This does not, of course, mean allowing technology to escape from analysis, as some have warned (Rose *et al.*, 1986; Clark *et al.*, 1988), but rather to suggest that the construction, usage and consequences of technology are all social. The key issue then becomes not so much what technologies 'can' or 'cannot' do, but the need to explain the underlying basis of claims made about the them.

In the context of 'going virtual', IT is pointed to as the means by which spatially concentrated organization structures can dissolve into new working relationships and (virtual) forms of organization. As such, we see information technologies represented as devices for 'transcending space'; for instance:

> For much of the productive work carried out in organizations, informa-
> tion and communications technology has made it possible to disconnect
> the place and time of work from the point at which the output is needed
> . . . the information age offers us the opportunity to adopt a radically
> different set of underlying assumptions on which to base the design of
> work.
>
> (emphasis added; Birchall and Lyons, 1995, p. 101)

Of course, to say that there is no ultimate and objective truth so far as representations of technology are concerned (only truths) does not mean that all such accounts are equally valid. There are concerns voiced here about the implications of this for the critical study of technological change (see McLoughlin, this volume). Woolgar (1993), however, points us to a fundamental methodological premise of textual analysis – that before we assert our own 'politically correct' accounts, we first need to know what counts as a persuasive reading. While some accounts of technology are more persuasive than others, they are still accounts – not 'definitive, uncontested and undeniable truths' (Grint and Woolgar, forthcoming).

As we will see, the persuasiveness of the 'space-transcending' interpre-tation of IT is given force if we accept certain underlying images of organization – particularly as a system for processing and communicating information. In many scenarios discussed here, such uses of IT may appear quite credible. For example, decentralizing work units to lower cost regions, and opening up new service frontiers by introducing remote services, such as 'telephone sales', may provide attractive innovation opportunities. Likewise, the flexibility offered by using IT to build 'virtual work teams' (Grenier and Metes, 1995) and project groups may offer many benefits. Indeed, Grenier and Metes argue that in the context of know-ledged-based competition, integrating a dispersed group of experts through IT may be the only way of tackling immediate problems and seizing short-lived opportunities. Before we explore the issues presented by the IT representations in these scenarios, we first need to examine the representa-tional facilities provided by IT.

INFORMATION WORK AND IT REPRESENTATIONS

The 'informating capacity' of IT, according to Zuboff, changes the basis on which knowledge is developed and applied in organizations – lifting it out of the body's domain and transposing it into the abstract domain of 'information' (or cyberspace). Of course, organizations have always involved a separation between, on the one hand, the embodied skills and knowledge of their workers (as data residing in the human memory or information processed through individual cognitive abilities), and on the other hand, the data, systems and techniques found in organizational files and manuals. However, where IT is interposed between individuals and work processes, co-workers and databases, the result may well be a greater transparency of data, as well as the integration of data sources and the systemization of data storage, retrieval and manipulation.

Examples of this can be seen with the introduction of client-server architecture. Such systems allow for a separation between (digitalized) data (as stored on shared, relational databases) and the local (and potentially dispersed) software applications used to retrieve, manipulate and communicate that information. Clearly, where data is stored and integrated according to formalized sets of data entities and attributes, networked computer systems may well make for greater centralization. Hence, rather than being the 'property' of individuals – and their filing cabinets, notebooks or even stand-alone PCs – data now 'belongs' to the computer system, or more accurately, to those who have the power to control the form and operation of 'organizational cyberspace'. So far as applications programs are concerned here, computer-mediation suggests a common set of software tools through which data resources are used. (Little scope may thus exist for local idiosyncratic and informal methods of managing data.) This would normally be the case, for instance, in a large insurance company. Typically, here, all data is 'pooled' on central servers, with standard applications used for accessing and storing data, as seen when setting up or enquiring into a customer's life insurance policy.

The contribution of IT to constructing organizational knowledge has been made elsewhere, of course. Orlikowski and Robey (1991) illustrate how IT is implicated in the modalities which link action (or work processes) to structure (that is, as institutionalized rules and resources [see Giddens, 1984]). In so doing, IT is taken to provide a set of interpretive schemes which represent reality and thereby help users structure and understand their world. This, Orlikowski and Robey go on to note, has profound consequences for power relations, since in providing a set of interpretive schemes, IT also institutionalizes those schemes by formalizing and encoding them.

Coombs et al., (1992) similarly show that while IT is the very medium through which social relations may be articulated, such is the way that forms of knowledge intersect with power, reproducing such discourse inevitably means engaging in a 'regime of truth', in which the world is made meaningful (represented) according to a particular set of interests. Such information resources are not divided equally in organizations, of course; hence, the introduction of IT to mediate data provision also serves to reaffirm an institutional order of authority (Orlikowski and Robey, 1991). According to Orlikowski and Robey, then, IT – through its embodiment of norms and provision of resources – is chronically implicated in the modalities through which structures of domination and legitimation are reproduced.

In providing representations of reality, 'informating processes' – as Zuboff (1988) conceives them – translate activities and material objects, dispersed in time and space, into a form which facilitates their control. According to Zuboff, IT is therefore the latest actor in the fundamental process of industrial bureaucracy – the rationalization and centralization of knowledge as the basis of control. This is echoed by Giddens (1987), for whom modern organizations are inseparable from the collation, storage and retrieval of information. For Giddens, organizations rely on their ability to stretch social relations across time and space. This requires, he suggests, the discursive recording and articulation of the conditions of organizational reproduction. The codification of words and numbers thus allows the past to be 'stacked', as manifested in tablets, files, documents, libraries and computer banks, such that organizations can reflexively monitor the conditions of their own reproduction (Giddens, 1981; 1987).

For Cooper (1992), IT thus encapsulates the three general functions of all formal organization: it makes transparent what is opaque, it makes present what is remote and it manipulates what is resistant. These functions are essential for understanding the role IT plays in representation, particularly its relevance, as Cooper sees it, to 'remote control', 'displacement' and 'abbreviation'. In remote control symbols and electronic devices substitute for direct human involvement (Zuboff, 1988). Processes of displacement illuminate Zuboff's observations of the way electronic texts infuse organizations. According to Cooper, organizational activity becomes, here, less a structure of discrete acts co-ordinated in time and space and more a series of transformations along informational networks. It is the infusion of data along informational networks (rather than by corporeal mediation in time and space) that captures the underlying issue of operating in a 'virtual' organization or cyber-business (c.f. Grenier and Metes, 1995; Barnatt, 1995).

Finally, IT abbreviates complexity by reducing a material world in time and space into electronic representations, available instantaneously on video screens or computer print-outs. These features, Cooper points out, are not unique to IT; however, they are, he suggests, hyperbolized there. The significance of this is that:

> Administrators and managers, for example, do not work directly on the environment but on models, maps, numbers and formulae which represent that environment; in this way, they can control complex and heterogeneous activities at a distance and in the relative convenience of a centralised work station.

> (Cooper, 1992, p. 257)

Where new information technologies, such as multi-media and VR devices, are introduced to refashion organizing processes, possibilities may well be conceived for enacting (c.f. Weick, 1979) ever more virtual organizational structures. In such cases, the organizations produced would involve a series of changes to their temporal and spatial constitution. It is to these issues that we now turn.

Representations of time and space

Many images we come across of organizations tend to be very reified ones. There is thus an intuitive sense of organizations as being solid, as things (for example, Sims *et al.*, 1993, p. 1; Morgan, 1993, p. 8). Such sentiments imply an 'absolutist' approach to time and space, involving seemingly 'objective' features, such as 'clock time' and 'physical distance' (see Gregory and Urry, 1985). By contrast, the discussion of 'elusive offices' and 'cyber-businesses' hints at a social world somehow outside time and space. In redressing this, we need to recognize that time and space are integral to all social processes and are therefore constitutive features of organizations (for example, see Jackson and van der Wielen, 1995). It is thus through human appropriation and experience that time and space are rendered social phenomena.

To untangle the relation between subjective experiences of time and space, and the time-space practices engaged in, we can turn to the work of Lefebvre (1974). According to him, spatial practices have three dimensions: first, material spatial practices – the interactions across space through which social life is produced and reproduced; secondly, representations of space – in the form of signs and significations which allow spatial practices to be understood and engaged in; and thirdly, spaces of representation – the intellectual creations and spatial discourses through which new meanings for space can be developed and expressed.

It follows from this that where the processes of social reproduction change, the qualities and meanings of space and time are also likely to change. Any move to transform the way material processes are produced and reproduced is thus linked to the social conceptions of both time and space (see also Lash and Urry, 1994). The ability to influence the way space is represented is critical, for example, in persuading workers that space is an open field of play for capital (Harvey, 1989). The same is true for time, of course; as Harvey notes: only in the context of rationalized and organized public time is it possible for personal senses of time and space to prosper. The power over representations, then, may well be as important as power over material practices. What is conceived of as un-social hours or days gives labour more legitimacy, and even the sanction of law, to refuse to work such times (Lash and Urry, 1994). The linkage between the realms of practice, representation and spaces of representation can be seen – as influenced by Lefebvre and Harvey – in Figure 9.1 (see also Jackson, 1995). This goes further than those, such as Giddens, who have concentrated

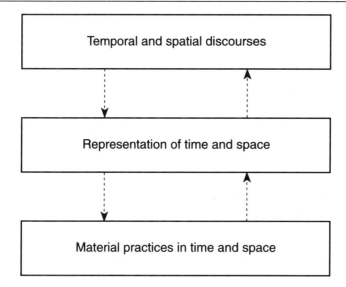

Figure 9.1 Representation of time and space

on issues of power (Pred, 1990) and illustrates the importance of the symbolic and normative dimensions of time and space.

In paid employment, for example, the work activities involved were traditionally bound temporally (as the working day) and spatially (at the work organization's office or shop-floor). In this instance, the meanings and normative values associated with 'going to' (or more accurately, 'being at') work, form a constitutive part of the work experience. To talk of 'work time' and 'work place' is therefore to signify and legitimize offices and shop-floors as the places where work 'should' be done, but fundamentally, the places where that cultural endeavour we understand as 'work' is performed.

So far as the dimensions of power are concerned here, we can see the key role 'concentrated' organizations – that is, those with factory premises and office buildings – play in producing and reproducing structures of domination within organizations. As Marglin (1974) shows with the rise of the factory, the need for a work place, as a recognized sphere separate from the domestic realm, was integral to the rise of an industrial culture. A concomitant part of this, as Thompson (1967) shows, was the corresponding separation of 'work' time from 'private' time – a juncture at which the notion of 'industrial time' was created, thus producing a distinct bifurcation between industrial and domestic temporal experiences. Foucault (1979) helps us to see that the creation of the central workplace and the 'enclosure' of workers within it afforded new opportunities for worker surveillance and thus work discipline.

We can see therefore that the practices and experiences involved in the central workplace involve a particular set of temporal and spatial norms, meanings and power resources. Any glib talk of 'virtualizing' organization necessarily implies something about the nature and importance of time and space to organizations. However, much of what is said tends to downplay not only the symbolic dimensions of organization, but also its normative and power dimensions. Where statements are made about organizational time and space – as found, for instance, when discussing their role in providing a social context for work – this is usually done in relation to an 'environment' for work interactions, not, therefore, as a constitutive social element which serves to produce the very experience of work.

Further issues about space crop up so far as remote communications are concerned. In this case, features of face-to-face interactions (such as body language and the opportunity to exchange corporeal documents and materials) is recognized (for example, Kinsman, 1987). Mostly, though, the key conception of space is an economic realm – that is, as a place that by its very existence involves costs – as overheads, leases, mortgages, ground rents and so on.

With these ideas in mind, we can now start to formulate a synthesized analytical framework with which to explore the information system metaphor in more detail.

THE 3 RS AND THE METAPHOR

If we draw together the aspects of representation just set out, we can see why the information system becomes a key metaphor for thinking about contemporary organizations, particularly where discussions of virtuality and teleworking are concerned. By taking a constructivist approach to technology, we have avoided the determinism characteristic of certain future work scenarios. Focusing instead on the way IT is represented, attention is drawn to the interpretive and rhetorical structures of those engaged in technological innovation.

This approach forces us to explain why certain readings of the technology are made – such as using IT to help create 'virtual work-teams' or to allow for greater home-based teleworking – and why some such readings are deemed more credible and attractive than others. Seeing IT as a means to overcome the locational constraints of concentrated organizations is a relatively easy observation to make, though. However, such a reading is also laden with a number of assumptions which prove more interesting. For example, there is the implication that IT-mediated communications can substitute for the face-to-face articulation of work relations. This may include the presumption that much of what is processed in an organization can be digitalized and represented electronically.

But there are further implications to this scenario. So far as the virtual organization is concerned, for instance, the absolutist approach to time and space – as conceived in the physical aspects of organizations, such as buildings, offices, furniture etc. – is challenged by a conceptual shift towards organizational enactment. Much of the imagery evoked in so doing draws on, and is legitimized by, the discourse of 'cyberspace' – an abstract domain where computer data is generated, stored and communicated. Organizations, here, are increasingly represented as being emptied of time and space, with working practices atomized into sets of individual activity.

It is in the context of 'emptied out' time and space, combined with an emphasis on representational processes, that IT's role in reconfiguring spatial organization is augmented. Indeed, discussions of organizational space may become conflated with cyberspace such that organizations appear to become synonymous with their information systems. As a result, new possibilities are seen to open up for working practices and forms of service provision. The construction of innovative opportunities thus happens concurrently with the identification of IT-facilitated responses. By construing organizations as information systems, a framework is created through which new opportunities can be conceived and solutions found. For example, interpreting IT as a means of integrating workers across space may illustrate the possibility of accessing new reserves of expertise. Where the Internet is concerned, the conception of a 'virtual market' (see Gates, 1995) may lead to innovations in the way a range of goods and services are advertised and traded (for example, Canter and Siegel, 1994).

In these examples, the wider context of organizational issues will clearly be crucial to decisions on IT-usage. As Coombs et al. (1992) illustrate, for instance, within a marketing department, IT may be seen as an instrument for product flexibility, while for administrators it may be interpreted as a tool to improve process efficiency. Likewise, Toffler's (1981) cosy notion of the 'electronic cottage', in which the emphasis appears to be on laudable issues such as community and quality of life, is unlikely to be a credible avenue for innovation in a situation where cost cutting and service improvements are sought. In these cases, what IT 'is' – either as a means of allowing work flexibility, as a competitive weapon, or as a means of cost-cutting – is constructed through different discourses, in which a variety of issues and rationales may be considered pertinent. Which discourse holds sway will be critical to determining the most persuasive representation of IT.

IT does not therefore lead ineluctably to certain applications, let alone the forms of working embodied in many of the new work concepts. The spread of computers, virtual reality technologies, and superhighway infrastructures, will not of itself lead to more 'virtual-teaming' or opportunities to peruse virtual markets. How we use such technologies depends critically on the way we construct and privilege issues and problems in a given context and form scenarios in which IT is used to address them. This in turn relies on our ability to envisage forms of IT configuration – or, put another way, to 'imaginize' innovative IT-related outcomes (c.f. Morgan, 1993). Such outcomes make implicit assumptions about information work and organizational constitution. In so doing, the complexity of organizational life is simplified, allowing certain features to be elevated. The information system metaphor thus reduces complexity by downplaying the social constitution of temporal and spatial practices and highlighting the ability to operate via IT-mediated representations of the world. It is against this background that we can draw on the space-transcending view of IT in imagining a range of possible futures, incorporating forms of organization, ways of working and types of services.

Having illuminated the theoretical pillars on which many approaches to IT-facilitated spatial innovations are based, let us now shed light on some of the key ideas which have been brought out. We will do this by looking at the importance of the above for each of the 3 Rs, starting with the treatment of IT.

Discussion of the 3 Rs

From the previous discussion, we have seen that the way technologies are read depends on each situation. Ideas like the 'electronic cottage' seem attractive, but the realities of organizational life means that in most cases, more pragmatic uses of IT are pursued. In the glamorized information age discourses, though, attention may still be given to the sort of change suggested here, but with such scenarios, it starts to become meaningless to separate IT from the wider alignment of entities implied. The electronic cottage, for instance, makes sense only if IT is understood as part of a broader canvas, involving communications infrastructures and domestic dwellings.

The problems of conceptualizing technology have been discussed elsewhere. For instance, Winner (1977) cites three levels at which we can begin to understand the term: the so-called 'apparatus', the techniques employed to use this, and the organization by which these are utilized. By taking a constructivist approach we are led to appreciate the mediating role of the actors in the innovation process. Of fundamental importance to this are the representational schemes involved in interpreting and negotiating over the technology. Such schemes in most work concepts draw on more than a narrow description of the apparatus. In many cases, therefore, the configuration of IT encompasses a broad set of entities. It is only through such a wider representational landscape – combined with the interpretive possibilities presented by cyberspace discourses – that particular IT-related scenarios become meaningful.

As part of these wider landscapes, a significant role is played by images of information work. But as with the so-called 'office of the future', new forms of spatial organization will not, of themselves, lead to an environment of highly skilled information workers (c.f. Dunlop and Kling, 1991). Moreover, while certain readings of the information system metaphor may appear to sound the death-knell for the traditional, bureaucratic organization, the result is not necessarily decentralized, democratic working. It has been argued that the very processes involved in organizing via IT may sharpen the need for formalizing representational schemes. The more formalization, the more those schemes are institutionalized and centralized, as with the standardization of software and documentation (c.f. Cooper, 1992). But while IT-mediated working may involve making the world more 'seeable' and manipulable across time and space, it also relies on localized actors drawing on and reproducing the same sets of interpretive structures. Given the problems even in concentrated organizations with attributing multiple meanings to the same sets of data (see for example, Walsham, 1993), there are evident difficulties here for intersubjectivity and organizational learning. Indeed, such matters shed doubt on the efficacy of dispersing many types of information worker (c.f., for example, Grenier and Metes, 1995; Birchall and Lyons, 1995). Taken together, this underlines the above argument for a constructivist approach to information systems. If we are to avoid the more simplistic parallels between manipulating artefacts and manipulating symbols, we must recognize the way human subjectivities are amplified when operating with representational facilities. While there may be benefits in forming virtual organizations and work teams, it relies critically on the shared stocks of knowledge which are used to interpret and agree the meaning of information employed.

Issues of meaning and normative systems apart, an extended reading of the information system metaphor also suggests major implications for power relations. There is an intuitive sense that the cyberspace implied in the information systems metaphor means that the new forms of organization operate in a politically neutral 'place' – devoid of the disciplinary qualities which Marglin (1974) and Foucualt (1979) help us to identify in supposedly more 'panoptic', concentrated forms. After all, how can a virtual domain have politics? But if we turn our attention not to the ontological questions surrounding these domains but to the way they are construed in discourse, we can come to some illuminating conclusions.

In accounts of the information age, organizations may well be represented as places empty of time and space, as notions such as virtual organizations and virtual communities suggest (c.f. Rheingold, 1994). The consequence of this for working practices is a separation of individual place (for example, a worker's work territory, denoted by a personal desk or work station) from organizational space (such as the office or factory). If we accept the significance of the norms and values which infuse the act of 'going to work', we must take care not to downplay the importance of temporal and spatial work routines to the meanings and practices involved in work activity. Given that time-space practices imbue such activities with symbolic significance, the result of 'virtualizing' organizations may be a transformation in the very meaning of work. In seeking to innovate so far as how work is done, therefore, the corollary may be a radical innovation in the phenomenon of work itself.

A key issue remains over the material consequences of recasting the temporal and spatial representation of work relations. The invocation of the information superhighway, and the concomitant imagery of a world market (for goods and labour) where the walls to economic transactions come tumbling down, is anything but neutral speak. The ability to construe the market for information workers as a virtual one raises the information superhighway to the level of a spectre – one which has dangerous consequences for capital and labour alike. That capital can be employed to utilize labour anywhere on the superhighway, may be used to increase worker anxiety and reduce their perceived market leverage. At a governmental level, such arguments are employed for keeping down wage costs and avoiding expensive social expenditure. In contemporary debates here, such notions are intimately linked to particular conceptions of the 'information society' and the need to develop government policies to deal with it. The British Labour Party, for instance, placed an advertisement in the national press which stated:

> The companies and countries that will succeed in today's global economy are those that equip themselves for the competitive and technological challenge of the new information economy.
>
> (*The Times*, 1 November 1995)

Drawing global dimensions to elevate the threat of competition, and couching the new age in information terms, may or may not be intellectually defensible; the important point for the present argument is that using such a discourse for framing industrial issues provides a powerful way of recasting the economic and political debate. The set of temporal and spatial dynamics which may be articulated here, if accepted, may have a crucial bearing on industrial and organizational outcomes.

Representations of time and space may also be used to break the emotive and symbolic link between the nation state and the socially responsible or 'fair' employer. No longer are wage differentials issues grasped in national or even provincial dimensions. Where workers are seen to operate within a virtual world market, the shadows of competition can be portrayed as stretching down the slip-lane to the superhighway.

In temporal terms too, organizations have been keen to enhance customer expectations of services. So far as dial and deliver goods, help-lines and other information services are concerned, expectations are increasingly embedded of ever wider frontiers of service. In the context of a '24-hour service society', all the hours of the day can be presented as open play for capital. Indeed, despite a few concessions over Sunday trading, we have already seen the boundaries between work and domestic time becoming more and more blurred – a blurring which exaltations invoking cyberspace and the information system metaphor can only accelerate.

CONCLUSIONS

This paper has argued for the key role of the information system as a metaphor for understanding many debates on modern organizational forms, particularly with respect to issues of 'virtuality' and 'teleworking'. It has suggested that the ideas and imagery associated with this have provided a central framework through which IT-related innovations can be conceived – especially where they concern new temporal and spatial processes.

To address these contentions, three analytical dimensions have been explored: representations of IT as space-transcending, the representational facilities involved in IT-mediated working, and the representation of organizational time and space. It can be concluded from this that much of the richness of organizational life – especially the constitutive role of time and space in work interactions – is downplayed in speculation on dispersed and 'virtual' forms of organization. Moreover, there is a growing tendency for organizational 'space' to be enveloped conceptually by cyberspace. Finally, it has been concluded that the representation of the virtual market, as embodied by the information system metaphor, provides crucial modalities for the articulation of power, as well as a key area for intellectual scrutiny.

References

Aglietta, M. (1979) *A Theory of Capitalist Regulation*, New Left Books, London.
Barnatt, C. (1995) *Cyberbusiness*, John Wiley, Chichester.
Bell, D. (1973) *The Coming of Post-Industrial Society*, Heinemann, London.
Benedikt, M. (1991) (ed.) *Cyberspace: the First Steps*, MIT Press, Cambridge, Massachusetts.
Birchall, D. and Lyons, D. (1995) *Creating Tomorrow's Organisation*, Pitman, London.
Boddy, D. and Buchanan, D. A. (1983) *Organizations in the Computer Age*, Gower, Aldershot.
Canter, L.A. and Siegel, M.S. (1994) *How to Make a Fortune on the Information Superhighway*, HarperCollins, London.
Clark, J., McLoughlin, I., Rose, H. and King, R. (1988) *The Process of Technological Change in the Workplace*, Cambridge University Press.
Coombs, R. and Jones, B. (1989) Alternative successors to Fordism, in *Information Society and Spatial Structure*, (eds H. Ernste and C. Jaeger), Belhaven, London.
Coombs, R., Knights, D. and Willmott, H. C. (1992) Culture, control and

competition: towards a conceptual framework for the study of information technology in organization, in *Organization Studies*, 13 (1), 51–72.

Cooper, R. (1992) Formal organization as representation: remote control, displacement and abbreviation, in *Rethinking Organisation*, (eds M. Reed and M. Hughes), Sage, London.

Davidow, W.H. and Malone, M.S. (1992) *The Virtual Corporation*, HarperCollins, New York.

Dertouzos, M. L. and Moses, J. (eds) (1979) *The Computer Age: A Twenty-Year View*, MIT Press, Cambridge, Massachusetts.

Dunlop, C. and Kling, R. (1991) Introduction: social controversies about computerization, in *Computerization and Controversy*, (eds C. Dunlop and R. Kling), John Wiley, Chichester.

Forester, T. (1989) Introduction: making sense of IT, in *Computers in the Human Context*, (ed T. Forester), Blackwell, Oxford.

Foucault, M. (1979) *Discipline and Punishment*, Vintage Books, New York.

Foucault, M. (1980) *Power/Knowledge*, Harvester, Brighton.

Foucault, M. (1982) The Subject and Power, in *Critical Inquiry*, 8, pp. 777–95.

Gates, W. H. (1995) *The Road Ahead*, Viking, London.

Gershuny, J. I. and Miles, I. D. (1983) *The New Service Economy: The Transformation of Employment in Industrial Societies*, Frances Pinter, London.

Giddens, A. (1981) *A Contemporary Critique of Historical Materialism*, Macmillan, London.

Giddens, A. (1984) *The Constitution of Society*, Polity Press, Cambridge.

Giddens, A. (1987) *Social Theory and Modern Sociology*, Polity Press, Cambridge.

Giuliano, V. E. (1991) The mechanization of office work, in *Computerization and Controversy*, (eds C. Dunlop and R. Kling), Academic Press, Boston, Massachusetts.

Gregory, D. and Urry, J. (eds) (1985) *Social Relations and Spatial Structures*, Macmillan, London.

Grenier, R. and Metes, G. (1995) *Going Virtual*, Prentice-Hall, New Jersey.

Grint, K. and Woogar, S. (1992) Computers, guns and roses: what's social about being shot? in *Science, Technology and Human Values*, vol. 17, no. 3, pp. 366–80.

Grint, K. and Woolgar, S. (forthcoming) *The Machine at Work*, Polity Press, Cambridge.

Gunton, T. (1983) Moving fast up the learning curve, in *Computing (Europe)*, special report on office automation.

Gunton, T. (1990) *Inside Information Technology: A Practical Guide to Management Issues*, Prentice-Hall, London.

Harvey, D. (1989) *The Condition of Postmodernity*, Blackwell, Oxford.

Heim, M. (1993) *The Metaphysics of Virtual Reality*, OUP, Buckingham.

Huws, U., Korte, W. B. and Robinson, S. (1990) *Telework: Towards the Elusive Office*, John Wiley, Chichester.

Jackson, P.J. (1994) *Telework: Theory and Issues*, unpublished PhD. thesis, Cambridge University.

Jackson, P.J. (1995) *Organising in Time and Space: A Theoretical Framework for the Study of Worker Dispersal*, Working paper series, Department of Management Studies, Brunel University.

Jackson, P.J. and van der Wielen, J.M.M. (1995) *Time, space and organisation*, presented at workshop, Action and Structure in Organisations, ESSEC, Paris, May.

Kaplinsky, R. (1984) *Automation: The Technology and Society*, Harlow, Longman.

Kinsman, F. (1987) *The Telecommuters*, John Wiley, Chichester.

Kling, R. and Iacono, S. (1989) Desktop computerization and the organization of work, in *Computers in the Human Context*, (ed T. Forester), Blackwell, Oxford.

Lash, S. and Urry, D. (1994) *Economies of Signs and Space*, Sage, London.

Latour, B. (1987) *Science in Action*, Open University Press, Milton Keynes.

Latour, B. and Woolgar, S. (1979) *Laboratory Life: The Social Construction of Scientific Facts*, Sage, London.

Lefebvre, H. (1974) *The Production of Space*, Blackwell, Oxford.

Lyon, D. (1988) *The Information Society: Issues and Illusions*, Polity Press, Cambridge.

Lyon, D. (1994) *Surveillance Society*, Polity Press, Cambridge.

Marglin, S. A. (1974) What do bosses do? The origins and functions of hierarchy in capitalist production, in *Review of Radical Political Economics*, 6, pp. 60–112.

Morgan, G. (1986) *Images of Organization*, Sage, London.

Morgan, G. (1993) *Imaginization: The Art of Creative Management*, Sage, London.

Orlikowski, W. J. and Robey, D. (1991) Information technology and the structuring of organisations, in *Information Systems Research*, 2 (2), 143–69.

Panko, R. (1984) Office Work, in *Office Technology and People*, 2, 205–38.

Peltu, M. (1980) New life at home for office workers, in *New Scientist*, 27 March, pp. 1004–8.

Phillimore, J. (1989) Flexible specialization, work organisation and skills, in *New Technology, Work and Employment*, 4 (2), 79–91.

Pinch, T. F and Bijker, W. E. (1987) The social construction of facts and artifacts in *The Social Construction of Technological Systems*, (eds W. Bijker, T. P. Hughes and T. F. Pinch), MIT Press, Cambridge, Massachussets.

Piore, M. and Sabel, C. (1984) *The Second Industrial Divide*, Basic Books, New York.

Porat, M. (1977) *The Information Economy: Definition and Measurement*, US Department of Commerce, Washington DC.

Prava, C. (1983) *Managing New Office Technology*, Free Press, New York.

Pred, A. (1990) Context and bodies in flux: some comments on space and time in the writings of Anthony Giddens, in *Anthony Giddens: Consensus and Controversy*, (eds J. Clark, C. Modgil and S. Modgil), Falmer, London.

Rheingold, H. (1994) *The Virtual Community*, Minerva, London.

Rose, H., McLoughlin, I., King, R. and Clark, J. (1986) Opening the black box: the relation between technology and work, in *New Technology, Work and Employment*, 1 (1), pp. 18–26.

Sims, D.M., Fineman, S. and Gabriel, Y. (1993) *Organizations and Organizing*, Sage, London.

Tapscott, D. (1995) *The Digital Economy*, McGraw-Hill, New York.

Thompson, E. P. (1967) Time, work discipline and industrial capitalism, in *Past and Present*, 38, pp. 56–97.

Toffler, A. (1981) *The Third Wave*, Collins, London.

Touraine, A. (1971) *The Post Industrial Society*, Wildwood House, London.

Turkle, S. (1987) Computers and the Human Spirit, in *Information Technology: Social Issues*, (eds R. Finnegan, G. Salaman, and K. Thompson), Hodder and Stoughton, Sevenoaks.

Walsham, G. (1993) *Interpreting Information Systems in Organizations*, John Wiley, Chichester.

Weick, K. E. (1979) *The Social Psychology of Organizing*, Addison-Welsley, Reading, Massachussets.

Winner, L. (1977) *Autonomous Technology*, MIT Press, Cambridge, Massachussets.

Woolgar, S. (1988) *Science: The Very Idea*, Tavistock, London.

Woolgar, S. (1991) The turn to technology in social studies of science, in *Science, Technology and Human Values*, 16 (1), 20–50.

Woolgar, S. (1993) What's at stake in the sociology of technology? a reply to Pinch and Winner, in *Science, Technology and Human Values*, 18 (4), pp. 523–29.

Zuboff, S. (1988) *In the Age of the Smart Machine: The Future of Work and Power*, Heinemann, Oxford.

Chapter 10

Babies, bathwater, guns and roses

Ian McLoughlin

INTRODUCTION

What is the relationship between technology and organization? Do technologies exert definitive independent influences over the organizational outcomes of change or is it organizational variables that largely shape technology and its effects? These questions have long exercised organizational sociologists and have become even more important as the pace of technological innovation has increased. However, theory and research on these questions remain at best 'ambiguous and conflicting' (Orlikowski, 1992) if not in 'extensive disarray' (Bedeian, 1980). The precise analytical role of 'technology' itself in understanding the organizational effects of technological change remains largely unresolved.

On the one hand, recent theory and research have contained strong arguments against 'technological determinism' and have instead stressed the role of social factors in shaping organizational outcomes of technological change (see e.g. Gallie, 1978; Boddy and Buchanan, 1983). While there are wildly conflicting views over how this occurs, some stressing the overriding and determinate influence of broader social structural factors (Braverman, 1984) and others preferring to emphasize the more indeterminate role of human agency (Wilkinson, 1983), there is common ground in the view that the capabilities and characteristics of technology itself are of little analytical interest.

Others have pointed to the danger of ignoring the analytical possibility of technology having an independent influence on organizational structure and behaviour (see Clark *et al.*, 1988; McLoughlin and Clark, 1994). In turn, this argument has been accused of being essentially technicist at its core. The origin of this attack is new work in the sociology of technology that has previously had little influence on debates within organizational sociology. The sociology of technology has stressed the need to understand technology itself, not just its organizational and societal outcomes, as socially shaped (see Introduction, this volume). From some vantage points in this perspective, 'technology' can only be understood as a social construct. It is from this angle in particular that much organizational sociology appears to adopt a determinist position.

The aim of this chapter is to explore this argument. It begins with a brief overview of the debate concerning the analytical role of technology in recent organizational sociology, in particular that taking a social and political process perspective (see Introduction, this volume). The 'technology question' is then explored from the point of view of the sociology of technology, or to be more precise, an 'extreme' or 'strong' relativist variant of it. The vehicle for this will be a recent debate that has focused on the question of whether artefacts – such as guns, roses or computers – have a definitive character and effect (see Kling, 1991a, 1991b, 1992a, 1992b; Woolgar, 1991a; Woolgar and Grint, 1991; Grint and Woolgar, 1992). As we will see, this debate strikes at the heart of the 'what does technology do' question in sociological analysis.

THE TECHNOLOGY BABY AND THE DETERMINIST BATHWATER

A major concern of much recent research on the organizational implications of new computing and information technologies has been to develop alternatives to what are regarded as 'technological determinist' modes of explanation. 'Technological determinism' is defined in organizational sociology as attributing to technology the status of a primary explanatory variable determining organizational structure and the behaviour of organizations members (see Rose, 1988, pp. 214–48). Such determinism is frequently seen as an endemic feature of previous analysis in the organizational/industrial sociology tradition. For example, Woodward's classic analysis of the relationship between production systems, management control systems and company performance is frequently held up as an exemplar of determinism, in so far as she concluded that particular forms of organization were appropriate to different types of technology (see Reeves and Woodward, 1970; Woodward, 1980). Similarly, there has also been a tendency to reject those attempts to counter technological determinism – such as Braverman's labour process theory and its derivatives – which remain in varying degrees faithful to the view that technology and the direction of technological change is largely determined by broader historical and economic forces (see Thompson, 1989).

In an important contribution to the development of an alternative to both these perspectives, Wilkinson (1983) has argued that organizations should be treated as, 'emergent entities dependent upon the conscious political decisions of actors and groups of actors' (1983, p. 9). As such, the introduction of new technology in organizations is best conceived as a process with indeterminant outcomes. Within this process a number of analytically distinct stages can be identified, each of which provide 'critical junctures' or opportunities for power-holders to make and modify 'strategic choices' in relation to particular issues highlighted by change. It is the nature of these choices, and the way these are contested by formal and informal negotiation by other organizational actors, that have the decisive influence on actual organizational outcomes (see Wilkinson, 1983; Clark *et al.*, 1988; Dawson, 1994).

Thus, the form of technology and work organization can be viewed, not as primarily a reflection of the capabilities and characteristics of production technology but, 'as an outcome which has been chosen and negotiated' within adopting organizations (Wilkinson, 1983, p. 20). From this social and political perspective, the search for an explanation of technological change's effects is therefore seen as moving from the nature of the technology to 'the processes of change within particular organizations and the manner in which management, unions and workforce are able to influence substantive outcomes' (Wilkinson, 1983, p. 21). Similarly Buchanan, suggests that 'to consider the impact of a particular technology is to consider the wrong question, or at best to consider only part of the issue' (Huczynski and Buchanan, 1991, p. 276).

Rejecting the argument that the characteristics and capabilities of technology determine organizational outcomes – or at least are the 'most significant contingency' shaping such changes – still leaves the puzzle of what role, if any, technology has to play. This issue has rarely been given any serious analytical consideration. However, a close reading of research findings of many studies which adopt a social and political process approach, even though rejecting technological determinism, seem nonetheless to point empirically to technology having an influence. For example, in his classic study of British and French oil refineries, Duncan Gallie argued that the forms of work organization in the four settings he studied reflected features of the cultural and institutional framework of the two societies rather than the technical capacities of continuous process production technology. Having said this, he also referred to particular observed influences that the technology did have at workplace level, such as being 'more conducive' to the adoption of semi-autonomous team working (Gallie, 1978, p. 221).

It might also be argued that it is a contradiction in terms to assume that technology itself is of little significance to the process of technological change. Indeed, if this were true there would presumably be little point in organizations ever introducing new technology. As Winner has argued: 'if [technology] were not determining, it would be of no use and certainly of little interest' (Winner, 1977, p. 75). One problem with the process approach, therefore, is that it runs the risk of the technology 'baby' being jettisoned with the determinist 'bathwater'. In other words, although not the single most important determinant, technology may still have influence over organizational outcomes. This raises the question of how 'technology' is to be defined, and its technical influences identified, if it is be incorporated as a variable in a process of change' model.

THE INDEPENDENT INFLUENCE OF TECHNOLOGY

This became a core question in research conducted by the author and colleagues (Clark *et al.*, 1988). This examined the effects on the work and skills of maintenance technicians of the computerisation of telephone exchanges by British Telecom. The study showed that the technical capacities of the telephone exchange systems were one factor shaping the 'design space' (Bessant, 1983) available to the various organizational actors in their attempts to influence the outcomes of change. It was argued that the exchange systems could be understood as engineering systems which comprised an architecture (system principles and overall system configuration) and implementation (physical realization in a given technology) (see Figure 10.1) (Clark *et al.*, 1988, p. 13). Two further secondary elements were also identified. The first referred to the way a system is dimensioned or configured to suit a particular installation (e.g. in physical layout of the hardware or customization of software). The second was the appearance of a system, that is its visible and audible features, ergonomics and aesthetics.

A key point here was that electro-mechanical systems were designed according to 'step-by-step' switching principles, where calls were switched or connected using electro-mechanical technology. In contrast, the computerized exchanges which replaced them were designed around a different telephony principle know as 'common control' whereby call connection

PRIMARY ELEMENTS	
Architecture	*Technology*
system principles	hardware
overall system configuration	software
SECONDARY ELEMENTS	
Dimensioning	
detailed design for a particular organizational setting	
Appearance	
audible and visual characteristics ergonomics aesthetics	

Source: Clark *et al.* (1988)

Figure 10.1 The concept of engineering system

was controlled electronically by a central 'computer' and the connections physically made by using far more reliable electro-mechanical switches.

The different architectures and implementation of electro-mechanical and computerized exchanges gave rise to different technical characteristics and capabilities. In particular, the new computerized exchange systems were more functionally interdependent, inherently reliable and had a degree of 'self-diagnostic' capability. Moreover, the virtual absence of serviceable moving parts meant the exchanges required far less routine preventive maintenance than their electro-mechanical counterparts. On the other hand, corrective maintenance tasks took on a new character. This was because of the functional interdependence of equipment and the need to rely on diagnostic information provided by the system and other testing aids. The latter were required to establish the nature of fault conditions in the absence of the visual and audible cues provided by the old electro-mechanical systems.

The technical character and capabilities of the two exchange systems had a strong influence on the changes in work tasks and skills. They also proved important in enabling and constraining factors in choices over job content, work organization and the control of work. For example, the new-found functional interdependence of the equipment meant that a significant proportion of corrective maintenance tasks were more technically complex. This tended to support a move away from individual to collaborative working among the technicians on the grounds that 'two heads were better than one'. It also represented a realization that errors could, in principle, affect far more of the exchange – *in extremis* leading to it 'crashing off the air'.

Similarly, whereas electro-mechanical systems designed on the 'step-by-step' principle enabled discrete areas of the exchange to be sectioned off into specific areas of maintenance responsibility, such a division of labour was less viable in systems based on the common control principle. Again this reflected the functional interdependence of the equipment in the computerized exchanges. In fact, just as Gallie found in his study of oil refineries, computerized telephone exchange technology was 'conducive' to team-based forms of work organization. As a result, a formal and fairly rigid division of labour, which was characteristic of electro-mechanical exchanges, shifted to a more informal team-based approach.

Moreover, the radical changes in skill requirements, from largely manual dexterities to new 'systems-based' skills, meant that the maintenance technicians enjoyed a new-found 'skill superiority' over their supervisors. Because they had little detailed technical knowledge or understanding, supervisors could not usually influence the day-to-day content, allocation and organization of work. This meant that team-based forms of work organization tended to be both instigated by the technicians (who had always enjoyed a high degree of 'individual autonomy') and subsequently operationalized by them through collective 'self-supervision'.

It must be emphasized that, in keeping with the process of change perspective, that technical influences were not claimed to be the sole determinant of these outcomes. Rather, the research stressed that roles of strategic choices at corporate level, made in the context of particular business conditions and industrial relations frameworks, and their mediation through 'political negotiation' by numerous stakeholder groups, such as local management, supervisors, workgroups and trade unions at national and local level. The technical capabilities and characteristics of exchange systems acted 'only' to enable and constrain this process of choice and negotiation, especially in relation to issues at the 'point of production' such as skills, job content and work organization. It should also be pointed out that the form of the technologies investigated being at some point 'socially shaped' was not denied. Rather, it was suggested that such social shaping, at least in this case, was primarily at work during the design stage, separated to a significant degree by both time and space from the implementation in individual exchanges. By the time the exchange modernization programme begun, any social and political choices along with technical choices were, in effect, 'frozen' in the final primary characteristics of the exchange system. Or to use Pinch and Bjiker's term (see Introduction), the technical system was 'stabilized' (1987). These prior social, political and technical choices, therefore, could be seen as providing the source of the technical influences which enabled and constrained subsequent choice and negotiation.

THE 'GUNS AND ROSES' DEBATE

Do technologies have specific technical characteristics and capabilities as claimed in this study of exchange computerization? A challenging argument against such views has been developed from one emerging school from within the sociology of technology. This suggests that to claim any sort of independent influence for technology is 'technological determinist'. The starting point here is the proposition that technical capacities are not fixed but 'essentially indeterminate' and open to 'interpretive flexibility'. Moreover, this is the case not only during the conception, design and development of a technology, but beyond when it is being adopted and used. According to Woolgar and Grint:

> . . . what a computer is for, what it can do and achieve, is also regarded as an interpretive issue on any occasion that it is described, planned, talked about, marketed, sold, used, reviewed, dismantled and so on . . . in other words, technological artefacts can be construed as texts that are *essentially* embedded in (and, at the same time, constituted by) their interpretive contexts.

> (Original emphasis, 1992, p. 370)

In this view it is mistaken to maintain that, at some point, artefacts can have a 'definitive character or effect'. This proposition has provided the focus for an illuminating debate between Woolgar and Grint (Woolgar, 1991a; Woolgar and Grint, 1991, 1992) and Kling (1991a, 1991b; 1992a; 1992b). Kling is open to the proposition that computing and information technologies may have technical characteristics and capabilities which, potentially, can facilitate social transformations. He argues that to establish how far this is the case requires a detailed examination of particular computing and information systems' technical capacities as well as the social aspects of processes of computerization. Woolgar and Grint take issue with Kling because, as in the study of exchange computerization discussed above, he sees technical influences as one possible factor shaping how a technology is designed and used. From the perspective adopted by Woolgar and Grint this is technicist and unacceptable. The debate is crystallized in a discussion of the relative merits of guns as opposed to roses as effective means of terminating human life.

Without, I hope, doing too much violence to their closely argued positions, Kling and Woolgar/Grint differ as follows. According to Kling:

1 Firearms have the unique technical capacity to wound, maim and kill human beings. As Kling puts it, 'it is much harder to kill a platoon of soldiers with a dozen roses than with well-placed high speed bullets' (1992b, p. 262).
2 This does not mean that the sale of every gun results in a violent act on a human being. How the technology is consumed or used depends on social factors. Guns, for example, might be acquired as 'trophies' which act as symbols of manhood to their possessors. However, guns give certain social groups – street gangs in Los Angeles for example – a superior technical capacity to ply their trade.
3 A sociological analysis might, therefore, reasonably attribute some independent influence on the social phenomenon of high murder rates in Los Angeles to the unique technical capacities of guns.

According to Woolgar/Grint:

1 Being shot is an essentially social phenomenon that can only be understood in the specific context of a killer being united with a gun. The human element (killer) and non-human element (gun) form an 'actor-network' and it is during the fusion of this network that the event 'being shot' is socially constructed.
2 The act of socially constructing 'being shot' can be viewed as comprising a number of onion-like layers. One interpretation is to assume that the onion has a technical core – the capacity of a gun once designed to maim and kill. A more radical view is to argue that this is illusory. For instance, the seriousness of the wound, the perception of the amount

of pain, the definition of if and when the recipient is 'dead', represent a series of social (re)constructions which will be contingent on social, cultural and historical context.

3 The fact that the recipient has a bullet hole in their head is dependent on this socially constructed knowledge of how it got there in the first place. That the hole was caused by the bullet is not an illustration of the technical capacity of the gun but the ability of the 'actor-network' to socially construct an interpretation that claims this to be the case.

Thus, from Woolgar and Grint's position, the application of the principle of interpretive flexibility, reveals that the linking of the 'gun' to a 'bullet hole' in someone's head is entirely a social construction. Rather like an Agatha Christie 'Whodunit?', the case that the gun is the technical source of the wound, has to be socially proven each time. Moreover, the principle of interpretive flexibility points to the possibility that an 'actor-network' could construct alternative accounts which would be equally plausible.

FALLING BACK INTO THE DETERMINIST BATHWATER?

Woolgar and Grint distinguish their approach, which they term 'thorough-going interpretivism', from the argument that technology is in some way socially shaped but at some point becomes stabilized, beyond which it can have independent effects. They term this latter approach 'restricted interpretivism'. Restricted interpretivism does not, as it claims, escape the trap of technological determinism, which Woolgar and Grint define as, 'the view that the artifact has a definitive character and effect' (1992, p. 370).

This is an important definitional point since the notion of technological determinism being employed here refers not to technology as a 'primary explanatory variable' but as a fixed independent category that can have any definitive 'technical influence'. What constitutes 'technological determin-ism', therefore, appears to differ for sociologists of technology – at least those of the 'strong' 'thoroughgoing interpretivist' position – compared to the position normally adopted within organizational/industrial sociology. As noted above, for the latter, 'technological determinism' is normally defined as a predisposition to give primacy to technology as the main causal or explanatory variable in the shaping of organization structure and behaviour. For the 'strong' variant of the sociology of technology, 'determinism' appears to arise as soon as any kind of independent influence is attributed to a technical variable. The technology baby and determinist bathwater are inseparable.

In this perspective, analytical attempts to 'rescue' the technology vari-able are inevitably misguided (Parayil, 1990). For example, returning to the argument made earlier concerning the role of technical influences on the organizational outcomes of the computerization of telephone exchanges, a 'thoroughgoing interpretivist' critique would run something like this:

1 The notion that telephone exchanges' technical capacities are defini- tively captured by terms such as 'engineering system', 'architecture', 'configuration', 'implementation' are illusory. These are means by which certain human and non-human actors constitute and represent their par- ticular version of how the technology works.
2 The principle of 'interpretive flexibility' argues that other equally plau- sible representations are possible. Indeed, it is not axiomatic that the telephone should be construed only as having the technical capacity to act as means of two-way personal communication. For example, at its inception, it was used to broadcast concert music and increasingly it is being construed as a means of transmitting non-voice data in digital form (Grint, 1991, p. 292).
3 The mistake is to privilege one particular representation of the 'technical capacities' of telephone exchanges over another. The fact that this particular representation was derived from an interaction between the sociologists and 'knowledgeable agents', such as telecommunications engineers, is irrelevant in so far as this is used to justify the superiority of the particular knowledge claim.
4 Rather, this version of the nature and capacity of a 'technology' should have been identified and construed as a 'text' constructed through dis- course by an actor-network of which the researchers were a part.

If the researchers had been thoroughgoing interpretivists they would have been more sensitive to other readings of the technology 'text'. Perhaps there were competing claims as to what constituted effective performance, why faults occurred, the best way to rectify them, how a telephone exchange actually worked, and so on. In this way, rather than demonstrat- ing definitive independent influences of a 'stabilized' technological system, the researchers would have realized the ultimately indeterminate character of the technology they were investigating. Thus, despite their claims to the contrary, those who argue for some independent influence of technology in effect 'fall back into the determinist bathwater'.

Discussion: the material limits of interpretive flexibility

Can the thoroughgoing interpretivist and process of change perspectives be reconciled, especially where the latter makes an explicit attempt to rescue the 'technology' variable? Kling is particularly dismissive of the thorough- going interpretivist position on two counts. First, the approach sidesteps the key question of how grievous bodily harm and murder could be accom- plished with roses rather than guns. It merely asserts that an actor-network could turn roses into effective weapons, but does not demonstrate how this might be achieved (1992b, p. 328). Second, the approach runs the risk of denying a 'critical dimension' to social analysis and its ability to challenge 'traditionally held views about the political neutrality of technologies and the links between social advantage and technological innovation' (1992a, p. 351). As such the sociologist may be rendered 'mute' on the key social issues raised by computing and information technologies. Kling argues that social analysts can also be 'reconstructive interpretivists' who construct 'new narratives about technological and social systems after they have examined the ways that important ambiguities are reified or taken for granted' (1992a, p. 355).

To be fair to the thoroughgoing interpretivist position, the approach claims to demonstrate the possibility of interpretive flexibility and does not set out to provide alternative interpretations on demand. Indeed, it is suggested that this is not the legitimate task of the technology sociologist any more than it is to adjudicate between different interpretations of technical capacity. A knowledge claim that roses can kill, if an actor-network made one, would be treated as just as plausible as the currently more popular common-sense perception that guns can kill. It is not the job of sociologists of technology to develop or legislate over such constructs (Woolgar and Grint, 1991, p. 41). Similarly, the approach does not accept that it is totally divorced from policy and critique. Indeed it is argued that the reflective analysis of the discourse of practitioners does 'not proscribe practical engagement in policy issues' but sets, 'it on a different' and 'ultimately more profound footing' (Grint and Woolgar, 1992, p. 36–68).

A major difficulty here is the analytical scepticism with which sociologists of technology in general, and thoroughgoing going interpritivism in particular, regard broader social and economic structures of power and interest. These 'material' or 'structural' phenomenon, just as with technological artefacts and systems, are it is insisted created anew by social actors within the context in which they act (see Williams and Edge, 1992). It is in this sense that Bruno Latour, one of the philosophical architects of the 'thoroughgoing interpretivist' position, suggests that factors such as class, power and politics should be seen as 'effects' and not 'causes' of social action (Grint, 1995). The problem, as Williams and Edge (1987) have noted, is that while 'opening the black box' of technology in an intriguing and potentially illuminating fashion, the sociology of technology, by apparently ignoring broader structural variables, in effect 'closes the lid' behind itself.

Appeals to the socially constructed nature of work and employment relationships have necessarily had only limited appeal for organizational sociology in the face of apparently clear and often conflicting influence of material power and interests. As Rose (1988) argues, too much emphasis placed on the socially constructed nature of industrial behaviour leads to a focus on the way organizational actors define their power position vis-a-vis their adversaries, rather than the material basis of such power itself. However, Rose argues that to view the exercise of power as purely symbolic is misleading:

> . . . many power-holders do not need to modify a subordinate's perceptions to have their own way: faced with difficult underlings, they simply threaten to cut their pay, demote them, sack them, send them to a psychiatric hospital, put them in prison, or shoot them, as the case may be.
>
> (Rose, 1988, pp. 276–7).

In other words to deny the material basis of power and instead focus purely on its symbolic aspects, places too much stress on the actor's ability to construct interpretations of the situation and not enough on the features of the situation which enable and constrain the actor's interpretive capacity (see also Russell, 1991). As Rose continues:

> Stress on the actor's own, on his *subjective*, definition of a situation, may lead us to play down unduly, or even ignore, the *objective* properties of the situation in which action occurs. These objective features *condition* action. This does *not* mean that objective features determine the subject's action: it *does* mean they can facilitate some forms of action while excluding others, and encourage some while discouraging others. To note the reality of the objective world is not to see it as deterministic or necessitarian, but to see how it shapes action. Of course the subject's perception of it can mediate his action. But subjects cannot choose to perceive what is not there, or to ignore what is there – at least, they cannot do this without suffering a penalty.
>
> (Original emphasis, 1988, p. 271)

In this view, exactly how engagement in policy issues is put 'on a more profound footing' by thoroughgoing interpretivism is, to say the least, unclear. At worst, as Rose states rather bluntly, we are left in, 'a relativist never-never land' (1988, p. 279).

The point then, is that 'interpretive flexibility' has material limits. As Orlikowski argues, there is a need to recognize the 'duality of technology' as both an 'objective reality and as a socially constructed product' (1992, p. 423) and that, 'the interpretive flexibility of any given technology is not infinite' and is partly constrained by 'the material characteristics of that technology' (1992, p. 405). Moreover, it can be added that this is so both during the production and consumption of technology within an adopting organization. As such, the idea of new technologies 'stabilizing' at 'critical junctures' during the process of change and thereby acting to enable and constrain subsequent social choices does not in itself constitute a regress to technological determinism. In fact, what is at issue here is not the claim that technologies have independent technical capacities, but whether these necessarily become fully 'frozen' or 'stabilized' at the point of implementation. In other words, the social shaping of technical capacities can occur post-adoption during implementation and operation within adopting organizations, but this in itself cannot be used to suggest the absence of 'independent technical influences'.

Indeed, the possibility that 'post-adoption' innovation or 'innofusion' (see Badham, 1993; Fleck, 1993; Webster, 1993) can occur once a technology has been adopted can itself be regarded as subject to technical influences which may enable and constrain such developments. The concept of engineering system outlined above implicitly allows for this by suggesting, as an important secondary characteristic, the dimensioning or configuration of the system to suit particular applications or implementations. For example, the common control equipment in the computerized exchanges was a specialised stored program control system. This comprised processing, storage and input/output devices and operated by constantly cycling through a program which enabled it to respond to incoming information in the form of instructions to other functional areas of the exchange. The program was not software based, but implemented in the form of more inflexible miniature threaded-wire units (see Clark *et al.*, 1988, p. 21). This particular technical characteristic acted to limit the immediate scope for post-adoption configuration of the exchange system. In contrast, the more advanced digital and semi-electronic systems which have subsequently been introduced implement their common control architecture in software form. The modular design and re-programmability of these systems might be expected to offer far more opportunities for post-adoption innovation and detailed dimensioning and configuration.

CONCLUSION

This chapter set out to explore the implications of some of the recent work in the sociology of technology for the organizational sociology of technological change. The conclusion is that the extreme relativist approach does highlight some important issues for organizational sociologists in investigating significant changes within organizations such as those involving computing and information technologies. However, in general, focusing exclusively on how organizational actors interpret organizational situations does not in itself provide a satisfactory basis for developing a convincing analysis, especially when considering the specific question of the relationship between organization and technology. Moreover, the proposal that we should see technologies as texts, if accepted *in toto*, would seem to disenfranchise the organizational sociologist in the hitherto key activity of developing 'alternative social narratives'.

Given this, it is difficult to see how the thoroughgoing interpretivist position can be reconciled with the process of change approach. However, this is not to say that an engagement with this position and other schools within the sociology of technology is not without benefit. For example, the notion of 'interpretive flexibility' is clearly of considerable use in trying to understand the scope for, and limits of, the social configuration and re-configuration of technological systems in both their production and consumption within adopting organizations (see, for example, Woolgar, 1991b; Badham, 1993). If we accept that the technical capacities of technologies are made sense of and given meaning through symbols it is, however, also possible to accept the 'the ontological status of physical objects as different from the ontological status of linguistic constructs' (Kling, 1992a, p. 362). Thus social action will be subject to, among other things, the material constraints and possibilities of particular technological systems.

The thoroughgoing interpretivist, while not denying that computers, guns, roses or telephone exchanges are real in a material sense, argues that knowledge of their technical capacities is entirely a social construct. Why, when someone wants to shoot somebody else they reach for a gun, when they want to talk to another person at a distance they pick up a telephone, or when they want to please a lover, they give a rose, is entirely a social argument. However, the position taken in this chapter is that the plausibility of the social narrative that explains these actions and their outcomes must rest, in part, on the technical capabilities and characteristics of the physical phenomenon concerned. Or to put it slightly differently, the reasons why roses make good gifts, bad weapons, and are lousy methods of conveying voice and non-voice data, do not lie exclusively in the persua-siveness of texts and their reading.

References

Badham, R. (1993) Introduction: New Technology and the implementation process, editorial for special issue of *International Journal of Human Factors in Manu-facturing*, vol. 3, no. 1, pp. 3–14.

Bedeian, A. (1980) *Organisations: Theory and Analysis*, The Dryden Press, Hinsdale, Illinois.

Bessant, J. (1983) Management and manufacturing innovation: the case of infor-mation technology, in *Information Technology in Manufacturing Processes*, (ed. G. Winch), Rossendale, London.

Boddy, D. and Buchanan, D.A. (1983) *Organisations in the Computer Age: Techno-logical Imperatives and Strategic Choice*, Gower, Aldershot.

Braverman, H. (1984) *Labour and Monopoly Capital*, Monthly Review Press, New York.

Child, J. and Loveridge, R. (1990) *Information Technology in European Services: Towards a Microelectronic Future*, Blackwell, Oxford.

Clark, J., McLoughlin, I.P., Rose, H. and King, J. (1988) *The Process of Techno-logical Change: new technology and social choice in the workplace*, Cambridge University Press.

Dawson, P. (1994) *Organizational Change: A Processual Perspective*, Paul Chapman, London.

Fleck, J. (1993) Configurations: crystallising contingency, in *International Journal of Human Factors in Manufacturing*, 3 (1), pp. 15–36.

Gallie, D. (1978) *In Search of the New Working Class*, Cambridge University Press.

Grint, K. (1991) *The Sociology of Work*, Polity Press, Cambridge.

Grint, K. (1995) *Management: A Sociological Introduction*, Polity Press, Cambridge.

Grint, K. and Woolgar, S. (1992) Computers, guns, and roses: what's social about being shot? in *Science, Technology and Human Values*, 17 (3) Summer, pp. 366–80.

Huczynski, A. and Buchanan, D.A. (1991) *Organisational Behaviour*, 2nd edn, Prentice Hall, London.

Jones, B. (1982). Distribution or redistribution of engineering skills? The case of numerical control, in *The Degradation of Work?: Skill, Deskilling and the Labour Process*, (ed. S. Wood), Hutchinson, London, pp. 179–200.

Kling, R. (1991a) Computerisation and Social Transformations, in *Science, Technology and Human Values*, 16 (3) summer, pp. 342–67.

Kling, R. (1991b) Reply to Woolgar and Grint: a preview, in *Science, Technology and Human Values*, 16 (3) summer, pp. 379–81.

Kling, R. (1992a) Audiences, narratives, and human values in social studies of technology, in *Science, Technology and Human Values*, 17 (3) summer, pp. 349–65.

Kling, R. (1992b) When gunfire shatters bone: reducing socio-technical systems to social relationships, in *Science, Technology and Human Values*. 17 (3) summer, pp. 381–85.

McLoughlin, I.P. and Clark, J. (1994) *Technological Change at Work*, 2nd edn, Open University Press, Buckingham.

Orlikowski, W.J. (1992) The duality of technology: rethinking the concept of technology in organizations, in *Organisational Science*, 3 (3), pp. 398–427.

Parayil, G. (1990) book review of Clark, J. *et al.* (1988), in *Science, Technology and Human Values*, 15 (1) 1990, pp. 124–5.

Pinch, T. and Bjiker, W.E. (1987) The social construction of facts and artifacts, in *The Social Construction of Technical Systems*, (eds W. Bjiker, T.P. Hughes and T. Pinch), MIT Press, Cambridge, Massachusetts, pp. 17–50.

Reeves, T.K. and Woodward, J. (1970) The study of managerial control, in *Industrial Organisation: Behaviour and Control*, (ed. J. Woodward), Oxford University Press, London, pp. 37–56.

Rose, M. (1988) *Industrial Behaviour: Research and Control*, Penguin, London.

Russell, S. (1991) *Interests and the shaping of technology: an unresolved debate reappears*, Department of Science and Technology Studies working paper no. 4. Wollongong University.

Thompson, P. (1989) *The Nature of Work*, 2nd edn, MacMillan, London.

Webster, J. (1993) Chicken or egg? The interaction between manufacturing technologies and paradigms of work organisation, in *International Journal of Human Factors in Manufacturing*, 3 (1), pp. 53–68.

Winner, M. (1985) Do artifacts have politics? in *The Social Shaping of Technology*, (eds D. MacKenzie and J. Wajcman), Open University Press, Milton Keynes, pp. 26–38.

Wilkinson, B. (1983) *The Shop Floor Politics of New Technology*, Heinemann, London.

Williams, R. and Edge, D. (1992) Social shaping reviewed: research concepts and findings in the UK, PICT working paper 41, Edinburgh University.

Winner, L. (1977) *Autonomous Technology*, MIT Press, Cambridge, Massachusetts.

Woodward, J. (1980) *Industrial Organisation: Theory and Practice*, 2nd edn, Oxford University Press.

Woolgar, S. (1991a) The turn to technology in social studies of science, in *Science, Technology and Human Values*, 16 (1), pp. 20–50.

Woolgar, S. (1991b) Configuring the user: the case of usability trials, in *A Sociology of Monsters: Essays on Power, Technology and Domination*, (ed. J. Law), Routledge, London, pp. 58–99.

Woolgar, S. and Grint, K. (1991) Computers and the Transformation of Social Analysis, in *Science, Technology and Human Values*, 16 (3) Summer, pp. 368–78.

General Index

Author Index